OUR AMERICAN PRINCES:
The Story of the Seventeen American Cardinals

OUR AMERICAN
PRINCES

The Story of the Seventeen American Cardinals

FRANCIS BEAUCHESNE THORNTON

G. P. Putnam's Sons New York

Library of Congress Catalog
Card Number: 63-9674

NIHIL OBSTAT:
Walter H. Peters, Ph.D.,
Censor Librorum

IMPRIMATUR:
✠ Leo Binz,
Archbishop of St. Paul
March 26, 1963

*To
Ray and Terry Hyer, and the Children
with Affection*

ACKNOWLEDGMENTS

Many kindly people (clergy and laity) have helped me in the long labor of completing the seventeen profiles of *Our American Princes*. I am deeply grateful to the following: The Most Revd. Leo Binz, D.D.; The Most Revd. John A. Donovan, D.D.; The Most Revd. Henry E. Donnelly, D.D.; The Most Revd. Alexander M. Zaleski, S.S.L.; The Rt. Revd. Msgr. Francis J. Lally; The Rt. Revd. Msgr. Franklyn Kennedy; The Rt. Revd. Msgr. Daniel Moore; The Rt. Revd. Msgr. Anthony L. Ostheimer, Ph.D.; The Rt. Revd. Msgr. Patrick Roche; The Rt. Revd. Msgr. William M. Drumm, J.C.D.; The Very Revd. Msgr. John M. Kelly; The Very Revd. Msgr. Joseph E. Michalski, J.C.L.; The Revd. Walter H. Peters; The Revd. Peter M. Shannon; The Revd. Bartholomew F. Fair, J.C.D., S.T.L.; The Revd. Nelson J. Curran; Mother Buck, R.S.C.J.; Mother O'Byrne, R.S.C.J.; Mother O'Connor, R.S.C.J.; Edward T. Foley, Esq.; Julie Kernan; Margaret Lavin; Margaret Judge; Monsignor Vittorio Bartoccetti; The Revd. Joseph J. Senger; Victor Ridder, Esq.; Ralph L. Woods, the distinguished anthologist, whose work was invaluable in researching the profile of Cardinal McIntyre, and Timothy Murphy Rowe.

"It is not the cardinal that ennobles a man;
it is the man that ennobles the cardinal."

CARDINAL GIBBONS

Photographs of the Cardinals will be found following page 160.

CONTENTS

Introduction

AMERICAN CATHOLICISM owes little or nothing to French and Spanish influences, although the first missionaries in the New World were French and Spanish Catholics. It was not until the English colonized the Atlantic seaboard that the Church, as we know it, began to assume its distinctive character in the United States.

The burning desire for religious freedom of the Puritans of Massachusetts was symptomatic of the feeling of other groups in England and Ireland, particularly the Catholics who lived under what has been described as "inhuman persecution." Like the other nonconformists, they too looked toward greater freedom in the new land. The Calverts established their colony in Maryland with an enlightened constitution that promised religious freedom for all groups that believed in God.

The situation seemed promising, but in the end the hoped-for gains were nullified by events in the mother country. First the struggle between the Puritans and Cavaliers led the Puritans in the colonies to take repressive measures against all other religious groups, particularly the Catholics. There was an easing of religious tensions under Charles II and his brother James II, but after the "Glorious Revolution" of 1688, in which William and Mary seized the English throne, persecution of Catholics was pursued with a new force and fury.

It is interesting to note that when New Amsterdam became New York, the Catholic governor, Thomas Dongan, initiated a period of toleration for all religions. Of course the "Glorious Revolution" put an end to such toleration, just as the struggle between Cavaliers and Roundheads had put an end to religious freedom in Maryland.

It is both creditable and noteworthy that in the two colonies where Catholics were for a time in control there was no religious repression of any sort. Catholics were not alone in this liberal attitude: Roger Williams founded Rhode Island to secure religious freedom for all, and William Penn established Pennsylvania in a true spirit of brotherly love for men of all faiths. American Catholics owe a great debt to the Quakers, because it was in Pennsylvania that persecuted Catholics took refuge and were able to begin the consolidation of their faith. From centers in Philadelphia and Conewago, the Jesuits ministered to their scattered flock in other states, they were also active in Maryland where they even made some noted converts.

The onset of the Revolution led to heightened toleration and bigotry. There was public outcry against the Quebec Act, which granted religious freedom to the French Canadians. Yet, at the same time, while the Continental Congress was passing resolutions condemning the Act, it was organizing a committee of which Charles Carroll and his priest-cousin John Carroll were members for the purpose of persuading the French Canadians to fight with them against the exactions of the Crown. It is, as John Tracy Ellis points out in his fine monograph, *American Catholicism*,[1] a sad but diverting example of human hypocrisy.

Catholics were but a small minority in the colonies on the eve of the Revolution, but there were among them men of substance and talent whose assistance was worth enlisting. This led the Virginians to pass an act of religious toleration in June, 1776. Before the year was out, Pennsylvania and Maryland did the same.

Prominent Catholics were quick to take advantage of the changing climate. Charles Carroll, Thomas FitzSimons and Daniel Carroll participated in the First Continental Congress.

---

[1] *American Catholicism*, John Tracy Ellis. Chicago: University of Chicago Press, 1956.

John Barry assisted in founding the American Navy, and Steven Moylan became Washington's mustermaster general. Others, like Robert Morris, lent their talents and fortunes to financing the struggle.

Washington himself was completely without bigotry, and his attitude played a large part in the growing spirit of toleration. More important still was the alliance with France, which brought ships of the French Navy and their chaplains.

The spirit of toleration became a settled pattern after the triumph of Yorktown. Both the Constitution and the Bill of Rights guaranteed the equality of all religions in the eyes of the law. Some of the thirteen original states did little more than pay lip service to these enlightened sentiments, but all eventually accepted the equality of all religions before the law. Catholic emigrants played a considerable part in building the new states on the frontier. As a result, prejudice and bigotry were not as forceful or prominent as they were in the older states.

In 1790, John Carroll journeyed to Lulworth Castle in England where he was consecrated the first bishop of the United States of America. Bishop Carroll would have preferred to see the American Church grow by slow stages into a well-organized and cohesive organization. However, this was not to be; in the middle of the nineteenth century, hordes of immigrants poured into the United States in hopes of making a better living and escaping the repressive measures they had endured in their homelands.

At first, the largest group came from Ireland. Its members were strong in faith but often intemperate and arrogant, frequently making trouble for bishops who were not of their own nationality. Other national groups were equally misbehaved and intemperate. In Philadelphia and Buffalo, a number of German and French Catholics completely defied their bishops and were in schism for some years.

But it was the battle over trusteeism that really jeopardized the Church. The growth of trusteeism in the United States has never been explained adequately. Did it arise from the fact that laymen in Colonial days had to stand between the priests and the law, while the Church was still a pseudosecret organization with no standing before the law? Did it grow out of a desire to be like the other colonists, who looked after their churches and hired or fired their ministers at will?

It would seem that the former was the case, because the appointment and removal of pastors and their assistants is strictly the prerogative of bishops. Since most of the work among the Catholics in the thirteen original states was done by Jesuits, we can hardly presume that they did not know what rights belonged to the laity and what rights belonged to the bishops.

The disgraceful quarrels between the Catholics of different nationalities and the struggle over trusteeism, especially in New York state, gave active fuel to the Nativists and Know-Nothings, who were determined to harry the Catholics out of the land. They argued that the struggle between Catholics and their bishops proved the bishops to be tyrants who oppressed their people and would oppress the rest of the country if they could once secure control.

History, it is often said, repeats itself. Just as Catholicism in the colonies had achieved its first measure of freedom and importance at the onset of the Revolution, so, too, the beginning of the Civil War brought approximately the same results. Once again it was seen that all Catholics, especially those of talent and substance, would be needed in the forthcoming struggle. For example, in New York the legislature repealed the notorious Putnam Bill, passed in 1855, forbidding Catholic bishops to hold property in their own name. In fact the Union Government asked the great Archbishop Hughes of New York to go abroad and dissuade foreign governments from aiding or recognizing the Confederacy.

Though bigots were especially active up to the time of the Civil War, we must remember that Catholics received "goodwill and help" from many non-Catholics of prominence. The national government and the Supreme Court kept a consistent watch over the rights of Catholics and "the citizenship of the foreign born."

The growth of the Church after the Revolution was truly phenomenal. By 1852 the 25,000 original Catholics had grown to almost 2,000,000. There were 1,421 priests in six archdioceses, 25 dioceses and 4 vicariates apostolic. These numbers might have seemed as anonymous as all statistics, but they were dramatized in May 1852, when the 32 bishops of the nation met in the first plenary council at Baltimore.

Americans were not the only ones astonished by the first plenary council. The minutes of its sessions were forwarded to Rome and were carefully examined by Pope Pius IX in 1853. The information and maturity he found in the report seemed so fantastically impossible that the Pope decided to send a special envoy who would give him a personal report and a true account of conditions of the Church in America.

For the mission he chose Cajetan Bedini, whose career as a papal diplomat had been long and distinguished. Bedini was accredited only to the American bishops, but he carried a letter to President Franklin Pierce.

Archbishop Bedini was met by Archbishop Hughes and a group of distinguished clergy when he arrived in New York in June 1853. They proceeded to Washington, where they were received ceremoniously. Hughes and Bedini then set out to make a complete investigation of the Church and her institutions. They traveled as far west as Milwaukee, visiting bishops, churches and charitable institutions.

Garibaldi's redshirts followed Archbishop Bedini to the United States, tried to murder him, and incited riots against him in Pittsburgh, Louisville and Cincinnati. Some Nativists aided them in these demonstrations, but the great mass of American Protestants viewed the archbishop's visit with complacency.

After a farewell audience with President Pierce, Bedini departed for Rome. His report to the Pope was most enthusiastic, and some of his comments are particularly worthy of note. He recommended the establishment of a nunciature at Washington, he praised the Irish and the zeal of the American bishops, and strongly recommended the appointment of native-born bishops in the future.

Equally important was his insistence that an American college should be established in Rome for the purpose of augmenting the number of American priests and training teachers for the American seminaries. The Pope donated the original building and founded an institution that was to have an incalculable effect on the American Church.

President Lincoln thought the American Church was important enough to have a cardinal, and he sent an envoy to Rome to make this point. In 1875, Pius IX elevated Archbishop McCloskey to the Sacred College.

From this time forward, the history of the Church in the United States is largely the history of her cardinals.

OUR AMERICAN PRINCES:
The Story of the Seventeen American Cardinals

John Cardinal McCloskey

---◆---

1810 — 1885

I r was the year 1810. James Madison was President of the
United States, then a nation of some 7,250,000. Of this
number there were about 100,000 Catholics. France, under her
triumphant emperor, Napoleon I, firmly controlled the continent of Europe and continued the old struggle with England.
The infant United States, caught between the two giant powers, suffered the confiscation and search of its ships on the high
seas. Public opinion was genuinely aroused, and the United
States was on the brink of war.

The Bill of Rights, ratified in 1791, and covering the first
ten amendments of the Constitution, guaranteed freedom of
worship to all religions. Catholics, long proscribed and con-
strained, were now certain of general toleration and protection
of the law. This added further luster to the appeal of the American frontier for all the oppressed people of Europe.

Not the least of the oppressed were the Irish. The Act of
Union—1800—had completely dispelled all hopes of Irish
freedom. Far more, it led to the harassment of an entire nation
and reduced the living conditions of the people to subnormal
standards. The result was a mass emigration to America such
as the world has seldom seen.

The hardship of the long sea voyage in crowded and
unhealthy sailing ships of any and every kind is a much-told
story. Scarcely less terrible was the condition of the Irish immigrants after their arrival. Too many of them crowded into

primitive slums or shanty areas in Boston, New York and other Eastern cities. For those who were able to find it, menial work was usually the only work available. The Irish became carters, drovers, carpenters' helpers, hod carriers, road menders—or just plain beasts of burden. Many of them, especially the women, went into domestic service.

Despite their poverty, these immigrants clung to their ancient religion, following it in their own peculiar fashion, with fierce pride. It was the same pride which on Independence Day and other holidays brought them out onto New York's Broadway in their cheap finery to mingle with the well-dressed festive crowds: the men in their skintight trousers and tail coats, ruffled shirts and square-topped beaver hats; the women graceful and elegant in their clinging Empire gowns topped with huge velvet poke bonnets gay with ostrich feathers.

It was against this backdrop of mingled light and shadow that John McCloskey was born in the little tree-bowered village of Brooklyn, on March 20, 1810. His parents, Patrick McCloskey and Elizabeth Harron, were both from County Derry, and belonged to the better class of Irish farmers. There was a tradition of learning in both families which could boast priests and doctors among their ancestors.

Patrick McCloskey was fortunate in being one of the rare immigrants whose education and background entitled him to a respectable place in this new land. He was a clerk in the firm of H. B. Pierrepont and had a position of some responsibility. Relations between the Pierreponts and McCloskeys were close and cordial.

Most likely due to the inclement weather, John McCloskey was not baptized until May 6, at St. Peter's Church in Barclay Street. The baby was carried down to the strand of the East River by his father. There the party took a rowboat or the primitive ferry which at the time linked Manhattan and Brooklyn.

Old St. Peter's, which had been opened with pomp and circumstance and many notables in attendance in 1786, was the mother church of the diocese. Its first years were plagued by quarrels between trustees and pastors and more than a little financial difficulty. Mother Seton and other famous converts had been baptized there, and testified to its glory and missionary zeal, but trustee troubles persisted, and as late as 1808 a violent anti-Catholic riot had added further difficulties.

In 1808, Dr. Luke Concannon was appointed the first bishop for the swiftly growing diocese of New York, but war between the French and English made it impossible for the new bishop to take possession of his see. Though he was forced to linger on in Naples, where he died in 1810, Bishop Concannon arranged for the appointment of Father Anthony Kohlmann, S.J., as administrator. Father Benedict Fenwick, S.J., was named assistant.

It is interesting to note that, beginning with his baptism by the future Bishop Fenwick, John McCloskey was intimately associated with many of the most important figures in the early American Church. It was largely through them and their appreciation of the boy's personality and talents that John's way was made easy in achieving the great responsibilities and honors that came to him later in life.

Elizabeth taught her son his prayers and the first facts of his religion, along with reading and writing, but John's formal education began with his attendance at Mrs. Milmoth's Brooklyn school in Red Hook Lane. Mrs. Milmoth was a retired English actress of considerable eminence. Her school attracted some of the best families in New York—the Pierreponts, Cornells, Cuttings and Lugers.

John's attendance there as a young child is clear demonstration of his family's status in the community, and very probably it also shows the continuing interest of the Pierreponts in the boy's future.

One can hardly doubt that Mrs. Milmoth's early training was of advantage to John to the very end of his life; he was widely known for the clear and precise beauty of his enunciation, which he later attributed to Mrs. Milmoth, and was equally notable for his poise and coolness under every circumstance, a quality in keeping with the actor's profession.

When John was about seven years of age the McCloskeys moved across the river to Manhattan, where they lived on Murray Street in St. Peter's Parish. By that time the War of 1812, with its flashing sea battles and Old Hickory's anti-climactic victory at New Orleans, was over. John was enrolled in the Latin school of Thomas Brady, whose own sons later became noted New York lawyers.

In 1820, Patrick McCloskey died at the early age of forty-five after a short illness of six weeks. This must have been a severe blow to John, just beginning his teens. In later years he recalled with gratitude the daily presence of the Jesuit Father Malou as a consoling and strengthening influence in this time of sorrow.

John was ready for college at the age of eleven. Many plans for the boy seem to have been discussed with his guardian, Cornelius Heeney, a former partner of John Jacob Astor. Should it be Columbia, Georgetown or Mount St. Mary's? During this time John's mother bought a farm near Bedford, in Westchester County—a fair indication that her husband's death had not left her in straitened circumstances.

The choice of a college was finally settled in a casual fashion, totally in keeping with the family atmosphere that characterized the Catholic community of those days.

Father Dubois, President of Mount St. Mary's, Emmitsburg, Maryland, and later bishop of New York, was visiting at the Catholic Orphan Asylum in Prince Street. At Heeney's suggestion, John McCloskey was called from Brady's Latin school. It must have been with some excitement that John hurried through the summer heat to an encounter that was so largely to influence his life.

No time was wasted in I.Q. tests or psychological probing. Father Dubois opened his breviary, handed it to the boy, and asked him to translate the Latin. It would be in keeping with Horatio Alger to report that our young hero came through the ordeal with blaring trumpets. Instead, after he had become the first American cardinal, John McCloskey used to relate that his translation was "not satisfactory." Whatever sting there was in the words was assuaged by the smiling assurance of Father Dubois that John's defects would easily be remedied at the "Mountain," as St. Mary's was affectionately known.

The following September, in 1821, John went to Baltimore by steamboat. Doubtless he visited the new Cathedral there— consecrated the previous May by Bishop Marechal—and marveled at its suave dome and lofty proportions, a source of justifiable pride to the infant Church in America.

From Baltimore, a stagecoach carried the boy up into the smoke-blue hills of Maryland. Whatever sense of loneliness went with John faded away in the presence of his sister, already in residence at Mother Seton's school in Emmitsburg.

Education at the Mountain was more than a brisk challenge. The school day began at the early hour of five o'clock, with meditation and Mass, followed by a simple breakfast and a long, demanding series of classes. There was little creature comfort. Even in winter, so the picture comes down to us from various sources, the boys made their morning toilets at a long wooden trough in the schoolyard. In winter the ice had to be broken before ablutions could begin. The smaller boys at the end of the line found the footing precarious as they bent like anxious cats above the ice-bearded edge of the trough and splashed the stinging water over their faces and hair.

There were high challenges for the mind in a thorough grounding in Latin and Greek, philosophy and mathematics. There was warmth for the heart in reading Walter Scott and Fenimore Cooper, and a special lift for Irish pride in the songs of Thomas More, more particularly in his exotic novel-poem, *Lalla Rookh,* which was still winning acclaim. Byron, too, had begun to cut his widest swath.

By graduation, in 1828, John was able to demonstrate that the Mountain had "remedied his deficiences" in no uncertain manner. The evidence comes down to us in a speech the fifteen-year-old boy delivered before the student body; it had selected him as best qualified to deliver the oration on patriotism, a then favorite subject, probably because of Lafayette's long visit and triumphal tour of the United States (1824-1825).

The seven closely written pages of the manuscript are a logical, graceful commentary on Horace's statement: "It is sweet and honourable to die for one's country." In the introduction, John asks to be judged leniently for his lack of years and mature judgment. Any comparison of his sentiments and their completely charming expression with the achievements of boys of like age today will illustrate the vast change in our educational system since 1825.

During his four years of college John had been surrounded with men of force and distinction. Father Dubois later became Bishop of New York; Vice-Rector Bruté, Bishop of Vincennes. One of his schoolmates, John Hughes, whose coadjutor John was to become twenty-three years later, was teaching Latin and mathematics in the college and was prefect of the study hall. Among his fellow students were John Purcell, eventually Archbishop of Cincinnati, and Father Constantine Pise, the writer and chaplain of the United States Senate. In John's graduating class were equally distinguished men, including three future bishops and a noted Jesuit.

Despite this hierarchical chorus, John returned to Bedford for the summer with no firm idea of what his vocation might be. Brady had fancied him for the law; others spoke of politics. John's mother wanted to secure a good position for her son in one of the big countinghouses, ancestors of America's powerful banking system.

John's mental uncertainty was resolved in a dramatic manner at his mother's farm during the winter of 1826-1827. The young man, then eighteen, attempted to drive a team of oxen drawing a heavy load of logs. The wagon overturned and the logs pinned him to the ground. He was found unconscious and carried to the house. For days he was completely blind and his situation critical.

The accident left its mark on his health for the rest of his life. During his convalescence, John decided that God wished him to be a priest. He returned to the seminary at the Mountain and began his new studies in the fall of 1827. An ironic commentary, for John's mother at least, was her success in securing his appointment to one of the great countinghouses, an appointment that might have meant so much two years earlier.

There can be slight doubt that the young man plunged into his new life with enthusiasm. In John's notebooks and papers for these years there is ample evidence of his high purpose and dedication. The notebooks record many things: unusual events, dramatic deaths of students or faculty members, seminary sidelights, notable occasions. Plans for meditation, aspirations, passages from books, all declare the dedication of the young student.

Among the entries is "a terse and full synopsis of the life of St. Francis de Sales," the only notation of its kind in any of the notebooks. It seems fairly obvious that the amiable Bishop of Geneva became John's model, both in sacred eloquence and the tranquil and good-natured manner in which he faced every crisis.

Toward the end of his seminary days John put himself under the spiritual direction of Bishop Bruté. He could hardly have done better. The bishop was deeply spiritual, but had a wide human wisdom and common sense.

By the time John had reached the end of his seminary training he was beginning to have a more precise view of his talents and how they could best be used in the service of the Church. It seemed to him that he was cut out to be a scholar or a teacher rather than a parish priest, and he tried to secure an *exeat* from the diocese of New York, which would have cleared the way for his new ambition.

Bishop Dubois' flock was growing at a fabulous rate, and there was an alarming need for priests. As a result, the bishop refused John's request to leave the diocese and become a teacher.

On January 12, 1834, John was ordained to the priesthood in "Old St. Patrick's Cathedral" on Mulberry Street. A furious snowstorm was raging, making it impossible for his friends to be with him; the dusky reaches of the church were almost deserted. While the wind rattled the windows, drowning the soft hiss of gas jets, John knelt in the luminous sanctuary for the long ceremony of ordination. The weather had also kept the usual throng of priests away. Except for the acolytes and the ministers at the altar, Bishop Dubois moved through the Mass unattended by his usual retinue.

But the joyful dedication of the new priest was obvious to all who saw him, particuarly to his mother and sisters, who were watching his movements with tear-dimmed eyes. Tall, erect, and frail looking as he appeared, there was an aristocratic sureness about him—the nobility of the thinking person who has mastered himself through reflection.

The esteem in which the young priest was held soon showed in the duty assigned him. John was first attached to the old cathedral in Mulberry Street. Added to his priestly duties in the busy parish was the task of looking after Bellevue Hospital and the cemetery on Eleventh Street.

With the opening of the small college and seminary at Nyack, New York, John got a speedy promotion by being named vice-president and professor of philosophy. Father John McGerry, who had been president of the Mountain, was called from Emmitsburg to assume the presidency of the new institution.

Bishop Dubois had fought for his college and seminary; argued with the high-handed trustees, Dr. Power, the vicar-general and many others. For the moment, the bishop seemed triumphant, but his triumph was short lived. Fire destroyed the seminary shortly after its opening in August 1834. There was no insurance on the buildings. The loss to the diocese was a terrible financial blow.

An interesting sidelight into the character and heart of Father McCloskey is to be found in his petition to the vicar-general in 1834, asking to be allowed to help in the work of caring for the sick and dying in the terrible epidemic of Asiatic cholera which was sweeping New York. The request was denied for obvious reasons, but the desire for such dangerous duty was typical of a man of sensibility and courage.

Shortly after the failure of the Nyack college, Father McCloskey approached Bishop Dubois for permission to study in

Rome. The bishop refused, but John was not daunted by the ✓
refusal. Mr. Heeney, his wealthy guardian, came forward with
a hundred persuasions, of which, along with his charge's poor
health, the strongest was the offer of John's mother to defray all
his expenses abroad.

In the face of the young priest's persistence, Bishop Dubois
permitted John to go for advice to Bishop Kenrick of Philadelphia. Kenrick had been a Roman student and could be expected to know a great deal about the expense and wisdom of
the excursion. When John assured Bishop Kenrick that he
meant to spend two or three years in Rome, the bishop advised
him to go.

In giving his final reluctant consent to the excursion, Bishop
Dubois acquiesced with outward good grace, but the following
letter written to Dr. Butler, President of Mount St. Mary's, on
October 7, 1834—a month before John's departure—reveals
the bishop's continuing doubts:

> I suppose, my dear Mr. Butler, that before this time you have
> received as answer from Mr. McCloskey, ordained February 7
> [*sic*], this year, informing you that he had made up his mind and
> applied to me for leave to go to Rome to complete his studies.
> I am far from approving this resolution, which is liable to more
> objections than he is aware of, and I earnestly urged him to go
> in preference to St. Mary's, but having promised him not to
> control him in his desire to improve himself, I could not oppose
> a resolution which he considers as the most suitable for his
> purpose. . . . I was the less inclined to contradict him, as his
> weak constitution is not likely to render him very useful, and
> may be improved by spending some time in Italy. He appears
> more inclined to a sedentary, studious, than to an active life,
> and I am afraid that he may thereby give the last stroke to his
> broken constitution. . . .
>
> Your devoted father in Xt.,
> JOHN, BP. OF N.Y.

John McCloskey's many friends came to the packet boat *Erie*
on November 3 to wish him *bon voyage*. A large number of
them offered their good wishes with sadness, for they thought

—from his pallor and fragile looks—that he had "consumption" and would never return alive. One wonders if John took with him the popular remedy of the day for consumption: "Into the yolks of 2 new laid eggs beat 3 tablespoons rosewater, then mix well in ½ pint of milk fresh from the cow, and sweeten with syrup of capillaire and a little nutmeg grated over."

From John's travel diary we have many sharply etched pictures of the trip to Le Havre, which lasted thirty days. The company he traveled with was distinguished but somewhat coarse in speech. John was often seasick, yet he found time to record a picture of a storm in which the mountainous waves impressed him with their tremendous majesty, particularly at night. On entering the English Channel, there were hours of tension on board the *Erie* over a near collision with another ship.

The overall spirit of the diary is one of joy and good health; the young man felt more and more vigorous with the passing days, which were spent "agreeably and profitably" in reading "travel books, Corneille's best tragedies, *The Life Of Mary Queen Of Scots,* part of Moore's *Life Of Byron,* and on Sunday, Masillon and the *Meditations Of St. Augustine.*"

The trip to Rome, across France by stagecoach to Marseilles and Nice, and thence by boat to Città Vecchia took over three months, during which John enthusiastically recorded his impressions of passing scenes and people.

The first glimpse of Rome, from a distance of twenty miles, threw him into a frenzy of delight. Great moments of its sacred history flashed through his mind as he gazed across the faded green distance to the golden bubble of St. Peter's dome and the Castle of Saint Angelo, glazed with the February sun.

The young student carried with him cordial letters of introduction to many influential people in Rome. Among these were Monsignor Angelo Mai, later Cardinal Mai, Secretary to the Congregation of the Propaganda, the aristocratic Cardinal Weld, and Dr. Cullen, Rector of the Irish College.

Through the good offices of Abbot Count Reisach, John was

eventually installed "in large and commodious quarters" in the convent of the Theatine Fathers, at Sant Andrea della Valle.

John's education was many-sided, and intellectually he made a long leap forward. Rising at six, he offered Mass at the Gesu, in the midst of its inspiring baroque beauty. After the usual Continental breakfast of rolls and coffee, John walked to the Roman College for the brilliant morning lectures of such Jesuits as Perrone and Manera. There was time for study before dinner at noon, and a period of bright chatter with his companion at the Theatine convent, Father Downes of Ireland.

John attended further lectures in the afternoon and found ample time to visit the famous shrines and churches of Rome, in the approved manner of good pilgrims who end all such excursions by visiting the Blessed Sacrament in one or several churches.

"Imagine that you see me [the busy student says in one of his letters] with a high-cocked hat, cassock, silk mantle or cloak according to the weather, and shoes with buckles, walking through the streets of this great city, minding nobody, and nobody minding me—quite at home."

The young priest's sightseeing excursions and close application to study, evidence of which remains in a great mass of manuscript notes, did not interfere with his sparkling social life. Friendships with many notables sprang up and flowered, in addition to those he had begun through letters of introduction; Lacordaire, Wiseman, and Channing, among the most famous, were to remain lifelong friends.

Not the least important of the new acquaintances was Cardinal Flesch, the uncle of Napoleon. John had been introduced to him by Bishop Bruté. It was through this introduction that John became an intimate of the French cardinal's household and met Madame Laetitia, Napoleon's mother. John saw her "propped up in bed eating her breakfast from a little table used by her son on St. Helena, the only article of furniture belonging to Napoleon she has."

Study, exploration of Christian and pagan Rome, excursions to Frascati and the environs of Rome in the heat of the summer, polite discussions with great personalities—it was scant wonder that John savored them all with delight and could consider them well worthwhile, even if he had spent "every cent of his inheritance."

The more than two-year sojourn in the holy city was not without a large dash of sorrow. John's favorite sister Elizabeth died in 1835; Father Anthony Kohlmann, his old friend and adviser, the following year. Though John grieved for both, he tried to accept the will of God and not repine, though he knew how much he would miss them in the years to come.

A picture of Father McCloskey, painted in Rome in 1835, gives us a very good idea of the man as he was seen by his contemporaries. The aristocratic head with its fine poise, wide forehead, classic nose, and shining eyes under well-defined brows, reflects the man of charm and self-possession. The picture also tells us a great deal about the many changes in clerical costume since 1835. The wide Byronic collar with its full black tie—much like those sailors wear today—sets off the wide-draped flowing lapels of the black coat framing the narrow expanse of white shirt front. A voluminous cloak of brown tweedy material is artfully draped over slanting shoulders, with a fashionably romantic carelessness—a far cry from the universal conservatism of today's clerics.

Father McCloskey seems to have been at home in the highest reaches of the Roman *ton* of his day: alert to catch the sparkle of new ideas, wonderfully adept at expressing himself with grace and force, spontaneous in affectionate response to kindness, and a good listener. The impression he made was an enduring one.

With regret, fully expressed in a letter written from Florence, Father McCloskey left Rome for a year's leisurely travel in France, Belgium, Germany, England and Ireland. He had left Rome without sitting for the examination for his doctor's degree; another mark of his independent cast of mind and aristocratic contempt for mere documents as proof of learning.

The land of his ancestors offered the traveler a warm welcome. Fires glowed, candles were lit; there was endless feasting and witty conversation. John accepted all of it with ease and warm gratitude. What interested him was the mind and heart of Ireland, and his love for the heritage showed later in everything he did as a priest, bishop and cardinal.

He was welcomed home by Bishop Dubois, who noted the deepened sense of poise and power in the young priest. As a test of his mettle perhaps, Bishop Dubois appointed John pastor of St. Joseph's Parish on lower Sixth Avenue.

This was the parish whose trustees scorned to receive the literary Dr. Pise, one of the most admired clergyman of his time. John's appointment to Dr. Pise's place, equally resented by the trustees, now brought the young priest into direct conflict with them.

Trusteeism which very likely had gained a foothold in the American Church in the days when Catholicism was proscribed in the colonies and priests had to be cared for and protected —since they had no status in the eyes of the law—placed all the real power in a parish firmly in the hands of the lay trustees. After emerging from the shadows, the infant American Church tried to adapt itself to this condition, although it ran counter to the entire spirit of the hierarchical system.

There was a further reason for enduring the nuisance: men of substance in the early church were not numerous; there was a necessity for dependence upon them. People being what they are, this dependence was often largely repaid by arrogance and self-importance.

When Father McCloskey arrived at St. Joseph's with his books and baggage, he found a barren rectory equipped with a few sticks of broken-down furniture. He was smiling as he put up his crucifix in the dingy office and set about preparing his first sermon, which he preached to a practically empty church.

Undaunted and serene, the pastor continued Sunday after Sunday with his beautifully balanced sermons on human respect, poverty and humility. There was no sharpness in them, but an objective sweetness of doctrine expressed in well-turned phrases.

Father McCloskey ignored the insulting notices the trustees left in the pulpit for him to read; he seemed equally oblivious of the fact that no salary was paid him, no one called to welcome him or consult him. Often enough he cheerfully walked the midnight streets on bogus sick calls planned to provoke and harass him.

Those who cared to pry saw him reading his breviary before the Blessed Sacrament, or busy at a deal table with his books. Once a week he sallied forth to dine with his old friend Dr. Pise.

At the beginning of the struggle, one of those who knew him best said of John McCloskey: "He will not fight but he will conquer."

So it proved to be. Within six months a group of parish women came forward to furnish the rectory; by the year's end the men had come around to make their peace with the gentle pastor who gave no sign that he had conquered. In his eyes the whole affair had been "a misunderstanding" aggravated by human pride. The correctness of the diagnosis was proved by the fact that his greatest opponents became his staunchest friends.

There was little time in which John could enjoy the undisturbed fruits of his triumph. A new force had come into the Diocese of New York with the consecration of John Hughes as coadjutor bishop in 1837. Hughes was a man of ideas, vigor and genuine bravery. One of his first projects had been an attempt to found a permanent seminary for the training of future priests. After a false start in the northern part of the state, Rosehill Manor was purchased at Fordham. The first building, staffed by the Vincentian Fathers, opened in 1840. It was called St. Joseph's Seminary. The second building, opened in June a year later, was known as the College of St. John. No one was surprised to read the news that the widely educated Father McCloskey had been nominated as its first president.

The position proved to be damaging to John's health and led to his return to St. Joseph's Parish in 1842. Two years later, very probably to Father McCloskey's dismay, he was consecrated Coadjutor Bishop of New York, a position to which *1844* he had been recommended by the fifth provincial council of Baltimore in 1843. The new coadjutor bishop of the largest diocese in the United States was only thirty-four. *34 y/o*

McCloskey's selection as a bishop indicated Rome's high respect for his prudence and mental maturity. That he was appointed *coadjutor* assistant had less meaning. Communications between Italy and the new continent were slow and uncertain In the event of war or some other disturbance, distant dioceses might be left without direction for months or years, an eventuality provided for by the appointment of a coadjutor with the right of succession.

Whether by design or mere chance, the consecration of Bishop McCloskey took place in the old St. Patrick's Cathedral in Mott Street, with great splendor on March 10, 1844. It was John's thirty-fourth birthday. We can imagine the joy of his aging mother and his sister Mary as they watched the splendid ceremony in which two other bishops were consecrated along with their beloved John.

There were seventy priests in the sanctuary of the cathedral; a crowd of almost 8,000 Catholics and Protestants jammed the church and spilled out into the surrounding area. The American Church had come a long way since its humble beginnings in Baltimore.

During the four years of his coadjutorship, Bishop McCloskey was busy with a visitation of the diocese. While the lionlike Hughes successfully fought the nativist politicians and the acrimonious battle with trusteeism, his coadjutor was busy strengthening the religious life of the people.

Noted converts of the stamp of Isaac Hecker, founder of the Paulist Fathers—inspired by Newman and the Oxford Movement—came to Bishop McCloskey for advice and encouragement. All confessed that they found him a learned, deeply spiritual man to whom they could completely open their hearts.

In his journeys about the vast diocese, Bishop McCloskey made known the needs of the college and the seminary; the generous response to his appeals assured a steady growth in both institutions. In the three important years between 1844 and 1847, the aggressive Hughes leaned strongly on the advice and unruffled encouragement of his youthful assistant.

The death of his mother brought Bishop McCloskey great sorrow in 1845, but like all his other sorrows, he bore it with a resignation in keeping with his Master and a doctrine which looked forward to the triumphant resurrection of the just.

At the sixth provincial council of Baltimore, Bishop Hughes asked that the northern part of the diocese be divided into the two dioceses of Albany and Buffalo. The building of the Erie Canal and a railroad had brought increasing numbers of Irish immigrants into the territory.

On April 23, 1847, the newly elected liberal Pope, Pius IX, who was to enjoy the longest reign of any pontiff in the history of the Church, erected Albany and Buffalo into separate dioceses. Bishop McCloskey was appointed the first Bishop of Albany, where he was solemnly installed by Bishop Hughes on September 19, 1847. In a written resolution passed by the board of Old St. Patrick's, the departing bishop was warmly commended for his services and given a gift of $800.

The seventeen years of the Albany episcopate were filled with endless labors. The diocese was like a country parish when Bishop McCloskey arrived. When he left it to become the second Archbishop of New York in 1864, it had grown into a splendidly organized diocese with a new cathedral, fine schools and many institutions which cared for all the social needs of the people.

The tremendous changes were largely achieved with light discipline and fatherly gentleness; Bishop McCloskey was their shepherd, they were his children. Priests and people grieved to see him go. Their grief was expressed in resolutions and tearful personal calls and in the princely gift of $4,000—a modest fortune in those days.

Proof of the bishop's spirituality and fatherliness are found in many documents. Less known but equally revealing of his alertness, self-possession and wit upon every occasion, are several stories that have come down to us from the Albany years.

On one occasion the bishop was traveling in a smoky coach of one of the early trains. Suddenly the conductor appeared in the doorway, shouting that the train was about to collide with some object. With the agility of a professional sprinter, the bishop dashed to the end of the coach. He was just getting off the platform when the collision took place. Though Bishop McCloskey injured his ankle, he had escaped the fate of a man in a seat nearby, who was killed.

More delightfully revealing was the occasion of the arrival at the bishop's office of a delegation from Utica, New York. This was a belligerent faction which disliked its pastor, Father McFarland, and wished to have him removed. Like most Irish, they were both vocal and explosive. Bishop McCloskey listened to the long-winded tirades in silence. His hands were relaxed in his lap, and had they been alert to more than their grievance, the accusers might have noted a twinkle in the bishop's blue eyes and a slight quirk coming and going at the corners of his mouth.

Silence fell at last. Then the bishop spoke in his elegantly modulated voice: "Gentlemen, your petition shall be granted very shortly. I have just received from Rome the bull appointing your pastor Bishop of Hartford." Then he left them to their consternation.

By the time the delegation arrived back in Utica, its members had all become ardent supporters of the new bishop; doubly important and proud of their ability to be the first to spread the good news of his elevation.

For Bishop McCloskey himself, the move back to New York at the height of the Civil War was distasteful. The Diocese of Albany had become very dear to him, and he was able to conduct its affairs with the gentle love of a true shepherd. When, after the death of Archbishop Hughes, on January 3, 1864, rumors began to mention McCloskey's name for the vacant post, the bishop took decided and vigorous action.

In a letter to Cardinal Reisach, the powerful head of propaganda, John roundly declared his "anxiety and fear" at the rumors. He begged the help of his old friend of Roman days in preventing his removal from Albany. The reasons advanced were the greater fitness for the post of Bishop Timon of Buffalo, or Dr. Spalding of Baltimore, and John's "misery" at the thought of being placed "in a position for the duties and responsibilities of which I feel myself both physically and morally, wholly unfit and unequal."

In evaluating this letter, it is customary to interpret it solely as an indication of Bishop McCloskey's humility and distaste for high office. There can be no doubt whatsoever that he shunned the limelight and had an intense personal distaste for positions in which he would be compelled to dictate to others. In this he was much like Pius X.

In Albany he had managed to create a warm family atmosphere in which affection and love were the touchstones. To move from this idyllic calm into the greatest city in the commonwealth—torn by internecine strife and still licking its wounds from the terrible antidraft riots of the year before in which over a thousand had been killed and wounded—seemed to demand a forceful genius for affairs that John could not find in himself.

But once the matter was settled and the official bulls had arrived, Bishop McCloskey steeled himself to obey the Pope's command. Archbishop McCloskey took the night boat from Albany on August 6, 1864, and arrived in New York the following morning. Accompanied by his secretary and Father Conroy, the archbishop proceeded to his new residence at 218 Madison Avenue, where he celebrated Mass at 9:30.

After Mass, he went down to the reception room; a woman was waiting to see him. To his enormous surprise, the agitated female, not knowing his identity, claimed to be his mother and assured him of her determination to live in his house.

By the time the police arrived, the stranger had locked herself and her trunk in the reception room. A policeman managed to enter by a balcony window, and the woman was carted off to the nearest police station.

When the archbishop arrived at the station to make his official charge, the bland-faced police captain, either because of bias or the aplomb of the woman, maintained that: "She told a very straight story for a crazy woman."

The woman was brought up from her cell, the charge was made, and the archbishop turned to leave. At this moment the prisoner began to rave and cry, "Are you going to leave me here with these rascals? They attempted to ruin me . . ."

Turning to the indignant scarlet-faced official, the archbishop said sweetly, "Yes indeed, she tells a very straight story." With that he left the police station.

Archbishop McCloskey's sermon at his installation outlined his goals clearly. He paid unstinting praise to the courage and achievements of the great Hughes and spoke modestly of his own competence. The primary emphasis of the oration was on peace, unity, respect for the hierarchical order of the Church, loyalty, and religious pride in the splendid things already achieved. In his conclusion, he spoke of the glory and influence of St. Patrick and prayed that his children in the new world "may never bring disgrace or dishonor on the name of their great saint."

For the remainder of the war and in the confused years of the reconstruction period that followed, Archbishop McCloskey gave a shining example in seeking to reconcile all the dissident elements in his diocese and the United States, whether from the north or south.

At home, with imperturbable good sense, he settled long-established misunderstandings with the Jesuits and other religious. It was also through his efforts that St. Joseph's at Troy, New York, became a successful seminary for the entire district, including New England.

Outside the diocese, the archbishop was a strong influence for reconciliation and order. The second plenary council of Baltimore was opened in October 1866 with 7 archbishops, 47 bishops and several abbots in attendance, accompanied by their aides and secretaries. They met in complete concord and fraternal respect, re-emphasizing the ideas of peace and harmony which they had stressed during the recent conflict.

The honor of preaching the opening sermon was given to

Archbishop McCloskey. In it he paid tribute to ideas of progress, the mystical body, the eternal youth of the Church and her infallibility. In his practical conclusion, the archbishop emphasized the spiritual nature of their work and the necessity of promoting proper ecclesiastical discipline.

The sermon was widely acclaimed by everyone, including Father Gibbons, the future Cardinal of Baltimore. Gibbons was the more astonished at the finished performance because he knew McCloskey had received a telegram announcing the burning of his cathedral just before he mounted the pulpit.

Gibbons' curiosity prompted him to question the archbishop the next morning about his wonderful self-control and composure under such trying circumstances. The reply was remarkable in its laconic simplicity: "The damage was done, and I could not undo it."

In the actual work of the council, Archbishop McCloskey strongly urged the necessity for education on the parochial level in industrial schools, and finally in a future Catholic university to be founded for the use of the whole United States. He was equally positive about the need for providing good children's books, and he desired parents to be on their guard against immoral literature of every kind.

Of all the archbishop's forward-looking and notable works, the erection of St. Patrick's Cathedral must be given first place. Bishop Hughes had laid the cornerstone of the building on the Feast of the Assumption in 1858. Seven bishops and 130 priests participated in the ceremony while 100,000 people watched. The Civil War put a stop to progress on the building. The project was dear to the archbishop's heart, and he spoke of it in and out of season. It was so vivid in his mind that he was able to make people see it as an accomplished and splendid reality that appealed to their pride and opened their purses. More and more of his own personal funds found their way into this building, so that at the end of his life he was almost a pauper.

Over and above his monetary gifts was the archbishop's continuing zeal for the beauty of this House of God; his own innate good taste, familiarity with the best on the Continent, and humility in consulting experts of every kind, played a large part in the final superb result.

Though Archbishop McCloskey appeared successful in everything he undertook, it must be emphasized that he had many sorrows and rebuffs, but his native tranquillity and spiritual orientation helped him to keep his private sorrows to himself.

In 1869, at the invitation of Pio Nono, Archbishop McCloskey, bearing expensive gifts from New York for the Pope, attended the Vatican Council with distinguished prelates from the entire world. Many of these were old friends, including Cardinal Reisach, one of the most important shapers of the council. Archbishop McCloskey was given an important post on the commission for church discipline.

The council opened with great splendor in the right wing of St. Peter's. Its first sessions led to important definitions concerning the Church and its organization. This period of cooperation and good-fellowship ended when the question of papal infallibility was advanced on the agenda. Feeling ran high on the subject. The infallibility of the Pope had been tacitly accepted from the earliest ages of the Church, but when it came to a question of being defined, many sharp divergencies of opinion began to be voiced with the utmost intemperateness. The liberals would have none of it; bishops of the right sought to overdo it. Between these extremes were many who believed that the time was not ripe for such a definition. There seems little doubt that Archbishop McCloskey was among the middle group. Yet after all the acrimonious debate, at the final vote, McCloskey voted for the much narrowed definition, along with the great majority of bishops.

It was the last public triumph of Pius IX. Shortly after, in 1870, the Franco-Prussian War began; the council was prorogued; Rome fell to the waiting troops of Victor Emmanuel; the Pope became the "Prisoner of the Vatican."

In the midst of the sorrows that came to the Church in the *Kulturkampf* in Germany, and the vilification of the Holy

Father in Italy, Archbishop McCloskey—following the example of Pio Nono—made a much publicized spiritual gesture by publicly dedicating to the Sacred Heart all the dioceses of his province.

The selection of the windows, altars and ornaments of his cathedral took up much of the archbishop's time in the following years, necessitating several journeys to France.

It had been rumored for almost a decade that an American would be named to the College of Cardinals. Dispatches in several papers—as early as 1864—had seemed to confirm the rumors.

Strangely enough, President Lincoln himself had suggested, through a special envoy to the Holy See, that it was high time the United States had a cardinal. Secretary of State Cardinal Antonelli had ridiculed the idea, but when the envoy quietly stood his ground, the thought of appointing an American to the Sacred College began to make real progress.

In a good-natured exchange of letters between Archbishops Spalding and McCloskey, each had tried to wish the honor on the other. One of Archbishop Spalding's letters about the rumor has a humorous cast which is quite in accord with the bigotry of the time.

> I presume [Spaulding wrote McCloskey] that the correspondent of the *Pall Mall Gazette* blundered fully as much in the assertion that there was any idea of my receiving the red hat as he did in saying that I was an Irishman! So far from receiving the red hat, it is not at all impossible—though I deem it scarcely probable—that I may have my black or purple one knocked off.

The persistent rumors were revived again in 1875, but this time they concerned Archbishop McCloskey alone. It was thought significant that Pius IX had signaled him out at the Vatican Council, and many considered this a clear indication of the coming honor.

The truth of the revived rumor was finally borne out in a message from McCloskey's agent in Rome, the Cavalieri Scalzi: "Congratulations on your elevation to the Cardinalate.

I await instructions in regard to meeting the expenses of Consistory, Briefs and Bulls."

The new cardinal received the astonishing news with tranquil common sense, since he felt the honor came to the American Church rather than to himself. Somewhat humorously, he exclaimed, "O, it was Cardinal Cullen got me into this box." If the cardinal was not overly excited, the United States was. Banner headlines proclaimed the news, thousands of congratulatory letters poured in, committees formed; in saloons and salons it was the burning topic of the day. Both Protestants and Catholics welcomed the honor as a mark of growing American prestige.

The original schedule for the conferring of the honor had to be changed because part of the cardinal's costume failed to arrive from France.

Finally on April 27, 1875, the ceremony of the bestowal of the biretta took place at the cathedral in Mott Street, which was jammed to the doors with all the outstanding figures in the city. The sanctuary blazed with light refracted colorfully from the dazzling uniforms of the participants and the two purple-draped thrones—that of the new cardinal on the right of the altar, and on the left the one for Archbishop James Roosevelt Bayley of Baltimore.

The Pope's legate, Monsignor Roncetti, attended by Count Marefoschi and Dr. Ubaldi in brilliant court uniforms, handed the scarlet biretta to Archbishop Bayley, who imposed it on the head of the kneeling cardinal.

It was a moment of personal joy for the two men. Father McCloskey had, years before, guided the confused Bayley into the haven of the Church and his present eminence; there had always been an affectionate bond between them.

The grave pageantry of the investiture was outdone on June 23 as Mount St. Mary's welcomed her most famous son. So great was the number of distinguished visitors that the students had to sleep in the barns, outbuildings or under the stars.

It was strictly an intimate, rowdily cordial and thoroughly family affair. When the cardinal rose from "his great satin throne, on the back of which was suspended a laurel wreath, and the top of which was tipped by a big bouquet of cardinal roses specially sent by the New York *Herald*, there was tremendous cheering.

When it had finally subsided, the cardinal, pointing his long finger at the clock, alluded to the shortness of time and then made a brief speech which concluded with the words: "Whatever I am, whatever I may be, under God's providence, I owe to this institution, more than any other here or elsewhere. Hurrah for the old Mountain!" He gaily waved his scarlet biretta as the cheers rattled the windows.

Cardinal McCloskey took possession of his titular church, Santa Maria Sopra Minerva, in a brilliant ceremony—and had several intimate visits with Pius IX—on August 30, 1875. Because of the illness of Pius IX, who died February 8, 1878, the new cardinal did not actually receive his red hat until March 20, 1878. Pope Leo XIII conferred the honor in a speech gracefully complimentary to both the cardinal and his swiftly growing nation.

The last years of Cardinal McCloskey's life were years of illness and pain, starred with great moments of his old vigor and joy. A splendid fair, held in the shell of the new cathedral in 1878, raised almost $200,000, which made it possible to dedicate the edifice on May 25, 1879.

The achievement was a real one. Who would have thought, in 1810, that in the span of eighty years, a weak and struggling community would have grown sufficiently in strength and substance to be symbolized by the most beautifully opulent church in the United States? It had come into being largely through the small gifts of innumerable poor immigrants, and it bespeaks their love and honor for all time to come.

The cardinal's last great burst of joy was on the occasion of the golden jubilee of his priesthood on January 12, 1884. Bishops, priests, and people paid him nation-wide tribute. Among the many beautiful gifts was a jeweled chalice from Pope Leo XIII.

All through 1885, the cardinal suffered bouts of fever, and

intense pain. For extended periods his sight was affected and he was unable to read. Those about him saw no change in the tranquil exterior he had always shown the world. He seemed content to pray in the quiet he had long desired. Those who stood at his deathbed on October 10, 1885 watched his quiet departure with anguish and were touched to note his youthful appearance after death. The body lay in state for two days in the lovely cathedral he had built. Over 150,000 people passed the bier to look upon the tranquil countenance of their good shepherd.

The Solemn Requiem Mass in St. Patrick's brought prelates, notables—and the thronging poor—to pay their last tribute. The cardinal had truly "won the hearts of the people," as Cardinal Gibbons said with vibrant emotion in his fine panegyric.

With the last absolution, the body was laid to rest under the high altar. Those with a sense of history knew in their hearts that never again in the history of the United States hierarchy would they see his like—a life reaching from the childhood of the American Church to its vigorous and full maturity; a momentous development in which John McCloskey had played a memorable and determining part.

James Cardinal Gibbons

1834 – 1921

O N a torrid day, July 23, 1834, James Gibbons was born in Baltimore, Maryland. Thomas Gibbons, his father, and his mother Bridget Walsh, came from a line of small farmers in Ireland. They had emigrated for political reasons, first to Canada and then to Baltimore, in the 1820's. Tom Gibbons was a man of enterprise and optimistic nature and soon became a citizen of his adopted country; in an equally short time he was the trusted employee of an import firm—a kind of peripatetic cashier who carried to the office the money brought by incoming clipper ships and the outgoing expense money for those about to sail.

A few days after James' birth, his godparents carried the newborn baby to the Cathedral of the Assumption nearby, where he was baptized. Andrew Jackson had been elected President in 1829, and the country assumed many of the rough homespun qualities of the man in the White House. With this came the snobbery of nativism, which gave rise to a hatred of all things foreign, particularly the Catholic Church. The bogus disclosures of Maria Monk fanned the hatred into riots and bloodshed. Along with the 100-percent Americanism, came a 100-percent bank panic, loss of savings, and wide unemployment.

For the Gibbons family, these trials were multiplied by the illness of their father, and on the orders of the family doctor, they stored their furniture with relatives and returned to Ireland.

The soft air of the green land did much to encourage the invalid, and he bought a small farm in Ballinrobe, County Mayo, and in his spare time also ran a general store.

When he was seven, James was sent to a small school in Abbey Street, in preparation for his entrance into a classical academy devoted to Latin, Greek and English literature. In keeping with the public-school spirit of the time, every boy was expected to take part in sports: wrestling, boxing, cricket, handball and swimming. James Gibbons was wiry and muscular; he enjoyed all sports with the kind of quiet, concentrated fury that characterizes the winner. In nearby Westport, James also came in touch with the Irish love of horses and racing for which he had an interest and fondness his whole life long.

It is interesting that Gibbons first close friend was a Protestant, Charles Clark, "a neighbor and one of the few Protestant families in the county"; an early introduction perhaps to the tolerant spirit and completeness of understanding which in later years enabled Gibbons to open the first intelligent dialogue between Catholics and Protestants in the United States.

James early learned to serve Mass in the parish church at Ballinrobe, made his First Communion at the usual age, and was confirmed while still very young.

Things were going well in Ireland when the dread blight and the ensuing potato famine struck the land. Hundreds of thousands left their despairing country in wave after wave of emigration. In the midst of this terrible time, Thomas Gibbons, never strong, died of cholera.

After his death, Bridget Gibbons kept the memories of America vivid in the minds of her children by telling them entrancing tales of life in Baltimore as they sat around the blazing peat fire in the long winter evenings.

She was determined to return to the United States, but the disturbed state of affairs forced her to delay for six years. Periods of bigotry and riot defaced the American scene; the revolutionary spirit swept governments in and out of power in Europe, including Pius IX, who was forced to flee from Rome to Gaeta, in the disguise of a country doctor.

Finally, in 1853, deeming the time ripe, Bridget split the family into two groups as a precautionary measure, and the voyage was begun. James, John and Bridget narrowly escaped death in the wreck of their ship off the Bahamas on March 17, but were finally united with their worried mother and her two other children in New Orleans.

Life was not easy in New Orleans. James found a job in a grocery store run by William Raymond. The salary was three dollars a week, but young Gibbons soon earned a small raise, due to his industry and ingratiating way with customers. In a short time his employer trusted him and looked upon him as a son.

The affectionate interest was providential, for yellow fever struck the city in an epidemic wave that took one in ten. People walked about with muffled faces; at night they shivered with fear as they heard the carts rumbling through the city and the piercing cry: "Bring out your dead!"

When James Gibbons became a victim, his sister Bridget devoted herself to him, scarcely leaving his side until the fever was spent. Each evening Mr. Raymond came to inquire about the young patient, bringing food and delicacies for the sick man and his family; he probably also paid the medical expenses of the long illness and convalescence.

The trial turned the young man's thoughts inward; he saw from his recent experience how short and fragile a thing life is. Prayer became a solace and an inspiration for him, and his thoughts began to center on the priesthood as he pondered whether or not God was calling him. The writings of Orestes Brownson spoke to the boy's heart of the greatness of the Church and the necessity for dedicated workers in the Lord's vineyard.

During the spring of 1854, his doubts disappeared. The city had been electrified by a Redemptorist mission given at St. Joseph's Church. The fiery preaching of Father Walworth, who was later, with Isaac Hecker, to found the Society of St. Paul the Apostle, revealed to Gibbons what he was and where his duty lay.

Each night he walked across the city to his home, more and more excited with the glorious prospect he saw opening before him. He undoubtedly discussed the possibilities with his family. In such a discussion, his mother and three sisters were sure to be on the affirmative side. In their minds no profession could compare with the priesthood. His strong-willed mother must have pointed out that his younger brother John was old enough to take over the principal burden of supporting the family; she and the girls would take care of the rest.

There were arrangements to be made with the Archbishop of Baltimore through the parish priest. There were undoubtedly hectic days preparing his wardrobe and the necessary supplies for his long absence, and the inevitable joyously tearful farewells as he boarded the river boat.

The journey to Baltimore took sixteen leisurely days up the Mississippi and Ohio to Wheeling, and thence by stagecoach to Baltimore and to St. Charles' College at nearby Ellicott City. Gibbons was a few years older than most of the boys in his class, but the thoroughness of his Irish training in the classics and literature put him far in advance of his fellow students. They might have resented the attainments of the smiling gray-eyed boy with the fair hair who seemed at once shy and so sure of himself, but once they saw him on the playing field and in the rough and tumble of college life, they discovered him worthy of respect and liking. Though he was only five feet, eight inches tall, Gibbons was like a coil of steel springs and played football with the ferocity of a mongoose.

Due to his Irish training and fierce determination, James finished his college course in two years. Those years had their joys and difficulties. The rules were monastic and strictly enforced. At first the friendly Gibbons had trouble with the rule of the great silence, from night prayers until after Mass next morning, and he sometimes set his will against the strongly individual eccentricity of some of his teachers. There were a thousand rough jokes to offset the disappointments.

On one occasion, a greenhorn Irish student was the reader for day. The book was *The Genius Of Christianity*. The nervous young lector announced the title of the work and alchemized the name of Chateaubriand into Kate O'Brien. The prefects had a hard time restoring order in the dining room that night.

Gibbons came to love and admire his teachers for their devotion to the stern rule they enforced, since he could see how completely they observed it themselves. The Sulpicians were to remain his favorite order through all the long years as Archbishop of Baltimore.

James graduated in the spring of 1857. Though not at the top of his class, his graceful manner of speaking and skill in rhetoric caused him to be chosen to deliver the commencement address.

That same fall he returned to Baltimore and entered St. Mary's Seminary on Paca Street, which bigots referred to as the "priest factory." A severe bout with malaria soon after his arrival almost finished his seminary career.

The four years that followed were brimful of mental activity in the intensive study of philosophy and theology. Prayer and meditation were largely the only recreations, except for a weekly walk into the country. These walks, taken by some forty young men in long black coats and silk hats, with a priest-prefect at the head and end of the long file, proved an incitement to the bigots. In addition to jeers and curses showered on them, there were frequent barrages of stones and an occasional gunshot. Looking back, we can admire the courage that refused to be intimidated by lawlessness, but we can doubt the wisdom of the provocation.

At the end of four years, Gibbons graduated with excellent marks and the highest tributes to his talent and industry. The Civil War broke out before he could receive the last of his major orders. Baltimore, like Gibbons himself—southern in heart, northern in head—went through a terrible time of riot and bloodshed. In May 1861, it was finally occupied by Union troops whose cannon dominated the city from Federal Hill. Martial law was proclaimed.

Early in June, Gibbons received the subdiaconate from

Bishop Kenrick in St. Mary's Chapel, and on the 13th he was ordained a priest. The learning, kindliness and love of children which the young priest saw in his bishop were the models he followed for the remainder of his life.

Soon after ordination, Father Gibbons received his first assignment, to Fells Point in Baltimore. The pastor, James Dolan, was a rugged individualist; the parish was a tough one. Dolan was highhanded and considered assistants a necessary and temporary evil. Gibbons lasted longer than most. At the end of six weeks, Father Dolan sent his assistant to St. Bridget's, a mission church he had established a year before in nearby Canton. The rudimentary rectory was built against one wall of the church, which was in the most dangerous neighborhood in the district.

On one occasion, Gibbons found a rum-fragrant soldier asleep in the church cemetery. Upon being awakened, the man grabbed a fence paling, and foaming and cursing, rushed toward the slight priest. Gibbons stepped neatly aside and felled his assailant with a single punch. The old boxing training in Ballyrobe had paid off.

In addition to St. Bridget's, Father Gibbons was given the care of St. Lawrence, about a mile across the Patapsco River. On Sundays, his duties there and in St. Bridget's were so demanding that he never had breakfast until one o'clock in the afternoon. In time, his naturally weak stomach sustained further damage, and for the rest of his life he picked at his food like a bird.

The plight of the soldiers and prisoners of war led Gibbons to volunteer as a chaplain at Fort McHenry and Fort Marshall. These duties brought him many difficulties because of his refusal to count loyalties where souls were concerned.

By the time the war was over, Father Gibbons had thoroughly earned the goodwill of Canton and the entire district. Devotion to duty, a mild and optimistic outlook, excellent sermons and abundant common sense had brought him to the attention of the new Archbishop of Baltimore, Martin Spaulding.

Spaulding, whose health was not good, needed an intelligent

secretary and he offered the job to Father Gibbons. James hesitated for a little and then decided that the burden was one sent by his Lord and he could not refuse it. Some measure of Gibbons' popularity and worth may be seen in the fact that a delegation from Canton waited on Archbishop Spaulding and begged him not to take Father Gibbons away from them.

In his new job, Father Gibbons made himself increasingly useful. Among other tasks, he helped with the priestly duties at the cathedral and gradually came to be known as the right hand of the bishop.

In 1866, Spaulding, with papal approval, summoned the bishops of the country to a plenary council in Baltimore. Many of the details of the significant meeting were left in the capable hands of Gibbons, who came to know most of the bishops intimately. After two weeks of discussion, the meeting closed with ecclesiastical splendor. All Baltimore watched the colorful procession going into the cathedral, and a murmur of surprise went through the crowd when the carriage of President Johnson arrived.

Among the acts of the council was the suggestion that a new Vicariate of North Carolina be created. Along with the recommendation to Rome, went the names of three candidates for bishop of the new office of vicar. Gibbons' name led the list. In forwarding the names, Spaulding described his secretary in warm terms.

James was at once disturbed and excited; he was reluctant to leave Baltimore and the amiable atmosphere of the bishop's house, but he yearned for his own diocese and the great possibilities of engrossing missionary work.

While he waited through the winter of 1868 for the necessary confirmation from Rome, Gibbons serenely carried on his duties and even found time to attend a reading and lecture by Charles Dickens, who loved American dollars as much as he hated American ways.

The consecration of Bishop Gibbons finally took place on August 16, 1868, in the Cathedral of the Immaculate Conception. Seven bishops were in attendance; the papers were filled with fervid praise of the "youngest bishop in the world." Bishop Gibbons was only thirty-three years old.

Everyone saw that the tasks before the new bishop would require heroism of the highest order. North Carolina was a Catholic zero; the new bishop had neither cathedral nor house; his few subjects were scattered in cities and pine barrens over a vast territory. It is significant that among the bishop's gifts was $100 from the crusty Father Dolan, along with a promise of two chasubles.

Gibbons arrived in Wilmington to find things worse than he had expected. The state was overrun by northern carpetbaggers and rascals of every stripe who were using the Negroes for gain and revenge upon the South. North Carolina was, as Gibbons said, "a desert." Of its 1,000,000 inhabitants, 700 were Catholic. Only three towns had churches, and there were but three priests beside the bishop to serve a territory of 50,000 square miles.

On a day of lashing rain, Spaulding installed his protégé in the Church of St. Thomas the Apostle, a poor brick-and-stucco church that was to be his cathedral. Bishop Spaulding concluded his hour-long sermon with a warm recommendation for Bishop Gibbons: "I know him well. He is beloved by all who knew him in Baltimore. I know you will like him. He improves with acquaintance. Though he will be found uncompromising in his principles, he will be charitable to all, assist all, irrespective of sect or creed."

Bishop Gibbons, accompanied by his eccentrically charitable assistant Father Mark Gross, began an apostolic visitation of his diocese that lasted for almost a year. By wagon, water, train, or on horseback, he was forever moving about, between returns to the poverty-stricken lean-to that served as his home base. He met bigotry and ignorance everywhere, but his mildness and his clear-cut sermons, his charm of manner and quick humor, made innumerable friends and turned difficult situations into triumphs for the Church. Many converts were made. Best of all, the bishop found that there was a reservoir of goodwill that could be tapped for the advantage of religion. Protestant churches, courthouses, village halls, garrets and taverns, all proved to be excellent launching pads for his apostolic zeal.

He found encouragement and humor in everything. Some of his stories are gems, such as the one about the North Carolina Irishman whose Baptist friends persuaded him to be immersed. After his immersion, he was requested to pray, and obligingly did so with a fervent recital of the Hail Holy Queen. Needless to say, he did not long remain a Baptist.

In September 1869, Bishop Gibbons was summoned to Rome for the Vatican council. The change from primitive life to the magnificence that is papal Rome was heartening, though there was still a strong spur to humility and a rumor of home in the cold austere cells of the North American College where the American bishops were housed. St. Peter's impressed Gibbons as few churches had. Perhaps it is better to say that he was completely enthralled with everything he saw in the Eternal City and so impressed with the council that he didn't miss a single session. It was a record few could match. His daily journals still remain one of the best accounts of what actually took place in the various sessions.

Pius IX had been severely criticized for calling the council at a time when the Church was under fire in Europe and the governments of the Continent were largely in a state of revolutionary turmoil. The criticism stemmed largely from a misreading of the character of this great pope and the meaning of his actions. It is so easy to say that he was a liberal pope until he was forced to flee from Rome, and a confirmed conservative ever after. Unfortunately this interpretation does not explain his actions and achievements with any degree of logic.

The flight to Gaeta proved to Pius IX that only supernatural and spiritual means were of value in combating the sickness and heresy of the times. He turned to the strengthening of dogmatic truth, a revivification of missionary zeal and activity the world over—especially in the Americas—and the creating of institutes and congregations fit for the spiritual work of the Church in our times. The political maneuvers he largely left to Antonelli.

The Vatican council was the climax of his massive effort to centralize and spiritualize the Church. The creation of the modern papacy is his greatest achievement. What seemed to be a defeat was in reality a conquest.

Gibbons saw and acknowledged how much good was done at the council. In regard to the doctrine of infallibility which, because of the intemperateness with which it was debated, came to overshadow other great accomplishments, Gibbons is objective and fair. He himself believed it, and so did a majority of the fathers. But most of the minority party—some of the brightest luminaries in the Church—felt the time was not ripe for such a definition. They were also convinced that the definition would prove to be a stumbling block to the well-disposed Christians in the Protestant world and in Eastern orthodoxy. The minority finally gave in with poor grace by absenting themselves before the final voting. In the midst of a furious storm of lightning and thunder that lashed the great church, infallibility became a defined dogma.

Bishop Gibbons, because of the needs of his diocese and its poverty, had considered asking permission to go home. With the onset of the Franco-Prussian War, his problem answered itself. The council recessed, the Piedmontese prepared to take over Rome, and the fathers of the council scattered to the four corners of the globe.

After a short tour of the British Isles and Germany, Gibbons made a special pilgrimage to Annecy to honor St. Francis de Sales, the saint of his heart and imitation.

The *City Of Brussels* bore him back to the United States on a furious autumn ocean of mountainous waves. He was happy to be home. His travels abroad had taught him many lessons, chief of which was a renewed love of the freedom and liberty found in his own country.

Sometimes it seemed to Gibbons that he was forever on the road visiting, begging, persuading, preaching, confirming, baptizing. Yet he was finding rewards in his work. A school system began to emerge, converts multiplied, churches sprang up as if by a miracle. There was a feeling of at-homeness in his cour-

teous reception almost everywhere by Protestants and Catholics, and he dared hope he was loved and admired—a climate
in which he always worked best. Hard work was good, but it
was much better and took on added gloss when it was appreciated.

In his absence, his people had built him a house. It wasn't
much of a mansion, but it was comfortable and snug. No more
would he wake on cold mornings to find that sprinkles of snow
or sleet had sifted in onto the floor and bedclothes.

One day he said to the unworldly Father Gross, "You know, it
would be a good thing if you were to write a book summing up
the truths and mysteries of our faith in a calm objective fashion. It would do incalculable good."

Father Gross looked at the bishop with the innocence of a
child. "Why don't you write it, Bishop?" he queried. "Everyone seems to like the way you explain things."

Gibbons chuckled. "I will write it," he said. Once the idea
had taken hold of him, he attacked it with his usual fury. He
finished the first chapter in a day, and a few months later the
entire work was done except for a few corrections made later
out of charity toward "our separated brethren."

The title, "Faith of Our Fathers," taken from Faber's celebrated hymn, summed up the work admirably. The antiquity
of history and scripture was there, and the perennial newness
that is the miracle of the Faith.

For over fifty years, the book dominated the field, and millions of copies were sold. Through its uncompromising but gentle persuasion, hundreds of noted converts came into the
Church.

The death of Bishop Gill of Richmond brought Gibbons
new responsibility. He was appointed administrator of the diocese in 1872, in addition to his already heavy responsibility in
North Carolina. His smile was a little grim when he realized
how amply he bore out the old saw, "The willing horse gets the
load." On June 30 of the same year he became Bishop of Richmond. It was a move up the ladder of ecclesiastical preferment,

but the diocese was poor and plagued with the same difficulties and poverty he had known so well in North Carolina.

The death of Archbishop Martin J. Spaulding on February 7, 1872, after a long illness, had brought to the See of Baltimore the aristocratic Bishop James Roosevelt Bayley, a noted convert from the Episcopal Church. Bayley was a chronic invalid. The climate of Baltimore did not please him, and his heart was still back in Newark where he had first been bishop.

Because of frequent bouts of illness, he had to call in Bishop Gibbons to assist him. As time went on, Bayley came to rely more and more on this willing and well-balanced helper. Appreciation warmed into affection, and Bayley finally requested the appointment of Gibbons as Coadjutor Bishop of Baltimore, with the right of succession. The papers came to Bishop Bayley in Paris during the beginning of his last illness, and were hurriedly signed and sent back to Rome. Bayley returned to Newark, and within a short time he was dead; Gibbons began his reign as Archbishop of Baltimore on October 3, 1877, at the age of forty-three.

He felt that he was much more than the Bishop of Baltimore. Washington was in his diocese, and the actions of the President and the Congress very much concerned him. Early in his reign, he began to accept Washington invitations to dinners and receptions. In this fashion he met the President and many cabinet members socially. His lack of pretense, easy manners, width of understanding and patriotic convictions, endeared him to many of his new acquaintances. Most of them had never seen a Catholic bishop at such close range. What they discovered in Gibbons was pleasing and memorable.

Thus the way was paved for his intervention with President Hayes in behalf of the Catholic Indians in 1878. The President went out of his way to compliment the work of the Catholic missionaries among the Indians, and the friendly conversation pleased Gibbons.

In the fall of the same year, he commended the observance of Thanksgiving to his priests and people. The pastoral letter caused a lifting of eyebrows; up to this time, the feast had seemed to be largely Protestant, and Gibbons' enthusiastic recommendation gave it a new slant and wider implication.

With the election of Leo XIII to the papal throne in 1878, new currents of thought and action began to appear. Word from the new Holy Father suggested that a plenary council of American bishops be held in Baltimore. Gibbons hesitated. Bigotry had abated somewhat, and he feared that such a council might be considered a provocation. Yet, on the Pope's wise insistence, he began the careful preparation for the significant meeting.

A thoughtfully prepared agenda was mulled over in Rome with Leo XIII and the bishops of the Curia Romana. It had been expected that Cardinal McCloskey would preside, but he was ill when the convocation day drew near, and the Pope appointed Archbishop Gibbons to be his legate. All Baltimore buzzed with expectation. On the opening day, the streets and rooftops were crowded with people watching the pageantry.

The work of the council, skillfully maneuvered by Gibbons, was important. The number of holy days to be observed by American Catholics, the strengthening of Church discipline and administration, and the settling of many points of protocol and procedure were crowned by first moves toward the establishment of the Catholic University.

The deliberations were carried forward in a spirit of notable amiability. Much of this was owing to the adroit Gibbons, who handled his firebrands among the bishops with a finesse that Rome thoroughly admired.

The guiding hand of Baltimore's archbishop was also seen in the pastoral letter issued by the council, praising Catholic patriotism and the American system in which the Church found the complete freedom so necessary for unhampered development.

Leo XIII was pleased with Gibbons, and his outspoken approval quite naturally led to rumors that Gibbons would be made a cardinal. These were renewed after Cardinal McCloskey's death in October, 1885.

After several false hopes—one of them sparked by no less a

personage than Archbishop Corrigan of New York—the news of Gibbons' elevation to the cardinalate on June 7 came from Denis O'Connell in Rome. Archbishop Gibbons received the red biretta from the hands of Bishop Peter Kenrick on June 30, 1886, and prepared to go abroad for the public consistory early in 1887, when he would receive the red hat.

The cardinal-elect was excited by the honor. There was a streak of vanity in him, but in this case his pride and pleasure came from his love of Baltimore and all the city meant in the life of the Church. Now the primatial see of the American Church had a distinction worthy of its role and place.

Aside from this honorable pride, Gibbons sailed with an anxious heart. A crisis had arisen in the Church's relationship with labor; the Knights of Labor, a pseudosecret organization, was fighting to raise wages and improve the frightful conditions of the working class.

The bishops of the United States formed into two groups: the conservative bishops, led by Archbishop Corrigan of New York, feared that the movement was the opening wedge of Communism; the liberal bishops—Ireland of St. Paul, Keane of Richmond, and Gibbons himself—heartily favored improvement of the workingman's lot and saw that a condemnation of the Knights of Labor would alienate their staunchest supporters.

The atmosphere was further embittered by the condemnation of the Knights by Cardinal-Elect Taschereau of Quebec, and the undignified public quarrel between Bishop Corrigan and one of his priests, Father McGlynn, over Henry George's book, *Progress and Poverty.*

Gibbons, who had long been urged to take a positive stand in Rome, was reluctant to do so. Ever the optimist and behind-the-scenes persuader, he had hoped for some change or some way of reconciling the two groups.

The moment had arrived when it was no longer possible to procrastinate. Once he went into action in Rome, Gibbons displayed his magnificent poise and plain speaking to the Pope and the Holy Office. So powerful was his intervention, in which Cardinal Manning supported him, that the Holy Office changed its decision on the Knights of Labor some eighteen months later, with the brief announcement that the Knights might be *tolerated*.

Gibbons received the red hat on March 17, and when, on March 25, he took possession of his ancient titular church, Santa Maria in Trastevere, he astonished the brilliant audience by giving a panegyric on the American system in which the Church is enabled to "blossom like a rose."

Gibbons' stature in the United States was immeasurably increased. People in his own town saw how worthy he was of love; that sentiment now spread through the great mass of workers who were the mainstay of the Church in the United States.

He soon had need of every inch of stature he could command. Hardly had the shouts of his triumphant welcome in Baltimore died away when a new and still more acrimonious battle took shape.

Peter Paul Cahensly, Secretary General of the St. Raphael Society, was convinced that German immigrants should retain their own language and customs and be ruled by bishops of their own race. Gibbons and the liberal group were equally convinced that such a movement would lead to division and a series of warring national churches. They were thoroughly convinced that everyone must learn the language of their country, and they deplored the divided mentality of those who refused.

The struggle was a fierce one, fanned into further fury by the inflammatory rhetoric of Archbishop Ireland of St. Paul. It was his tragedy to be a hundred years ahead of his time in his liberal views, but completely and ferociously intransigeant where his convictions were concerned. Gibbons fought the transplanted nationalism with his usual common-sense approach and clearly stated his position to the Pope and the papal court.

Cahensly carried the battle to Switzerland. At the international meeting of the St. Raphael Society, he drew up an overbalanced and prejudiced memorial on the subject, which was sent to Leo XIII. The shrewd pope was not in favor of the arguments, and that news was diplomatically conveyed to Gibbons.

Gibbons' chance meeting with President Harrison at Cape

May, New Jersey, revealed that the President and cardinal were
in complete agreement on the subject. Gibbons was permitted
to forward the President's views to Rome, and in doing so gave
the final *coup de grâce* to the "national" movement.

The victory was almost entirely of Gibbons' making, and can
be summed up in his own words, delivered with dramatic intensity on the occasion of conferring the pallium on Archbishop
Katzer of Milwaukee in August, 1891:

> Woe to him, my brethren, who would destroy or impair this
> blessed harmony that reigns among us! Woe to him who would
> sow tares of discord among the fair fields of the Church in
> America! Woe to him who would breed dissension among the
> leaders of Israel by introducing a spirit of nationalism into the
> camps of the Lord! Brothers we are, whatever may be our na-
> tionality, and brothers we shall remain. Loyalty to God's
> Church and to our country—this is our religious and political
> faith. Next to love for God should be love for our country. The
> Author of our being has stamped in the human breast a love
> for one's country and therefore patriotism is a sentiment com-
> mended by Almighty God Himself. Let us glory in the title
> of American citizen. We owe our allegiance to one country and
> that country is America. We must be in harmony with our
> political institutions. It matters not whether this is the land of
> our birth or our adoption. It is the land of our destiny.

The two intemperate struggles made Gibbons yearn for
peace, but there was no peace in sight. In fact a violent struggle
was shaping up on the question of public schools. The liberal
and conservative bishops were again sharply divided, and the
enemies Ireland had made in fighting Cahenslyism swung their
influence to the side of Corrigan and the conservatives. In time,
it was to tell.

Though the third plenary council of Baltimore had insisted
on the building of parochial schools with dispatch, the fathers
saw that many Catholics would have to attend the public schools.
The burden of supporting a dual school system was seen to be
both unjust and financially burdensome.

Ireland admired the public schools and was ahead of his time

in realizing how difficult it was going to be to support the parochial school system as the years went on, and he tried to work
out a compromise. Taking as his model the Poughkeepsie Plan,
which was fairly widely followed elsewhere in the country, he
made an arrangement in Fairbault by which the city authorities
rented the Catholic schools for a dollar a year. During school
hours the nuns, in their religious garb, taught the regular subjects; after school hours they taught religion. The city was responsible for paying their salaries.

The Fairbault plan and Ireland's hot defense of it occasioned
a great outcry among many of the conservatives, particularly the
bishops of German descent, who had no love for the Archbishop
of St. Paul.

Ireland was denounced in Rome, and Gibbons was quick to
defend his friend. He first wrote to Denis O'Connell, the rector
of the North American College, extolling Ireland's virtues as
a bishop and an American. Later he wrote a ten-page letter to
the Holy See, explaining the complexities of the question. It
was at once a clear explanation of the realities involved and a
defense of the American system which Ireland was attempting
to use in a fashion that would break down prejudice and benefit
the Catholic community.

Ireland went to Rome in defense of his plan. After a long delay, he received the equivocal response, *"tolerari potest,"* which
is equivalent to "it may be permitted."

The dispute continued with malice and name calling, even
after the Pope had given his decision. Leo XIII now saw his
chance for imposing peace and establishing his apostolic delegate in Washington. Most bishops were against a delegate, fancy-
ing his presence meant a curtailment of their power.

The United States had asked the Pope for some priceless
fifteenth-century maps for the Columbian Exhibition in Chicago.
In the fall of 1892, the Pope graciously sent the maps in the care
of Archbishop Francesco Satolli, the noted Thomist scholar.

After arriving in Baltimore, Stolli attended the archbishop's
annual meeting in New York, at which he presented a fourteen-

point program. He reiterated the Pope's "toleration" of Ireland's school plan, refused to condemn the American school system, and though calling for an expansion of the parochial school system, explicitly forbade American bishops to punish parents who sent their children to public schools.

In January of the following year, Archbishop Satolli was appointed apostolic delegate to the United States on a temporary basis. The cardinal and bishops accepted the unwanted delegate with what grace they could muster. Gibbons, though among the reluctant, was grateful for the promised end to the important but disgraceful controversy on the school question.

The liberal bishops seemed to be triumphant. Satolli at first appeared to be firmly on their side. Dr. McGlynn was rehabilitated and freed of censures. Ireland, whose French was fluent, became the darling of the French Republicans to whom he preached the superiority of the American separation of Church and State. The Catholic intellectuals of the continent, bolstered by conservative opinion everywhere, despised American optimism and smugness and bided their time.

The first blow came in 1893, with the papal condemnation of the Knights of Pythias, Oddfellows and the Sons of Temperance. Cardinal Gibbons fought against the decree, but his opposition was in vain.

The liberals opened new doors for criticism by participating, with papal approval, in a ten-day Chicago meeting of the World Parliament of Religions. Cardinal Gibbons gave the opening and closing prayers; Ireland and Keane read papers on Catholic doctrine.

This first attempt at the now widely accepted necessity for dialogue was far in advance of its time. Prejudiced critics on both sides of the Atlantic interpreted the participation as indifference or excessive toleration.

Signs of the temporary eclipse of the liberal bishops began to appear. The first was an encyclical letter to the American bishops, praising the "vigor and devotion of the American Church," to which Leo XIII appended the warning that "it was erroneous to presume that the separation of Church and State in the United States was the most desirable status of the Church or that it would be universally lawful or expedient for Church and State to be, as in America, dissevered and divorced."

Soon after, in the same year, Archbishop Satolli reported Gibbons to Rome for "insubordination," because he had not published the decree against the condemned secret societies.

Gibbons, still hoping to reverse the decision of the Holy Office, went to Rome. There he found that Monsignor Denis O'Connell, his loved and valued protégé, had been asked to resign as Rector of the North American College. The conservative bishops were no longer willing to support a rector who consistently planned the Roman strategy of the liberals, and also did much to inoculate the students with his width of outlook —quite often at variance with the views of their own bishops.

During the next year, Bishop Keane was asked to resign as Rector of the Catholic University of America, for much the same reasons. The climate of malice and gossip intensified, and the time was now ripe for one of the strangest battles in the history of the American Church.

In 1891, Father Walter Elliot had written a life of Father Isaac Hecker, the founder of the Paulist Fathers. At first the somewhat ponderous book caused little stir, either at home or abroad; it had an imprimatur, and a glowing introduction by Archbishop Ireland.

A French translation of Hecker's life, by the Abbé Felix Klein, was published in 1897. It had a long and often inaccurate introduction and caused a sensation in France, going through seven editions in a short space of time. The ultraconservatives began to find in the book more than a taint of heresy. Hecker was falsely accused of placing too much reliance on the private inspiration of the Holy Spirit, of exalting the doer over the thinker, the active over the contemplative life, and of the watering down of Church doctrine for the sake of making converts.

European hatred of everything American received fresh im-

petus during the lightning-swift war with Spain in 1898, which
Gibbons had tried to avert.

At this juncture a new volume, *Is Father Hecker A Saint?*
appeared in France, with a Roman imprimatur granted by Al-
berto Lepidi, O.P., Master of the Pope's Palace. The book was
written by the unscrupulous and abusive Abbé Charles Mag-
nien, under the pseudonym Charles Martel. It was a jumble of
accusations and distortions which caused a great outcry to the
Holy Office for the condemnation of this heresy of Americanism.

Gibbons indignantly saw the complete injustice and malice
of the attack which he denounced with scorn in a formal letter
to Cardinal Rampolla, the Secretary of State.

Gibbons pointed out that the enemies of the United States
were using the word "Americanism" in a perverse sense in order
to make it seem ". . . erroneous and even heretical . . . All
this is false, unfair, slanderous . . . I have no hesitation in af-
firming that you have not in the whole world an episcopate, a
clergy, and believers more fundamentally Catholic, firmer in
their faith and more wholly devoted to the Holy See. The imprimatur given to this libel gives it the meaning of a serious
work and one worthy of confidence."

The Pope, who had been alarmed by the controversy, was
shaken by Gibbons' letter, and reserving the matter to himself,
silenced all further controversy. An Apostolic letter, *Testem
Benevolentiae* (Proof of Our Love), was sent to Cardinal Gibbons on January 22, 1898.

At the time, the encyclical was considered a strange letter. In
it the Pontiff referred to the erroneous opinions described as
Americanism in the French life of Father Hecker. These opinions, if they did exist, should be condemned, but the Pope was
careful not to state that they did exist and he made no reference
to the specific political and social characteristics of the American
people which were the good marks of the term "Americanism."

Looking back from a distance, the encyclical letter is not as
strange as it must have seemed at the time to those liberal bishops, who loved both church and country with flaming intensity.

It was characteristic of Leo's subtle mind, and so ambiguously phrased that it condemned what was heretical if it existed, while nowhere stating it did exist.

On March 17, 1899, the twelfth anniversary of his elevation to the Sacred College, Gibbons sent his formal reply to the encyclical. After respectfully thanking the Pope for his concern and for having cast light on these questions, Gibbons made it amply clear that the "Americanism" ascribed to the American Church by her critics and enemies was both "extravagant and absurd" and had never existed.

Gibbons' prudent but firm protest had its desired effect. Bishop Keane became Bishop of Dubuque in 1900, and two years later Denis O'Connell was named rector of the Catholic University of America and later Bishop of Richmond. Both appointments brought tremendous joy to the cardinal.

The struggle over phantom "Americanism" was the last great battle of Gibbons' life. The peace he had so desired had at last arrived. The dawn of the new century found him the first citizen of Baltimore and one of the outstanding men of the nation, admired and loved by presidents and people.

In 1903, Cardinal Gibbons made ready to go to Rome as the aged Leo hovered between life and death. Accompanied by Father Patrick C. Gavin, Gibbons arrived in time to participate in the election of Giuseppe Sarto as Pius X.

It was a dramatic conclave and the first in which an American cardinal had participated. Cardinal Rampolla, the favorite, was vetoed by Austria, to the outrage of the Sacred College. The votes of the electors gradually shifted to Cardinal Sarto, but he seemed adamant in refusing the honor. As this juncture, Gibbons personally intervened by reassuring the weeping candidate of the warm and vigorous support of the American Church in all the problems of his reign. Cardinal Sarto still refused. Then Gibbons persuaded Cardinal Satolli that the Patriarch of Venice must be *made* to accept the will of the Sacred College.

For the intervention, Satolli took with him Cardinal Ferrari, Sarto's oldest friend among the cardinals, and Cardinal Agliardi. By the use of a shrewd combination of spiritual argument and a veiled threat of the divine wrath should he refuse, Cardinal Sarto was convinced that he must accept his greatest cross. Next morning he was elevated and chose the name Pius X.

The twilight of the cardinal's life was as radiant as the first hint of dusk falling on his beloved Baltimore. Now that his place was secure and his battles were over, he found time for writing, advising the many who called upon him for assistance, strolling about the city, jesting with the altar boys, visiting with his oldest friends the Shrivers, at Chapel Hill. His was the common touch, informed with homespun wisdom.

Above all, there was time to spend in securing and forwarding the Catholic University of America. It was the very apple of his eye, and no one in its long history ever worked so unremittingly that it might become the important institution that it is today.

The celebration of the cardinal's golden jubilee in 1911 gives us some clue to his popularity and eminence. President Taft and his Cabinet, the Justices of the Supreme Court, and many other government officials joined with the bishops of the church in paying tribute to Baltimore's cardinal.

With the onset of the First World War in 1917, the eighty-two-year-old cardinal moved the bishops of the country to pledge the loyalty of their people in the struggle. Up to the time of his death on March 24, 1921, he remained vigorous and in full possession of his remarkable faculties.

After his death, the flood of tributes from world leaders and the common people were as moving as the tearful throngs that passed his coffin as he lay in state.

Some revered him for his patriotism or his humanity, some for his priestliness or wisdom. Few were able to see, as we can now, that the American Church as we know it today is largely his creation.

That priests and people are one, that patriotism and religion go hand in hand, that prelates of any stature are capable of rising above their racial bias, that separation of Church and State assists the Church in "blooming like a rose," that dialogue is possible and necessary between all who worship God, that understanding and love of the common people is the cornerstone of progress, all these he had fought for and built into the consciousness of the American Church.

It was difficult to imagine how any American prelate coming after him would have either his opportunity for greatness or the discerning, unmovable prudence that made him supremely great in action.

John Cardinal Farley

1842 – 1918

THE STORY of John Murphy Farley's early years seems lost in a haze of legend and timid statements.[1] James J. Walsh says: "Farley's family were farming people in reasonably comfortable circumstances, able to afford their children a good education. One of his brothers, Edward Farley, emigrated to New York and became a rather prominent merchant in the city. His maternal uncle, Patrick Murphy, was for years a member of the well-known firm of Solomon & Son. The future cardinal's preliminary studies were made near his native home, but Irish schoolmasters have ever been known for their thoroughness, and he secured an excellent grasp of Latin and Greek and of fundamentals in mathematics."

To this Spartan summation of twenty-two years, Brendan Finn, in his *Twenty-Four American Cardinals*, has little enough to add in two sentences; "Orphaned when still a child, John was educated through the generosity of an uncle. He received his first beginnings in Latin and Greek at St. McCartan's College, Monaghan, Ireland."

Both authorities are in agreement on the date of Farley's birth, April 20, 1842. Both further agree that the young man emigrated to America at the height of the Civil War in 1864. 22 y°.

In the face of this strange economy of facts concerning Far-

---

[1] The name of Cardinal Farley's father was Philip Farrelly; Cardinal Farley changed the spelling of his name to conform to the family pronunciation. His mother was Catherine Murphy Farrelly.

ley's early life, we may hope to understand something about his development by an attempted reconstruction of the times and circumstances in which his formative years were lived.

Newton Hamilton, about forty miles from Belfast, where Farley was born, was a small town in the west central part of the County of Armagh, which is squeezed in between the counties of Monaghan and Down, at the edge of the Mourne Mountains of northern Ireland. Like all small Irish towns in 1842, its whitewashed cottages straggled along the narrow main street.

Beyond the town, to the west and north, stretched the green fields with their staggering hedgerows marking off garth and tillage. To the south, the lofty top of Mount St. Gullion dominated the hilly landscape; beyond it was the higher reach of Mount Carlingford, looking out on the Irish Sea. On days of wind and rain, the mist closed in from the sea, veiling the mountaintops from view and making this small world seem smaller still.

Irish Catholics in this district were under the firm dominance of their Protestant overlords and neighbors. Time and bloody persecution had made Catholics cohesive and secretive, taking the Mass and education where they could find them, though by 1842 they no longer had to resort to the fields and hedges.

The old legends of the great days of Maeve and Cuchulainn flitted through their minds, to be retold around the turf fires at night, but the abortive successes of the Young Ireland Movement made them less nostalgic for the past and more hopeful for a free future unblighted by famine and economic strangulation.

John would first have learned to read and write at home. There, too, the great truths of the faith became shining realities. To specific teaching was added the moving recitation of the beads each night, with their association with the great mysteries of the faith, while the firelight played on bent heads and minds were filled with glowing love of Mary and her Son. This world of immortal romance found its complement in the exciting world of nature with its own rich wisdom. There were mountains to be explored and climbed with childish wonder and delight, culminating in a final view of the world spread out below like a magic carpet.

Excursions farther afield led to the edge of Lough Carlinford, a deep bay of the Irish Sea, and ecstatic summer hours of swimming and fishing. Market days at the thriving town of Dundalk or Monaghan and county fairs offered moments of high excitement.

Everyone was expected to work. Even the smallest boys helped with mattock, hoe and shovel, trying to scratch the simplest living from the soggy soil. There was peat to be cut and stacked; twigs from the forest to be tied in bundles for convenient kindling to the accompaniment of witty comments on life and people.

Irish love of learning was deep and universal. Priests and schoolmasters were honored as much for what they knew as for what they were; for though the new masters might sneer at the "pig in the parlor" and "Paddy dear, and did yez hear?" the people remembered the tradition of ancient studious days that had cast its glow from the Ireland of saints and sent scholars to enlighten all of Western Europe in the sixth century. This great past in the works of Irish literature was, even as early as 1842, beginning to emerge from the riddle of Erse.

It must have been with a sense of complete dedication that Farley entered St. McCarten's. There in a primitive and ascetic atmosphere, learning was only a shade less firmly enshrined than the Sacrament on the altar.

Studies were not mere tasks in which unwilling schoolboys fought to gain a "credit"; they were exciting excursions. Latin and Greek opened the riches of the past and provided enduring examples of graceful speech; mathematics demonstrated the laws on which the world turned; philosophy explained the reasons of things; theology their divine glorification.

Discipline was a problem easily solved by the pandy bat, mercilessly applied at sensitive points, or the burdensome translation of fifty or a hundred lines of Ovid or Virgil. Few mavericks survived the treatment.

Whether it was the recurring famines or the thirst for op-

portunity that drew Farley out of his suffering land, he mi-
grated to the United States in 1864. The young student was not
long in making his talents felt in the country of his adoption.
One year spent at Fordham University served to reveal the dazzling promise of the stocky but handsome youth. He wrote facile
poetry and prose and showed himself far in advance of his classmates in philosophy and languages. The demonstration and
certitude of his call to the priesthood led to his entry into the
provincial seminary at Troy, New York. Once again, after a
single year of residence, his general brilliance and the enthusiastic approval of the college rector moved Archbishop Mc-
Closkey to select John as a candidate for the newly established
North American College in Rome, at one of the most "exciting"
periods of papal history.

The opportunity was a splendid one. Those who visit Rome
today and find it fascinating would have been immensely more
charmed and interested in the Rome John Farley knew between
the years of 1867-1870.

Pius IX was still the Pope-King of the whittled-down Papal
States. Soldiers of the Emperor Louis Napoleon were at last
leaving for France. Their duties in manning the walls and polic-
ing the city were being taken over by smart groups of papal
Zouaves, recruited from all over the world, who comprised the
Pope's army under the command of General Kanzler. Their
presence in the Holy City was the last frail barrier preventing
the seizure of all that remained of papal territory, including
Rome. Victor Emmanuel and his United Italy Government
were settled in Florence, impatiently awaiting a change in the
fortunes of France, which would clear the way for the long-pre-
pared march on Rome.

The atmosphere in which John found himself might well be
called the Indian summer of the Papal States. Pius IX was preparing to summon the bishops of the world to the Vatican council. There was excitement in the air as elegant state carriages
flashed through the streets bearing princes and bishops to audiences with the Pope.

The Pope himself might be seen almost anywhere in the city.

Sometimes the wide-eyed students observed the memorably graceful white-clad figure conducting visiting cardinals on a tour of the churches, or attended by a single chamberlain, moving along in his gilded carriage toward the Pincian Gardens where he took his daily walk, and in his merryhearted fashion exchanged pleasantries with princes or peasants.

After the frenetic newness and bustle of New York, Eternal Rome possessed a glamorous serenity that could completely capture the heart of any young student with an inquiring mind. Its classic ruins, blending subtly with the monuments of papal Rome, provided perpetual contrast and surprise. They also furnished endless opportunity for recreation after the heavy schedule of lectures in dogmatic and moral theology and canon law.

Since Count de Rossi's significant work in archaeology, every foreign student had become something of an armchair archaeologist as he visited the newly uncovered catacombs of early popes and saints or the gorgeous remains of villas once owned by Roman emperors and magnates.

Great lectures, great architecture, great art—these offered golden opportunities to any ambitious student, as John could easily see. To seminarians, there were added attractions in being able to learn lessons for their coming ministry through the observation of Christian government at its best and social service at its most brilliant.

There were adequate schools and colleges for all who desired to learn. Good industrial schools for teaching trades were under the special patronage of the Pope, who had spent his early training as a priest in such institutions. Homes for the orphans, the insane and the aged, were conducted with an intelligent kindness and understanding that no other government in the world could equal at that time.

That Farley learned these lessons well is amply illustrated in his important work for parochial schools and Catholic social institutions, as bishop and cardinal.

The important events of Farley's Roman years are almost too numerous to mention. First among these was the 18th centenary of Sts. Peter and Paul, celebrated with unexampled splendor in 1867. The vast crowds knelt in prayer as the Pope was borne through the streets in magnificent state, carrying the Blessed Sacrament on the Feast of Corpus Christi. During the continuing celebration, the Pope blessed the sumptuously restored church of St. Paul's Outside the Walls and canonized 205 of the martyrs of Japan. The illumination of the city and its innumerable churches, colorful processions, and the fervor of visiting dignitaries and pilgrims, turned the days into a wonderful tapestry.

The year promised to end on a note of alarm when Garibaldi's redshirts invaded the last papal territory south of Rome. Kanzler and his papal Zouaves, with powerful French aid, roundly defeated Garibaldi at Mentana, and triumphal celebrations were added to the many religious festivities.

For John Farley, the year 1870 had a personal meaning and importance that was to make it memorable for the rest of his life. With the triumphant conclusions of his examinations behind him, he was ordained to the priesthood on June 11, by Cardinal Patrizi, the Pope's vicar-general.

The spiritual joy of the occasion has not come down to us in any written form, but John's love of St. Philip Neri, the great Renaissance saint, which had been important in molding his life and his piety, would have insured his careful preparation for the great event and the delight that came with its accomplishment.

That same year, Farley attended the Vatican council where he observed the democracy of the Church, debate (often heated) in the formulation of necessary dogmas and disciplinary laws.

He was fortunate in having an inside view of the gathering due to the presence of Archbishop McCloskey, who because of his important position on the committee for Church discipline and his many friends among the cardinals, was able to open every door to the young student.

So we may picture Father Farley looking on in St. Peter's at that moment of storm and intense drama when the doctrine of infallibility was promulgated to the delirious shouts of the vast crowd watching the proceedings.

Near the end of August, Father Farley left Rome for the return voyage to America. Thus by a few short months he missed the drama of the fall of Rome, one of the highlights of which was the impetuous offer of the students of the North American College to take up arms in defense of the pontiff's person. It was a request that would have warmed the hearts of frontier America.

The first assignment given the young priest was that of assistant to the pastor at New Brighton, Staten Island. Father Farley must have been stimulated by the change from the magnificence of Rome to the austere simplicity of a country parish. Staten Island was thoroughly bucolic in 1870. A rickety ferry connected the island with Manhattan. Except for that unreliable link, Father Farley might have been back in Newton Hamilton.

With a simplicity that characterized his entire life, Farley threw himself into the affairs of the parish: the visits, sick calls, office consultations and services of the altar that fill to overflowing the first years of young priests in the active ministry.

There was ample time to go through his books once again for the consolidation and evaluation of the knowledge he had gained in Rome. It is easy to picture the grateful pride of country parishioners who congratulated themselves on having this unusual priest in their midst; one who intimately knew the Holy Father and all the famous cardinals about whom he related personal stories with the warmth and verve of an eyewitness. Years later they still remembered him with gratitude and undimmed admiration.

The rustication of Father Farley lasted two years. In 1872, with the elevation to the Diocese of Albany of Father McNierney, Farley was made the archbishop's secretary. By training and character he was well fitted for the job.

A bishop's secretary is an important person. He not only has to make the bishop's appointments with a discerning eye, but he also has to know canon law thoroughly and all the modes of protocol and address which are proper in dealing with the highest officials of the Church.

Farley was the ideal man for the position. It was his task to make all the arrangements for McCloskey's reception of the red hat in 1875, and he accompanied the cardinal to Rome in 1878 for the actual reception of the red hat and the renewal and consolidation of the old friendships of his student years.

In 1884, a year before Cardinal McCloskey's death, Farley was created a papal chamberlain, an unusual honor at the time, which clearly marked him for future preferment.

Then, in August of the same year, in order to clear the way for Bishop Corrigan's rule of the diocese—already in practical effect due to the cardinal's ill health—Monsignor Farley was moved to the pastorate of St. Gabriel's Church on 37th Street.

The parishioners were mostly workers and clerks. Farley made himself at home with them, sharing their simple joys and sorrows with all the warm humanity of a country boy born in simple circumstances.

Now the lessons and work in Rome began to bear fruit. The parish debt was paid, the church was refurbished and beautified, the parochial school was improved to such a point that it outrivaled the public schools of the district. A parish hall was built in which the dignified monsignor could meet his people for group action and parish festivities. A parish census and regular visits to his people rounded out Monsignor Farley's program.

While all this was taking place during Farley's seventeen years as pastor of St. Gabriel's, he was moving into public view as a man of creative ideas. He spoke on Catholic education and social service with force and spirit, and his comments on the great encyclicals of Leo XIII were quoted with approval. The perfect ordering of his parish revealed his genius for organization.

These were the most important reasons for his appointment as Vicar-General of New York in 1891. The new honor automatically brought with it the chairmanship of the Catholic school board.

The next year, Monsignor Farley demonstrated his talent for public relations by organizing the famous Catholic school parade. Bigots had maintained the inferiority of the parochial school system; now, for the first time, New Yorkers were able to gauge the massive Catholic effort in the vigorous march of nuns and their pupils through the streets of the city.

Two years later, Farley followed up this demonstration with a city-wide exhibition of the work produced in Catholic classrooms. Protestants were surprised at the showing, and many Catholics were equally amazed. The exhibition led to Monsignor Farley's elevation to the highest rank of the monsignorate, prothonotary apostolic. No one was surprised when he became Auxiliary Bishop of New York a few years later.

One of Bishop Farley's first successes was a drive that liquidated the $300,000 mortgage on Dunwoodie Seminary, in honor of Archbishop Corrigan's silver jubilee in 1898. Archbishop Corrigan died on May 5, 1902. In September of that year, Bishop Farley became Archbishop of New York.

The United States was full of bounce and vigor at the time. Teddy Roosevelt had become President the year before, after the assassination of McKinley. The Panama Canal act had been passed by Congress. The Floradora Sextet was saying a temporary good-bye to Broadway.

The last years of Archbishop Corrigan's reign had been anything but peaceful. New York was split into many political factions; economic and ethnic groups were at loggerheads with each other. Archbishop Corrigan had been on the wrong side in the Knights of Labor dispute and in the outcry against Henry George, whose theories several prominent priests of the diocese supported.

Archbishop Farley was the ideal man for the times. Working quietly behind the scenes, he succeeded in bringing the various warring groups into cooperation and harmony. Those who knew him best in those years learned to respect his talents in gracefully but firmly saying no without hurting the feelings of anyone. With his soft voice, twinkling eyes and courteous explanations, without compromising either his dignity or his office, the archbishop forged a new unity of purpose for his people.

Among the older members of the clergy, the unity of purpose was partly brought into being by the official recognition of their work. This came in the form of the creation of many monsignors. Up to this time, the honor had been given to very few, and Farley's generosity in this regard was widely applauded. The rash of red rabies also led to many jokes, among the best of which was the quip Archbishop O'Ryan made to Farley himself: "Ah, Your Grace, I understand that since your recent trip to Rome half of your diocese has become purple, the other half blue."

Farley's studies and observations in Rome had taught him the value of publicity, at which Pius IX was a past master; the Roman years had also given him a sense of solidarity with all the joys and sorrows of the Pope.

When, at the turn of the century, irreligious politicians secured control of the French Government, an immediate attack was mounted against the Church. Religious orders were persecuted and laicized. Ancient abbeys, schools and shrines were seized. These and many other intolerable abuses in keeping with the malignant disease of statism so evident in our own day in the works of Hitler and Stalin led to a direct and prolonged battle with the new pope, Pius X.

Archbishop Farley was quick to show his sympathy for the Pope by organizing a mass meeting of Catholics in the Hippodrome to protest the persecution in France. It was attended by a huge throng which packed the building and spilled out, some 30,000 strong, into the surrounding area.

Noted Catholic laymen denounced the religious persecution with passion, and exposed the truth of what was taking place in France. The atmosphere of the evening was both electric and dramatic. New York's newspapers gave the gathering the widest possible coverage, and news of the protest meeting went out over the whole world. It provided one more weapon for the Pope and helped the papacy materially in its eventual triumph over the insensate irreligious group recruited mostly from the ranks of the Grand Orient, the intellectual leaders of European Masonry.

The exposure of evil and evil men, the archbishop saw, was but one facet of the Church's struggle in the modern world. With this in mind, Farley mounted a positive attack against world-wide ignorance of the Church and her teachings by organizing the publication of the *Catholic Encyclopedia.* Committees of scholars were set up—the archbishop started the fund-raising with a subscription of $5,000—and through his encouragement of the project in other dioceses across the country, he became the leader in bringing the undertaking to a triumphant conclusion in 1914. Every aspect of Church history, teaching and sanctity, thus became available to the public in an easy and palatable fashion.

Farley, himself a clever writer, contributed articles to the *Encyclopedia.* His intelligence and ability with a pen are easily measured by the two books which he published: *The History of St. Patrick's Cathedral* and *The Life of John Cardinal McCloskey.*

In the crisp pages of the cathedral history, Farley illuminated his facts with many charming insights. It is genuinely good reading. His biography of Cardinal McCloskey is even more remarkable. Farley lets McCloskey tell most of the story himself from letters, diaries and the important pronouncements of his long and distinguished career. What emerges is a massively charming picture of this shy but unusually talented prince of the Church, shot through with humor. Farley's great love for his subject distinguishes the genuine biographer from the bookwright.

Archbishop Farley devoted a great deal of attention and time to the priests of his diocese and the candidates for the priesthood. He made frequent visits to the senior seminary at Dunwoodie, and spoke to the students with great fervor about those qualities that distinguish the good priest.

As a spur to numerous vocations, Cathedral College was organized to prepare young men for the senior seminary through a course of solid study and testing which gave students ample time to discover whether they were fitted for priestly life. The first rector of the new college was Father Patrick J. Hayes, a young priest of the diocese whose piety, zeal and executive talents had marked him for swift advancement.

Remembering his own experience, Archbishop Farley usually sent his newly ordained priests to the country parishes of the diocese. Through this arrangement he let them discover the depth and warmth of their vocation in the simple neighborliness and family atmosphere prevailing in country places. In these circumstances, young priests learned that parishioners are *people*—a lesson of enduring value when they were later moved to the big city parishes with their complex life and unavoidable tendency toward formalism in relations between priests and parishioners.

Following the splendid example of Pius X, Farley initiated a monthly day of recollection for reading, study and the spiritual life. Such gatherings also gave the priests of the diocese a chance to know each other better, and aided the discussion of problems common to all.

There was nothing parochial in Archbishop Farley's respect for the priesthood. He was the soul of hospitality to visiting clergy, he received missionaries into his diocese and permitted them to collect funds for their enterprises.

When the Catholic Foreign Mission Society was founded by the "modern apostle" Father James J. Walsh, Farley warmly welcomed the new community in establishing its mother house and training center at Maryknoll, near Ossining, New York. The cardinal materially assisted the infant organization with prudent advice, praise and money.

The hundredth anniversary of the New York Archdiocese, celebrated in 1908 with great pomp and oratory, revealed Farley's supreme grasp of public relations. By this time New York had become largely an Irish enclave, and this was reflected everywhere in the city's life and politics. The archbishop's invitation to the Cardinal Primate of Ireland, asking him to preside at the Solemn Mass celebrating the occasion, brought to New

York Cardinal Logue, Archbishop of Armagh. It was a subtle blending of Irish nostalgia for the Old Land and its glory, along with a sentimental glance at the province from which Farley had come to the United States. The New York Irish needed no cue to read the lesson aright; from Bishop Concannon to Archbishop Farley—in spite of seemingly insuperable obstacles—the past hundred years had been a continuous triumph for the Irish of the Diaspora.

Two years later, in 1910, the last and most permanent fruit of the centenary, the consecration of St. Patrick's Cathedral, took place in an atmosphere of jubilation and splendor. His Eminence of Armagh returned for the celebration, and the beloved Cardinal Gibbons of Baltimore lent his purple and sparkling presence to the occasion along with many prelates from all over the United States, and most important of all, Cardinal Vannutelli, the Pope's legate.

It was scarcely a year later that New York newspapers had a fresh occasion for banner headlines when they were informed that Cardinal Merry del Val had summoned Archbishop Farley to Rome to be made a cardinal. Apostolic Delgate Falconio and Archbishop O'Connell of Boston had also been nominated for the same high honor. All the ceremonies of elevation were to take place in Rome, as swift communications between the two continents—along with the fact that the United States was no longer a missionary country—now permitted such an arrangement.

Farley and Falconio left New York on the S.S. *Kronprinzessin Cecilie*, accompanied by their suites and a large number of noted clergy and laity from New York and Washington, D.C. In compliment to the distinguished guests, their ship flew the papal flag at its masthead.

Upon their arrival in Rome, the three American prelates received their formal letters of nomination on November 27, 1911, at the North American College, after the secret consistory of the morning during which Pius X had given a deeply moving sermon concerning the mounting attacks on the Church.

In keeping with protocol, the ensuing two days were taken up with the solemnities attending the conferring of the red birettas and the *cappae magnae,* which actually took place on the afternoon of November 29. The Pope recalled with pleasure a visit in Venice with Cardinal Farley when he was Auxiliary Bishop of New York.

The ceremonies were completed on November 30 in a public consistory in which the three American cardinal-priests actually received their great red hats and were assigned their titular churches. Cardinal Farley's, to the delight of all, proved to be Santa Maria Sopra Minerva, which had been the titular church of Cardinal McCloskey; a subtle reminder to the world that the first two bishops of the diocese of New York had both been appointed from this Dominican mother house.

These connecting links were put into gracious phrases on December 10, 1911 as Cardinal Farley took formal possession of his church. In addition to the acknowledgment of the great debt New York owed to Santa Maria Sopra Minerva, Farley paid a glowing tribute to Cardinal McCloskey and all that outstanding prince of the Church had accomplished.

The welcome home in New York was a delirious succession of parades and banquets, signalized by the somewhat orotund oratory of the day and notable for the cooperation of the Protestants and Jews in making the welcome memorable. When the S.S. *Berlin,* flags flying, arrived in New York Harbor on the unusually mild morning of January 17, 1912, she was met by countless numbers of small craft lavishly decorated for the occasion. All the way to her pier in Hoboken, whistles and horns filled the air with ear-numbing sound. This chorus was answered by the deep bass of the *Berlin*'s foghorn.

A gaily decorated boat carried the resplendent cardinal and his suite to the Battery. There the cardinal entered an open carriage for an almost five-mile drive through shouting throngs of Catholics waving papal flags, augmented by thousands of New York citizens of many faiths. It is estimated some 500,000 took part in the welcome.

The press of the crowd around St. Patrick's Cathedral called for the best efforts of New York's Finest in keeping decorum and order. Mounted policemen, every button flaming like the sun, trotted up and down along the barricades.

When the cardinal's carriage arrived, there was a frenzied shout. As a kindly concession to popular ignorance of what a cardinal's hat really looked like, Farley had donned its betasseled medieval splendor for the parade. At the door of his cathedral, the cardinal was met by the ecclesiastical procession prepared to escort him into his church.

He uncovered his head, knelt and fervently kissed the cross tendered to him by the crossbearer. Then, to the jubilant strains of *Ecce Sacerdos Magnus,* the procession entered the cathedral.

The banquets and meetings of congratulations that followed were in a sense anticlimactic, but they served to reveal the pride of all New Yorkers in the honor that had come to one of their own. The cardinal, with praiseworthy humility, constantly insisted that the honor was due to their efforts and achievements rather than to his worth or importance.

One of his acts at this time brought him tremendous personal delight. The lovely palace of the Mastai-Ferretti family in Senigallia, where Pius IX had been born and brought up, came on the market after a series of financial reverses. Cardinal Farley at once stepped forward with the necessary $10,000 for the purchase of the noble old house and its art treasures. It was an act of pure gratitude and love that brought back to the cardinal all the unalloyed happiness of student days and the many occasions on which he had experienced at first hand the radiant charm and benevolence of the last Pope-King.

Today the palace is a beautiful American memorial to the pope who did so many significant things for America. Its art treasures have appreciated over the years, and the value of the palace today is multiplied fabulously.

In 1914, Monsignor Patrick J. Hayes was appointed Auxiliary Bishop of New York. The appointment was a welcome one. Hayes had been the cardinal's secretary and closest collaborator for many years and knew the diocese intimately.

Farley's elevation to cardinal's rank consolidated his position in the diocese and the city. When the First World War drew the United States into the conflict, the cardinal quickly threw his weight and genius for organization into the war effort. The first step was the establishment of the New York Catholic War Council. This group was responsible for the opening of canteens to serve both men and women of the armed forces, and a hospital for shell-shocked veterans.

Bishop Hayes became the first military bishop of the United States. In the creation of the military ordinariate, Hayes showed his positive talent for organization. Before the war ended, the ordinariate had recruited some 1,500 priests to serve the armed forces.

The various war bond drives brought the aging cardinal into the war effort personally. His mere presence on any platform was a guarantee of a large turnout. On the many occasions when he spoke, it was with the same warmth and graceful common sense that moved men to contribute generously.

Many thought it unfortunate that Cardinal Farley did not live to see the triumph of the Allies that came with the signing of the Armistice on November 11, 1918. At the very time when the final struggle was at its height and American boys were dying by the thousands on the Meuse-Argonne front, Cardinal Farley died peacefully on September 17, 1918.

The newspapers trumpeted praise of the dead prelate, citing his many achievements for the city and the country. The thousands who loved him filed past his coffin. On the day of the funeral, the sanctuary of his debt-free cathedral blazed with the varied purples of three cardinals, the apostolic delegate, and many bishops and monsignors.

The dead cardinal had assumed the rule of the diocese at a time of division and political confusion. He had resolved these differences with a firm hand, and then moved on into a future in which the beauty, intellectual and cultural influences of the Church could be demonstrated to the world. Prudence and peace were his watchwords; he acted with imperturbable firmness and massive dignity.

Despite his large talent for affairs, Farley remained a pastor at heart—the dignity, holiness and love of the priesthood were always his first concern. That was why his undivided heart demanded respect and got it; that was why he had been able to accomplish so much.

William Cardinal O'Connell

1859 - 1944

I N *Recollections of Seventy Years,* Cardinal O'Connell has given us the story of his life as he saw it. The book is carefully written and meticulously documented; it cannot be ignored, but it is bound to be subjective rather than objective, and the reading of its four hundred pages leaves not the slightest doubt that it is a full-dress portrait in which the lights and shadows are artfully planned to achieve a general effect of massive greatness. In discussing the cardinal's life, his autobiography must be consulted; it must also be interpreted.

James Buchanan was nearing the final phase of his four-year term as President on December 8, 1859, the day on which William O'Connell, the last of eleven children—the son of John O'Connell and Brigid Farley—was born in Lowell, Massachusetts. It was the Feast of the Immaculate Conception.

The year 1859 had begun optimistically with the discovery of the Comstock Lode in Nevada. It gathered excitement in the stirring new tune "Dixie" composed by Dan Emmett, which set everyone to jigging, and ended on a note of tragedy in the death of John Brown after his abortive capture of the arsenal at Harpers Ferry.

William was the baby of the family of seven boys and four girls. The father was a millhand in one of the Lowell textile mills. They were fiercely and proudly poor.

In his early childhood, the sturdy boy was the inseparable

companion of his mother. In the late afternoons when the chief household tasks were over, he sat on a stool at his mother's feet as she sewed and mended for her large family. The yellow glow of the lamp made a nimbus of her graying hair. The child listened to stories of Ireland, which seemed to him more glamorous than any fairy tale. They were heavily spiced with hilarious episodes that made them both laugh. These hours forged a bond between mother and child that grew ever stronger with the years.

The life of the family, though straitened with poverty, was colored by moments of joy as they sang and jigged and made merry on great feast days. St. Patrick's day easily ranked with Christmas and Easter as one of the important days of the year. On the eve of that great day, the house would be fragrant with the smell of the Irish "cake" and a great saddle of mutton baking in the oven. Next morning they would all go to church and then watch the huge parade of the Ancient Order of Hibernians as it went through the streets with deafening bands and flying green banners. The remainder of the day was sacred to song and dance and liberal libations of potheen. The mill-owners, who held the Irish in conditions very near to slavery, dared not interfere with the celebration in any way. Even without interference, there were brawls and broken heads before the feast was over.

When William was four years old, tragedy struck the family with the fatal illness of their father. The child was wakened and brought to his father's room in the middle of the night. The circle of lamplight around the bed revealed his father's drawn face and his mother's kneeling figure. She was weeping bitterly. When all the children were assembled, Mrs. O'Connell, prayer book in hand, led the prayers for the dying, which the children answered.

Suddenly the agony was over. The mother pulled the sheet up over the white face and returned to her knees and prayers for the faithful departed. At their conclusion, she rose, dried her eyes, and said to the children, "The holy will of God be done."

Her resolution and courage in facing the future and eking out the family resources by personal service in the homes of well-to-do families of the district impressed her son as no other heroism ever had.

William's grade-school days were unhappy. The atmosphere of the public schools of the time was one of narrow bigotry. The Catholic children, particularly the Irish, were treated with harsh contempt by most of their teachers. The bitterness increased at times as the No-Nothing Movement brought gangs of toughs into the streets to threaten Catholic churches and convents.

By the time William reached high-school age, some of the antagonism had abated. The boy avidly began to learn for the first time, except in his courses in English history which was presented as an anti-Catholic tract. With rage in his heart, the boy heard his Church and its heroes abused and vilified.

He found what comfort he could in learning to paint modestly good water-colors and in mastering the piano and the organ. Music, next to his religion, was to be William's great solace until the end of his life.

In his twelfth year, young O'Connell attempted to hold a summer job in one of the textile mills. He lasted one full day in the unhealthy atmosphere which had looked so glamorous from a distance, with its clacking machinery and floating bits of cotton fluff in the dusky atmosphere.

With his mother's firm support, the boy pointed his course toward the College of St. Charles at Endicott City in Maryland, in September, 1876. En route to school, he stopped in Philadelphia where the Centennial Exposition was in progress. To one who had hardly been out of his district, the buildings, music and excitement of the exhibition were like a glimpse of Paradise.

The first sight of the college and its massive towers impressed the boy. In the two years he spent with the Sulpician Fathers, he was firmly grounded in Latin and science. Greek did not appeal to him, and he did less well at it.

Far more important to his future was the influence of John

Bannister Tabb. Father Tabb, a convert from the Episcopal Church, was a noted poet. In his classes, O'Connell found a love of language and poetry that completely enchanted him, especially since all of Tabb's intuitions were liberally salted with wit. The bond between pupil and teacher was strengthened by Tabb's proficiency in music. Through him and his tremendous enthusiasm, William came to love the great masters and their works, and his progress at the piano and organ was swift.

In spite of the country atmosphere of the school, O'Connell's health began to fail in his second year. There can be little doubt that separation from his mother had a great deal to do with his "breakdown."

Once at home and enrolled in Boston College, in its old quarters on Garrison Avenue in the South End, O'Connell's health began to improve. He rode a spirited little horse named Billy in the late afternoons. The brisk daily exercise brought the color back to his cheeks.

He was his mother's favorite confidant, and he came to her with all his anxieties, joys and sorrows. Her sage advice and guidance played a large part in his triumphant graduation at the head of his class in June 1881, with three gold medals in philosophy, physics and chemistry, and several prizes in poetry and rhetoric.

During the college years, mother and son spent many hours discussing William's vocation. The young man felt that God was calling him to the priesthood, and the delighted mother warmly encouraged him and doubled her own prayers for her favorite child.

When Archbishop Williams was approached, he enthusiastically accepted his new recruit. "Your record is fine, my boy," he said, "the place for you and your studies is obviously the North American College in Rome."

Mother and son dreaded the long separation, but in spite of her fears, Mrs. O'Connell hid her feelings and encouraged her son. In September 1881 William departed for Rome on the Cunard liner *Marathon*. Visits to Ireland, England and France fired his romantic mind with inspiration and pleasure. Ireland lived up to his great expectations; England was less stimulating; Paris a distinct anticlimax. The French mentality and hard sense of reality did much to dim his memories of the dramatic squares and parks, Notre Dame and the tomb of Napoleon.

The first years of Roman study were exciting. Great teachers like Satolli and Agliardi impressed and inspired the young student; sightseeing in Rome and in the Alban Hills filled his mind with glowing pictures of the antique world and of the Renaissance. The atmosphere of the college was dark and cold in winter, the food was poor in quality and badly cooked. But what were such minor inconveniences compared with all the shining benefits that flowed from being at the very heart of the Christian world?

O'Connell worked hard, painted many water colors, took charge of the college choir, and identified himself completely with the jocosely happy life of the students. His appointment as first prefect is an indication of his standing with the college authorities.

After his ordination in St. John Lateran on June 8, 1884, at the beginning of his third year, the young priest looked forward to the achievement of his doctor of divinity degree and threw himself ardently into his studies. Before the year was out, a near pneumonia undermined his health. Father O'Connell was sent out to the bracing air of Anzio Beach. Recuperation was rapid, but early in his fourth year a serious bronchial congestion forced him to return to the United States without his degree.

The story of Father O'Connell's departure from the North American College, as he tells it in his autobiography, is saturated with emotion and disappointment. The loss of his degree was obviously a terrible blow to him.

The reunion with his mother and her joy in him and his priesthood had a tonic influence. After a happy week in Lowell with the family, Archbishop Williams assigned Father O'Connell to a small parish in Medford. The pastor, Father O'Donnell, was amiable and easy-going. Parish duties were not onerous, and O'Connell was able to spend many quiet hours walking and studying. He was completely restored to vigorous health within two years.

In October 1886, Father O'Connell was transferred to the "largest and busiest parish in the diocese," St. Joseph's in the West End of Boston. It was mostly a tough slum area, generously peppered with saloons and gambling joints, but in spite of his many parish duties and the shabby atmosphere, Father O'Connell read omnivorously and pondered the problem of the rapidly growing Church in America. The acrimonious disputes between eminent groups of bishops, who didn't hesitate to differ publicly with each other over the school question and politics, was something of a shock after the order and discipline of Rome.

Almost ten years went by in a busy round of parish duties. With every lull in parish activities, Father O'Connell went straight to the family home in Malden. There, over a cup of tea, he regaled his mother with amusing stories of parish affairs and received in return intimate rundowns of family joys and sorrows. It grieved the young priest to see her increasing feebleness.

In 1893, while visiting the Chicago Exposion, Father O'Connell had a premonition that all was not well with his mother. Cutting short his visit, he took express trains first to New York and then to Boston, arriving there in the late evening. Without waiting for morning, he hurried out to Malden where his mother greeted him with joy. In a few hours she was dead. The shock was tremendous. She had been his best inspiration and adviser. Looking back much later as honors and fame came to him in abundance, he found a certain emptiness in them all because they lacked the intimate stamp of her joyous approval.

Concealing his grief as best he could, Father O'Connell returned to his duties at St. Joseph's. When a change came, it was as staggering as it was welcome. A telegram from Cardinal Ledochowski announced that Father O'Connell had been appointed Rector of the North American College.

O'Connell received the news with some trepidation, since he knew very well that the man he was replacing had been drawn into the controversies of the times and was no longer welcome in Rome. If he were to take on the job, would he, too, be forced to take sides, or would he be given a free hand in running the college in a manner approved by his "immediate superiors in Rome"?

Archbishop Williams saw the wisdom of O'Connell's question and advised him to take up the matter with the other three archbishops of the board of directors of the college. Cardinal Gibbons acquiesced, and the archbishops of New York and Philadelphia agreed warmly with O'Connell's point of view. Having secured their blessing, Father O'Connell departed for Naples.

He found Rome changed; it had grown into a great city and had lost much of its country atmosphere. Servants and students welcomed him warmly at the college, and he started to feel his way into his new responsibility. If he had had any romantic or ambitious dreams about it, they were shattered in his first interview with Pope Leo XIII. Leo informed O'Connell that he expected great things of the college under his rectorship. The Pope closed his general remarks with one of the incisive personal comments for which he was famous:

"You are young and strong, I see. That is good! You will need all your strength. Yes, you're rather young—but old enough if you follow good advice."

The rector began his reign with hard-headed realism by establishing cordial relations with his immediate superiors Monsignor Cisca and Cardinal Ledochowski. Next he got an increase of funds from the American bishops, which made it easier for him to conduct the college in keeping with the standards of comfort, elegance and hospitality which are the marks of Roman courtesy.

The students were quick to note the changes. They were more comfortable, the food was of better quality, the cooking improved. Father O'Connell, noted for his excellent preaching in Boston, now turned his talent to good advantage. Seated at a small green-baize covered table in the chapel, he gave the students biweekly instructions that were in accord with the width of his own culture and spirituality. They found him trenchant, witty and urbane, and they grinned a little, as students will, at his mannerism of putting on his pince-nez in moments of seriousness and then dropping it with a little jingle when he was amused or making an emphatic point.

O'Connell's youth was also an asset. The students took his advice and correction as if it were from an older, interested brother. At first apprehensive when he joined them in walks and excursions, they learned to enjoy his good-natured companionship and wide knowledge of the riches of Rome and Italy.

They were vastly pleased, too, when almost by a miracle he found and bought a summer villa for them—the Villa Santa Caterina, adjoining the papal villa at Castel Gondolfo in the Alban Hills.

Within two years, the Pope expressed his approval of Father O'Connell by making him a domestic prelate. The honor did not turn O'Connell's head, but it did mark him in Rome as a future celebrity in the American Church. People began to cultivate him; the cardinals of the Curia consulted him on questions affecting the United States; the great Roman princely families received him into their homes; he was a respected guest of the enormously rich Americans who lived in the Holy City between visits to the spas of Europe. Though many of the latter were not Catholics, they came to admire the shy young prelate for his wit, urbanity and bottomless knowledge of history, which did so much to enliven their boredom.

Music, which they all loved, was a further bond. On many occasions, the glacial atmosphere of puritanical politeness was warmed into a semblance of hilarity as their favorite monsignor sat down at the Steinway grand and let his fingers ripple over the keys.

Among O'Connell's closest friends was a young monsignor

by the name of Rafael Merry del Val. By background and talent, Merry del Val was destined for a great career in the Church, and his easy ways, facile English and charming personality, endeared him especially to all the students of the North American College.

After six years as rector of the college, Monsignor O'Connell was named Bishop of Portland, Maine. All his Roman friends rejoiced, though they realized how much they would miss his affable companionship.

In May 1901, O'Connell was consecrated bishop by Cardinal Satolli in the splendor of the Corsini Chapel in St. John Lateran. The crowd of celebrities overflowed out onto the geometric floor of the great church as the long ceremony progressed.

The bishop's welcome in Maine was astonishing; the governor gave an official reception in his honor, and Protestants and Catholics flocked to welcome him. The vast diocese soon felt the shock of his vigor and thoroughness as he visited every parish. Everyone was charmed with his masterly sermons.

With the death of Leo XIII in 1903, Cardinal Sarto of Venice became Pope Pius X, and Bishop O'Connell's good friend Merry del Val was made Secretary of State. The effects of the appointment, as far as O'Connell was concerned, were soon manifest.

On his first visit to the new pope, the Bishop of Portland was received with affection by a man who had few peers in unaffected warmth. Pius commended Bishop O'Connell for his good work and presented him with an exquisite reliquary of the true cross.

At the end of the audience, the Pope said, with a beaming smile, "You are young and strong, dear Bishop. Soon we shall have a great deal of work for you to do."

In the following year, Pius fulfilled his promise by appointing Bishop O'Connell papal envoy to the Emperor of Japan. The appointment was a shrewd one. In the recent Russo-Japanese War—in which the United States had exercised a benevolent neutrality toward the Japanese—Americans had achieved a certain popularity among them. Yet the termination of war had led to an outbreak of violent hostility to all foreign missionaries, particularly those from Europe.

The appointment surprised and terrified O'Connell. He had long been intrigued with the studies of Oriental art and customs, and he realized, as few men in his time did, the importance of maintaining face. It was easy to envisage how foolish he would look trying to keep his dignity while accommodating his huge frame to floor mats and tiny furniture. The fear at once haunted and amused him during the long sea voyage with his secretary, Father Collins, and Father Supple of Boston.

Upon his arrival in Tokyo, the bishop's fears melted away like swamp mist in the rising sun. A new liberal party under Prince Katsura had come into power while the papal legate had been at sea. O'Connell was received with deference, his quarters were splendidly furnished in Western fashion, the German Ambassador loaned him a smart victoria with two spirited bay horses.

On the day of his audience with the Emperor Mutsuhito, the glittering imperial carriage came for him. Resplendent in his full purple, the bishop, accompanied by his aides, swept across the moat and into the courtyard of the imperial compound.

Emperor and bishop liked each other at once; the exquisite politeness of the host was matched by the massive decorum of the visitor. All phases of Church problems were discussed through animated interpreters. As a mark of Mutsuhito's admiration, O'Connell was awarded a decoration—the Grand Cordon of the Sacred Treasure—and on his last night in Tokyo was entertained at a state banquet by Prince Katsura. The bishop drank a toast to his Sacred Majesty; Katsura returned the courtesy with a toast to the Pope.

In his report to Pius X in Rome after returning from the Orient, O'Connell gave the Holy Father an exhaustive description of the state of the Church in Japan. One of his points recommended the establishment of a Catholic university in Tokyo.

Two years later, Pius X established the school, which was placed in charge of the Society of Jesus, widely admired in the Orient since the days of Matteo Ricci.

O'Connell's successful mission received an immediate reward. Merry del Val personally informed his friend that he had been appointed Coadjutor Archbishop of Boston, with the right of succession.

Archbishop Williams received his coadjutor on April 3, 1906, in a brilliant ceremony at Holy Cross Cathedral. The aging prelate cordially welcomed his vigorous assistant. O'Connell, in his turn, offered the bishop his "complete devotion" and the "loyalty of a son to his father." To the people and priests, he promised no copy of his great predecessor but "his simple self."

The coadjutor had full need of his strength and courage. After a forty-year reign, Archbishop Williams was tired and ill. Almost immediately, he turned over burden after burden to his assistant. In a little more than a year he was dead, and O'Connell succeeded him on August 30, 1907.

The new archbishop had, even as a young priest, chafed at the careless way in which the diocese was run. Archbishop Williams had been a true father to his priests and people, but he had no mind for detail and was amiable to a fault. O'Connell, with his wide-ranging mind and directive talents matured in Rome at the American College, saw at once how much there was to do. He resolved to make the diocese a model based on the reform directives laid down by Pius X himself.

It was a tough decision, and the archbishop carried it out with tough-minded objectiveness. In his memoirs, O'Connell minces no words about the incompetence and confusion he found, and he minced no words in making radical necessary changes. Many were hurt; many resented his efforts.

One of his first acts was to place all charitable work under the direction of the Catholic Charitable Bureau. Within a few years, everyone was ready to commend his change. Expensive financing was cut to a minimum, overlapping efforts were ruled out, directorates were shaken up and reordered. The result was a comprehensive and practical effort that for the first time in its history met the social needs of the diocese. Institutions prospered and grew, and other bishops came to study O'Connell's plan and methods.

Colleges, schools and parishes all felt the change. Whatever criticism the archbishop voiced, in retrospect at least, was seen to be constructive. New colleges sprang up like mushrooms. Boston College and the other educational institutions of the diocese found themselves with new plans and increasing funds with which to execute them.

In emulation of Pius X, the archbishop found that charity begins at home; the chancery was efficiently reorganized, canon law was firmly enforced, the major seminary was refurbished, and plans for a minor seminary took shape.

On the purely spiritual front, the archbishop aided the Passionist Fathers and the Ladies of the Cenacle in opening retreat houses to which men and women could retire for an evaluation of their faith and devotion. In his own mind this was one of the most important moves in his long reign.

So wide was the swath cut by the Archbishop of Boston, so great was his impact on American life, that few were surprised when he was summoned to Rome for the reception of the red hat in the autumn of 1911. The cardinal-elect was not yet fifty-two years of age, a fact that gives us some measure of his stature as a prelate. Rome does not move with haste.

Boston took the new honor and the man to her heart. The respect and admiration for his native talent and dynamism were now lifted into adulation. The cardinal's word could make or break men in such an atmosphere. Politicians recognized this, and even the redoubtable Curley walked softly in the great presence.

The people realized that the cardinal was firmly on *their* side and that all his labors were for them and the Church. At heart he was the boy who sat at his mother's feet and wished Catholics to be a shining light to a culture that had once despised and underestimated them. He was jealous for them with the jealousy of Jehovah for his chosen people.

With the death of his beloved Pius X in August 1914, Cardinal O'Connell moved heaven and earth to get to Rome in time for the conclave. His ship rushed toward Italy under full steam, and the Italian Government put a fast train at his disposal in Naples, but he refused it and elected to go by car.

The effort was in vain. Cardinal O'Connell, along with Cardinal Gibbons, arrived shortly after the voting was over. The learned Della Chiesa had been elected and had chosen the name of Benedict XV. For O'Connell there was only one candidate, his great friend Merry del Val. It cannot be doubted that O'Connell's enthusiasm for his candidate led him to hope that his presence might have swayed the election. But Thomas Morgan's somewhat gossiping *Speaking of Cardinals* has magnified the disappointment beyond reasonable limits. O'Connell did strongly protest to the new pope that more time than ten days should be allowed for the arrival of distant cardinals. He might utter his discontent in a moment of pique, but he was far too shrewd to put himself in the position of becoming *persona non grata* at the papal court by casting doubt on the wisdom of the election.

Yet he sensed a change in the climate with Merry del Val's pseudoretirement. Never again would he have the sense of complete confidence in being at the heart of things in formulating Church policy. Later still, with the appointment of Bishop Spellman as his auxiliary, the cardinal felt himself supplanted by one who far outshone him in influence with the papal Curia.

Beyond such clashes of personality was the enduring reality of Boston. In the thirty years that remained, Cardinal O'Connell became a symbol of the new Boston that had come into being. It was not by chance that the wits among the Irish, traditionally "agin the government," gave him the title of "Number One." It was well merited. No single man of his time had done such outstanding things for so many people in Boston.

Every phase of Catholic life was ordered and organized. The guilds for professional men—beginning with St. Luke's guild for doctors—came into being, and guilds for social service workers and business people soon followed. The old medieval pride in craft and profession which the cardinal so warmly admired in his study of history became a living modern reality under the moral leadership of the Church.

The apostleship of the word was always near to the cardinal's heart. Few prelates of his time equaled him as a pulpit orator; fewer still had his complete understanding of the importance of communication and dialogue.

Early in his reign, he bought the Boston *Pilot*, made famous by John Boyle O'Reilly, and turned it into one of the finest diocesan newspapers in the United States.

From his experience as a lecturer in the Catholic Summer School, he organized a lecture bureau and the Catholic Truth Guild. By these means, the public was positively educated in Catholic belief and practices. In the light of such truth, many prejudices and old wives' tales withered and died.

Some of the cardinal's outstanding social improvements are well worth remembering. Through his Guild of St. Apollonia, he provided adequate dental care and supervision for all the parochial schools of the diocese. In the Catholic Guild for the Blind, he was even more of a pioneer. In cooperation with the famed Perkins Institute, he immeasurably furthered the teaching and care of the blind for the entire United States.

His diocese was his main preoccupation, yet there was nothing provincial about the man. In the struggle for Irish self-determination, he spoke out forcibly and bluntly for his people and lent his enormous prestige to the collection of funds through which this struggle was brought to a triumphant end.

The width of his love for all was demonstrated amply during the terrible influenza epidemic of 1918. Without a moment's hesitation, the cardinal turned the seminary, colleges and many other Catholic institutions, into infirmaries for the sick and dying, without reference to creed or color.

O'Connell was equally alert in seeing the need for missionary activity in the great world that did not know Christ. The Society for the Propagation of the Faith was strengthened under the inspired direction of Father Cushing, and its fund-raising activities were notable among the generous charity of a generous nation. Vocations for the missions were constantly and intelligently fostered. Father James A. Walsh, a priest of the diocese, was encouraged to found the Foreign Mission Society, which has become the miracle of Maryknoll.

As a man, Cardinal O'Connell was basically gentle and fatherly with all those who appreciated those fundamental virtues. When crossed or opposed, he could be truculent and punitive. The rules he made were strict, and he permitted no exceptions. Those who saw him in the company of the cultured and witty beheld the complete man; his knowledge and appreciation of art, music and literature were both deep and wide, his conversation had a tinge of droll humor, and his phrasing was worthy of a *salonnier.*

One must read his autobiography to savor his sentimental side—the powerful love he had for his mother, Our Lady and his dearest friends. The record is an honorable one that any man could be proud of. He wore neither his faith nor his patriotism on his sleeve, but evidence is there for both, massive as stone.

The cardinal was a brilliant pianist. He could compose music as well, and was a fair poet, as several good hymns bear witness. In his later years he spent many quiet hours at the piano, living over again the joys of his youth. One wonders if his tremendous bulk in those years was not an annoyance and a cross to one who had climbed mountains with his brood at the North American College and had shown competent horsemanship as he galloped through the meadows on his pony Billy.

In his last illness, the indomitable cardinal fought bravely against the pneumonia that threatened his life. He was eighty-five, the wonder drugs had not been discovered, the struggle was one of the few he had ever lost. Death came on April 22, 1944. The cardinal was conscious to the end, answered the prayers for the dying and gave a final blessing to the faithful members of his intimate household.

In a sense, his funeral was the triumph of his life. The eulogies poured in, the tears flowed, thousands upon thousands came to look upon him and do him reverence. What he had accomplished was the living memorial.

Dennis Cardinal Dougherty

———◆———

THE year 1865, despite the close of the Civil War, was a year
of sorrows. In April, the flags of the whole land were at
half mast as the crepe-decked mourning train bore the body of
Abraham Lincoln to his last resting place on the green prairie
of Illinois.

Later in the same month, the steamer *Sultana* exploded on
the Mississippi River. Seventeen hundred men of the 2,300 on
board perished; sadder still, they had been returning home
from gray days in southern prison camps.

In the quiet Pennsylvania Dutch towns above Allentown,
the black-bordered newspapers heralding these events were
reverently folded and put away in tin trunks for future generations. The war years had brought considerable affluence to
the district; the need for coal and iron in the pursuit of victory
provided work for everyone and brought to the old-fashioned
towns and villages new names and faces, many of them Irish.

Among these emigrating from County Mayo, were Patrick
Dougherty and his wife Bridget Dougherty. To them, the year
1865 was irradiated with quiet joy in the birth of their son
Dennis on August 16 in the village of Homesville. The village
scarcely deserved that title, since it was a collection of a dozen
frame houses in the environs of Girardville, most of whose inhabitants were in some capacity attached to the anthracite mines
of Schuylkill County.

The Irish were an ambitious lot, fiercely determined to give their children every possible advantage in the land of their adoption; they were ardently religious and depended for advice on Father Michael A. Sheridan, Pastor of St. Joseph's Church in Girardville.

It was Father Sheridan who baptized Dennis and in the years of his early growth detected in the stern-mouthed boy with the dark hair a quickness of mind and will and a devotion to his duties as altar boy that marked him as a candidate for the priesthood.

The record of those early years is a thin one. We know that the sturdy boy attended the public school in nearby Ashland until the age of ten, and after that went to high school in Girardville until 1880. In that year, at the age of fourteen, Dennis applied for entrance into Overbrook Seminary.

The seminary authorities considered him too young for admission, but Archbishop Ryan, who knew a promising young man when he saw one, sent the boy to St. Mary's College, which was run by the Jesuits, on Bleury Street in Montreal.

The long train trip north was an exciting experience for Dennis; equally electrifying was the revelation of the cosmopolitan city with its ancient churches and culture, so different from everything he had known in the Pennsylvania hills.

We have no record that he had difficulty adjusting to the ascetic life of dormitory and study hall and the strange cadences and complex verbs of the French language, but it can scarcely be doubted that there must have been initial moments of loneliness and discouragement, fought down and consumed in his driving ambition to learn everything he could with utmost thoroughness. The fact that he was from a large family had prepared him for discipline and amiable fellowship.

A solid grounding in the classics and a complete mastery of French that was to mark him in all the ensuing years had prepared Dennis to pass the entrance exams to Overbrook in 1882. His record in these examinations was so brilliant that he was permitted to skip the first two years of training. In the three years of his residence in Overbrook, he easily surpassed everyone in his classes and proved himself a born leader.

In 1885, Archbishop Patrick John Ryan did more than voice his appreciation by sending the stocky young man on a long slow sea voyage to Rome, where Dennis entered the North American College in September.

The twenty-five-year reign of Leo XIII was just breaking into full flower. Once again the world was looking up to a pope who resembled in intellect, force and grace, the most admired popes in history. However, the anticlericals still were powerful in the Holy City, and it was with something of a shock that Dennis heard himself cursed by a cabbie or endured being spit upon by passing priest-haters.

The North American College on Humility Street was a little cosmos of its own: bare in its cells and creature comforts, lovely in its baroque chapel, famous in its young rector, Monsignor Denis O'Connell, the intimate advisor and pawn-mover of Cardinal Gibbons and Archbishop Ireland of St. Paul. One of the senior students of the college, a great broth of a man named William O'Connell, was senior prefect, directed the choir, and was said to have a brilliant future.

To one of Dougherty's fierce ambition for self-improvement, Rome was heaven. There was a wealth of learning, culture and religious perfection waiting to be assimilated. He fell on his studies with zest, and in rambles about the city and its ancient churches, fairly crammed his mind with antiquity and beauty.

Among the teachers at the Urban College one man stood out with unusual power—Francis Satolli, who brought to his teaching of St. Thomas Aquinas inspired and eulogistic qualities that gave his lectures a pyrotechnic quality. Dougherty's acquaintance with Satolli ripened into an admiring friendship which lost no lustre through the years and was to play a large part in Dougherty's advance up the ladder of preferment.

Those who knew Dennis best admired the tough quality of his mind; he examined ideas minutely from every side, was able to comprehend them in their totality and express them in excellent Italian, Latin, French or English. Scholarship was almost a mania with him, but he was equally dedicated to sports and the practical application of religious truths to life.

Needless to say, he made an excellent record in his studies, which, a few weeks after his ordination on May 31, 1890, brought him the degree of doctor of divinity for work actually done and carefully examined.

Ordination took place in St. John Lateran and was performed by Cardinal Parrochi, the fatherly vicar-general of Leo XIII. Father Dougherty found the devotion of his Roman years amply rewarded by special permission granted him to offer his first Mass at the hallowed altar of St. Peter's Chair. Bernini's baroque gloria above him was symbolic of the transcendent joy in the young priest's heart.

It was almost with a sense of loss that he returned to the raw power of the American melting pot, with its striking exuberant roughness and fluctuating financial health. The very year after his return to Philadelphia, the Bank of America failed, causing the failure of several other banks and the American Insurance Company.

The reunion with the family in Girardville was a happy one for the young doctor. The Irish community turned out to a man for his first Mass and reception. They all felt a surge of prideful joy that one of their own had reached such a towering eminence of place and learning at the age of twenty-five. Friends and neighbors had a thousand questions to ask about the great Pope Leo, whose oleograph picture hung in most of their lace-curtained parlors.

Bishop Ryan appointed his glossy young doctor of divinity to a professorship at St. Charles Seminary in Overbrook, where he was to remain for thirteen years. We can gain some idea of the range of Dr. Dougherty's talents when we discover that at different periods he taught Greek, Latin, French, Hebrew and dogmatic theology.

Students found him strict and demanding. He did not tolerate fools gladly. Lack of preparation or excuses were met with his favorite maxim, *Labor vincit omnia* (work conquers every difficulty), enunciated with the dead-pan humor of a Chinese sage. They respected him for his scholarly solidity—not without charm—that demanded their devotion and best efforts.

That it was no mere pose, they could see from his own daily devotion to books and mental tasks that often appeared in scholarly articles in learned Catholic journals.

During his teaching years, Dr. Dougherty saw the last battles being fought by Cardinal Gibbons, Archbishop Ireland and their supporters, for a liberal American Church well-disposed toward labor, the public schools and ardent patriotism, as opposed to transplanted nationalism. The furor over false Americanism was hotly debated; Dr. Dougherty was on the liberal side himself, though his liberalism was tempered by his deep knowledge and wide experience of the Roman outlook.

Another event not so closely connected with his scholarly preoccupations, but central in the effect it was later to have on his life, was the Spanish-American War. The United States was in a jingoistic mood that crystallized into belligerence with the sinking of the battleship *Maine* in Havana Harbor in 1898. The war was soon over, but it left the United States with headaches that were to persist for many years to come, and it saddled the country with an imperialist reputation that still haunts us throughout the world.

One of the worst headaches at the turn of the century was the Philippines. We had annexed them from Spain and were trying to pacify the Islands whose guerillas were fighting us as they had once fought Spain.

As is usual in such a disturbed situation, the Church is the first sufferer. The natives mistrusted and persecuted their Spanish bishops of the old regime, and the result was religious chaos. Rome saw with hard-headed realism that it would be necessary to replace the Spanish prelates with American bishops.

Dr. Dougherty was the first to be chosen for appointment to the ancient diocese of Nueva Segovia at the north end of Luzon, with its capital at Vigan, about twenty-seven miles from Manila. The announcement of Bishop Dougherty's elevation came to Archbishop Ryan by telephone at Overbrook on the Tuesday of Holy Week, April 7, 1903. With some astonishment, he walked into Dr. Dougherty's study with the news. "You've been appointed bishop of Nueva Segovia in the Philippines. Do you accept?" he inquired in his booming voice. "You must be quick about it. The delegate is waiting for your answer."

Father Dougherty paled. "May I have a few moments to pray in the chapel?" he asked.

Permission was granted, and the archbishop waited out the short interval until his return.

"Your Grace," Dougherty said, with a slow seriousness that implied all he didn't know about his new assignment and its difficulties, "a priest should always obey the Holy See. I will go."

The bishop-elect was summoned to Rome for his consecration at the hands of Cardinal Satolli, who had obviously played a large part in Dougherty's nomination for the post.

It is some measure of the esteem in which Dr. Dougherty was held throughout the diocese that in the brief interval before his departure for Rome the archbishop and the priests of the diocese gave him a dinner at St. Malachy's Rectory and presented him with a check for $11,000 to which was added a second check for $550 from his friends among the laity.

Two days later, Dr. Dougherty sailed to Rome from New York on the liner *St. Paul*.

The consecration ceremony took place in the beautiful basilica of Sts. John and Paul, not far from Santa Maria Maggiore. In keeping with Rome's habit of dramatizing and inspiring her promising sons, the ceremony was carried out with splendor in the Chapel of St. John of the Cross, founder of the Passionists and one of the greatest missionaries of modern times.

It was a happy thought, for the young bishop was to find in the Philippines a set of circumstances that would have discouraged anyone but the most dedicated and virile type of priest.

Bishop Dougherty, thoroughly briefed and instructed, returned to the United States as speedily as the times permitted. Archbishop Ryan generously allowed him to recruit five priests as the core of his faculty in attempting to rebuild his ruined seminary in the Philippines. With canny wisdom, the bishop chose Fathers Daniel J. Guercke, John B. McGinley, James J. Carroll, James B. McCloskey and Edgar W. Cook. Except for Father Cook, who died a few years later in Philadelphia, all were to become bishops, either in the Philippines or in the United States.

Throngs of priests and people milled about the railway station on August 24, 1903, as the little band waited the departure of the Pittsburgh Express.

At last they were off in a flurry of cheers and good wishes for the trip to San Francisco. There were a few days for sight-seeing and visiting friends before departure from San Francisco on the S.S. *Corea* on September 3.

During every spare moment on the long voyage across the Pacific, the bishop paced the deck with a small Spanish grammar clutched in his big hands. There was much laughter among his confreres as they tried to match him in their understanding and pronunciation of the language.

The trip was far from being all work and no play; they enjoyed shuffleboard and other deck games, and joined in the concerts and merriment customarily found on shipboard, where people feel drawn swiftly together by the limited space and the loneliness of the sea about them.

The bishop and his priests left the *Corea* in Hong Kong, proceeding to Manila by smaller steamships. News of their arrival on October 6 had preceded them; the dock was crowded with American and Filipino celebrities led by Archbishop Guidi, Apostolic Delegate to the Philippines. Bands of school children waved tiny flags and sang out a shrill welcome. For about two weeks, the bishop and his group saw the sights of the big city, rested, and were carefully informed about the colossal tasks that awaited them in Vigan.

Yet in spite of the thorough briefing, they were hardly prepared for the reality they found on October 22, 1903, as Bishop Dougherty entered Vigan and took formal possession of the Diocese of Nueva Segovia. The cathedral was scarred by war and sadly in need of repairs, both outside and in. The bishop's house was in fairly good condition, but it had been entirely stripped of its furnishings, and the chapel had been used to stable a native general's horse.

The large seminary was in a state of complete disrepair; it had been despoiled of all its furnishings, and the many books in its excellent library had been appropriated by native shops and stores as wrapping paper. Bishop Dougherty was appalled, but he had not changed much from the stern-mouthed boy of his childhood. "It will improve," he said. "We'll beat it."

It wasn't merely repair of diocesan buildings of which he spoke. The native war against the Spanish, which had been going on for years, had unleashed a spirit of rebellion among the native clergy. One of them, Father Gregory Aglipay, had gone into schism with large numbers of his followers, and had taken over a great many church lands and buildings.

On his first visitation, Bishop Dougherty had doors slammed in his face and was threatened with bodily harm; he also found some of the half-ruined churches locked against him. First attempts to recover alienated property proved abortive. He next brought pressure to bear on the United States Governor in Manila, William Howard Taft, who advised him to resort to the court for redress.

It was first proposed that the bishop be prepared to prove Church ownership of the project involved, which he shrewdly rejected, maintaining that in justice it was Aglipay and his group who were the aggressors and must show title for the property they had taken. The United States Government in the Islands and the courts accepted the bishop's summary, and—after years of protracted litigation—most of the stolen lands and buildings were returned.

Bishop Dougherty quite unashamedly begged from every important person and organization he knew in the United States. Among his greatest American benefactors was the young Extension Society which on one occasion cabled him a large sum of money it was not quite sure it had in the treasury. Also, despite the explosive quality of Filipino emotion, Bishop Dougherty was fearless in approaching personally every family in Vigan that was financially able to help the work of restoration.

Gradually things began to fall into shape. The cathedral was repaired and beautified; pastors were found and trained for work in 110 parishes. The once-flourishing academy for girls was restaffed by the Sisters of St. Paul of Chartres and soon attracted the daughters of all the responsible families.

Best of all for the future, the seminary was thriving. During the war and first pacification of Luzon, American troops had occupied the building. The United States Government appropriated generous damage funds that helped the institution to new life and health. Compensation was also made for the church buildings damaged in the war.

The sorties to the courts in Manila and the demanding paperwork and correspondence of the large diocese were all done under the most trying conditions, between diocesan visitations by boat and horseback.

We can gain some idea of the bishop's stamina and labor if we recall that on one extensive visit he confirmed 70,000 people in a matter of weeks. Furious heat, towering mountains, cloudburst rains—nothing deterred him. He had the stamina and dedication of the greatest missionaries.

The crown of the bishop's work in Nueva Segovia came in the convocation of the provincial council of Manila in 1907, which he had largely inspired and prepared. Abuses and problems of the province were debated, new rules of conduct were drawn up, and a plan of action was laid out for the future.

Near the end of the year, Bishop Rooker of the large Jaro Diocese in the middle islands died. Rooker had been consecrated in Rome the same morning that Bishop Dougherty had received consecration, and though he had accomplished much, he lacked the driving energy of the Bishop of Nueva Segovia. On April 19, 1908, the Holy See asked Dougherty to move up to the larger see. It was in a sense a promotion, but the problems to be solved were far greater than the honor involved.

The bishop wouldn't have been human if he hadn't commented to himself and intimates about the "willing horse," but he accepted the new burden with the suavity that characterized him all his life. Besides, he had grown fond of these people; they were quick to hate, but equally quick to love, and their needs cried aloud for the help he could give them.

There were over 1,500,000 Catholics in Jaro, with only 52 diocesan priests and 72 priests of religious orders. Over half the parishes were without pastors. Illoilo welcomed the new bishop with joy. He spoke to his new flock fluently in Spanish, was affable, loved their children, and several times went to the United States to raise large sums of money for diocesan building and charities.

In the seven years in Jaro, he found pastors for most of the parishes—even from as far away as Mill Hill in England—built schools and thirteen new parishes, beefed up the seminary and academies of the diocese, and visited even the most distant barrios and the long-forsaken leper colony.

Both the bishop and his people were proudest of all of the large new hospital built in Illoilo, and staffed by the expert Sisters of St. Paul of Chartres.

On the occasion of Bishop Dougherty's silver jubilee on May 31, 1915, Jaro turned itself inside out to honor its shepherd. In the pale green of first dawn, exploding firecrackers announced the beginning of the great day. For the Solemn Pontifical Mass in the cathedral, the best musical talent in the Islands had combined with memorable results. All elements of the community were represented, whether Catholics or not, and the Illoilo *Enterprise-Press*, in a glowing front-page article, paid tribute to Bishop Dougherty for his zeal, amazing accomplishments and sterling manhood. The day ended with a grand reception and a brilliant display of fireworks embroidering the black velvet of the tropic sky.

In reply to the outpouring of extravagant praise, Bishop Dougherty replied briefly in Spanish, deprecating his own efforts, gracefully passing the credit to his priests, Sisters and the entire community. The great throng gave the speech a standing ovation of cheers and applause.

The *Enterprise-Press* had voiced the hope of Jaro that

Bishop Dougherty would still be among them for his fiftieth anniversary. Rome decreed otherwise. Advice came by wire from Philadelphia, on Tuesday, November 30, 1915, that Benedict XV had appointed Dougherty Bishop of Buffalo, New York, to succeed Bishop Charles Henry Colton. The news caused consternation in Jaro. There were affecting farewells. The bishop himself was sad to leave his warmhearted flock; he could remember with a grimace the hard days of endless confirmations as the perspiration rolled down his face in rivers, but he also remembered the beautiful soft faces of the country district children who had followed him, adoringly clutching at the hem of his cope and even the staff of his crozier. The bishop realized, too, that it would be a tonic shock to be shifted from this lush green paradise to one of the windiest and coldest cities in the United States.

Buffalo welcomed Bishop Dougherty with northern verve and vigor. On May 16, 1915, when he was installed in his beautiful cathedral by Cardinal Farley of New York, 50,000 men escorted him to his residence.

The new bishop, despite the cold, threw himself into the work of the diocese with almost shocking completeness. A quick survey showed him that there were many things to be done. The chief problem was the diocesan debt—over $1,600,-000—most of which had been spent on the lovely new Cathedral of St. Joseph—with its rumors of Chartres and San Marco in Venice. From hard experience in the primitive atmosphere he had known, the bishop saw only too well that a debt-ridden bishop is unable to meet the challenge of new situations or the demands of service to his people.

In a straightforward series of affable meetings with all the pastors of the diocese, Bishop Dougherty informed them that each parish would be assessed a tax in keeping with its size and means, which would be used to pay off the debt and meet the needs of expansion.

In the two remaining years of his tenure of office as Bishop of Buffalo, he began the complete reorganization of the Catholic schools and charities, established fifteen new parishes, and freed the diocese of debt. When the United States entered the First World War, he ardently supported the drives and social services with speeches and personal appeals.

On May 1, 1918, Benedict XV promoted Bishop Dougherty to Philadelphia, to succeed Archbishop Prendergast, who had died. Bishop Dougherty was the first native son to become archbishop of the see.

Buffalo was sorry to see him leave, but the City of Brotherly Love outdid itself to welcome its distinguished new leader on July 9, 1918. From every section of the huge diocese came large delegations; all of the numerous national groups and parishes were represented. Some brought their own bands and choirs; all bore resplendent banners and service flags.

At 6:45 P.M., the church bells pealed out a call to assemblage. The bishop's special train arrived at 8:27, and an enthusiastic reception took place on the flag-decked platform. A procession of seventy-five cars formed and proceeded along Broad Street through six miles of cheering people. The press of excited crowds was so thick that police lines were broken and the archbishop did not reach his residence on Race Street until 11 P.M. Visibly affected, he thanked everyone for the warmth of his welcome in words of sincere simplicity:

"I am very glad to be in Philadelphia after an absence of many years. I do not know of any place in the world where I would rather live than among the good people of Philadelphia. I am especially gratified with this splendid, but unmerited, reception."

The scenes of enthusiasm were duplicated on the following morning with the formal installation of the archbishop in his cathedral. The big church was jammed; thousands were massed outside in Logan Square and on the parkway.

The ecclesiastical procession from the rectory to the cathedral was of great splendor. Spectators pushing against the barriers pointed out the famous figures of the hierarchy as they passed, and a loud cheer went up when the frail crimson-clad form of Cardinal Gibbons was recognized.

The cardinal installed the archbishop in the gracious old

ceremony and paid high tribute to his talents and labors in the mission field. In reply, Archbishop Dougherty, after thanking everyone for their part in the ceremony, went out of his way to voice a panegyric to the cardinal, as the chief architect of the Church in America.

For days after, there were banquets, speeches and visits of ceremony. Among these, a visit to Girardville evoked a new peak of enthusiastic response.

The cardinal's sisters and two of his brothers had attended the ceremonies in Philadelphia. Once again they were at his side, and when the long reception was over, they escorted their distinguished brother to the frame house in which his aged mother waited with the warmest welcome of all.

The archbishop began a careful survey of his diocese and its needs. Before it was well underway, the dread influenza epidemic struck Philadelphia in 1918. The archbishop at once placed all the buildings and facilities of the diocese at the service of the city and state officials. Nuns and nurses worked around the clock, seminarians dug graves, every lay organization committed itself to the desperate struggle. When it was over, the mayor and governor paid the warmest tributes to the archbishop and his people.

The end of the war, on November 11, 1918, brought many French and other foreign visitors who came to thank Philadelphia and its archbishop for their generous charity. Among them was the noted Cardinal Mercier, Primate of Belgium.

On Tuesday, May 6, 1919, the cathedral was again of city-wide interest as handsome and princely Apostolic Delegate Archbishop Bonzano conferred on Archbishop Dougherty the sacred pallium in confirmation of his authority.

The archbishop was proceeding with a vast diocesan reorganization when, on February 13, 1921, the Philadelphia papers' headlines announced Archbishop Dougherty's elevation to the College of Cardinals. Rejoicing at the news was state wide. Officials and men of all faiths took pleasure in the honor.

The cardinal-elect, resplendent in a sleek silk hat and the

glossiest of black kid gloves, embarked on the *Nieu Amsterdam* with his suite on February 19, 1921.

The papal Undersecretary of State came to the North American College with the *biglietto* of nomination on March 7. For almost a week, the splendid pageantry of elevation to the Sacred College unrolled. After his reception of the great hat at the hands of Benedict XV on Thursday March 10, the cardinal sent two messages to his people, blessing them and referring the luster of the honor to his country, state, and all its people "irrespective of creed or race."

Receptions and festivities of the most glittering kind followed until Palm Sunday, March 20, 1921, when Cardinal Dougherty took possession of his ancient titular church SS. Nereus and Achilleus.

The cardinal participated in the ceremonies of Holy Week and had several audiences with the Pope. A dinner had been scheduled for Easter Monday, but it was canceled when the news of Cardinal Gibbons' death flashed over the wires. Cardinal Dougherty at once issued a statement filled with praise of his friend, beginning with the words: "By the death of Cardinal Gibbons the Church in America has lost one of the greatest men in its history, and our country a foremost citizen."

Cardinal Dougherty returned to the United States on the *Olympic,* to be greeted in a series of festivities and a torrent of praise such as few churchmen have ever received. His Eminence went through the barrage with serene good humor and continued self-deprecation; he did not forget his mining ancestry. The final reception at Girardville topped everything in delirious joy. Seldom had a papal honor been so liberally shared by all from the governor to the humblest citizen.

At the age of fifty-six, Cardinal Dougherty had moved from the poor mining section of Pennsylvania to the pinnacle of Church preferment. In his almost thirty-year reign as Philadelphia's cardinal, he had reached the peak of service to his city, the nation and the world.

In his sermon on the cardinalate on April 29, 1921, he had

said: "Whilst exalting the office, let the man be humbled. Let
him be filled with confusion that such as he should have been
thought of for so high a place." This humble summation gives
us a key to the cardinal's tremendous achievements over thirty
years. He had been signally honored, but the honor demanded
the utmost in service to the American Church and the Holy
See.

When Benedict XV died in January 1922, Cardinal Dougherty hurried to the conclave. The S.S. *Lorraine* was delayed by
storms, and the strong but scholarly Achille Ratti had already
been elected pope by the time Cardinal Dougherty reached
Paris on February 7.

The new pope received the cardinal in several lengthy audiences and promised that the papal constitutions would be
changed so that American cardinals would be given sufficient
time to take part in future conclaves.

The cardinal celebrated his episcopal silver jubilee in June
1922. Once again the hierarchy of the nation and officials of his
state and city participated in a brilliant series of ceremonies
culminating in the blessing of the magnificent new seminary of
Saint Charles Borromeo which had been building for eighteen
months.

The day of dedication, Sunday June 10, dawned bright and
clear as thousands of buses and cars converged on Overbrook.
Sixty thousand men, marching sixteen deep, were led by
contingents of the armed forces with flying banners, and twenty-
five bands and drum corps passed by the cheering thousands
along the way.

Apostolic Delegate Archbishop Fumasoni Biondi blessed the
Escorial-like gray granite buildings, the cardinal pontificated at
the Mass in the superb chapel, and a luncheon for the distinguished company was served in the refectory, with endless
speeches and warm felicitations. Then admiring thousands in-
spected the buildings.

In the years that followed, everywhere the cardinal went in
the United States and abroad on pilgrimages or required *ad
limina* visits to Rome, he received top news coverage, notably

at the eucharistic congresses in Chicago in 1926, Dublin in 1932, and Budapest in 1938.

Though only 5 feet 8 inches in height, he had a massive dignity. Along with his impressive appearance went a rangy mind, brilliant scholarship, and the ability to express himself in several languages—all of which made him perennially popular.

His reception in Eire was particularly warm, because of the large part he had played in helping Ireland achieve her independence. During the Black and Tan troubles after the First World War, the cardinal had permitted a collection in his diocese which had brought in almost $100,000 to support the Irish people in their struggle.

Of all his appearances abroad, the most notable was at the eucharistic congress in Manila, which was in a sense his second home. The announcement by the press in October 1936 that Pius XI had chosen Cardinal Dougherty to be his legate *a latere* to the thirty-third eucharistic congress in Manila caused wide comment, since it was the first time an American had been selected for such a mission.

Cardinal Dougherty journeyed to Rome with an imposing suite. All along the way he was treated like a reigning prince. Having received his instructions from the ailing pope, he took the S.S. *Conte Rosso* at Naples on June 10. The ship, which flew the papal flag, had been placed at the disposition of the legate and a huge throng of pilgrims.

Twenty-one days later, the *Conte Rosso* sailed into Manila to a welcome that would have warmed the most jaded. The cardinal was one of their own; many remembered him and his labors for the Islands. Guns boomed, gaily decorated launches and boats shrilled horns and whistles, an enormous crowd, led by the president and all the dignataries of church and state, waited on the dock. Following the reception, the legate and his suite were housed in the presidential palace.

Weather and the times had combined to make every act of the Congress a brilliant success. The huge amphitheatre at Luneta Park echoed to the hymns and prayers of millions led by their bishops from all over the Christian world.

On Sunday, February 7, the climax of the devotion was the eucharistic procession. Two hundred thousand marched in groups through some 600,000 spectators. At 9:00 P.M., after the closing benediction, the voice of the Holy Father was heard giving his apostolic benediction to the assembled crowds.

En route home on the *Tatsuta Maru*, Cardinal Dougherty stopped in Tokyo, where he was feted by the government and had a cordial audience with Emperor Hirohito. The cardinal, accompanied by the Archbishop of Tokyo and the apostolic delegate, visited the Shinto shrines and prayed for the Japanese servicemen buried there. This act put an end to a controversy that had troubled Vatican-Japanese relations for years.

Another facet of Cardinal Dougherty's prominence on the world scene came from his early devotion to the Little Flower. Long before she was widely known, Bishop Dougherty had read her life with amazement and had espoused her cause. On his many trips to Lisieux, he came to know the Sisters of Therese, and in visits with Pius X and succeeding popes had supported her cause warmly. In time, everyone in and around Lisieux looked on the stout American prelate as the Cardinal of the Little Flower. From 1913 until the canonization of the saint in 1935, he made frequent trips to her shrine, and it gave him great joy to assist at the dedication of the great Basilica in Lisieux—to which he had been a generous contributor—in 1937.

The world-wide prominence of Philadelphia's cardinal and his many journeys did little to slow his work at home. In all the years he lived at the cathedral rectory, he said the six-o'clock Mass and preached the Sunday sermon. Saturday afternoons and evenings saw him in his confessional, like any humble curate.

Everyone in his official family knew how hard he drove himself in long hours of paperwork in the simple chancery, in public appearances, confirmations, church and school dedications, which were but a sampling of his labors. There was not a committee for the cultural or physical welfare of his state and city that was complete without him. In great celebrations such as the sesquicentennial celebrations of independence in 1926 and the adoption of the Constitution in 1937, he brought out the Catholics of state and city in thousands, to glorify patriotism and love of America.

The first flock he had shepherded had been dark-skinned children, and he loved and tended them with a complete devotion that in his new eminence was channeled into massive aid for American Negroes and Indians. His encouragement of Mother Catherine Drexel in her apostolate, his massive aid to the Extension Society and the Indian missions, give us part of the magnificent story. More telling still was his encouragement of Doctor Anna Dengel and her associates in their Medical Misson Society with its headquarters at Fox Chase. The cardinal's two compelling memoranda moved the Holy See to open up a completely new field of missionary activity for Catholic women by granting qualified Catholic nuns permission to practice medicine.

In the twenty-two crowded years as Archbishop of Philadelphia up to the celebration of his golden jubilee, the accomplishments of Cardinal Dougherty were more than remarkable by any standard of judgment.

The statistics—106 new parishes established, 75 new churches built, 22 others renovated, 20 new ecclesiastical buildings—mostly for the wide-flung social services—146 new schools and academies, 7 homes for the aged, 7 orphanages, 3 retreat houses for women, 1 for men, and the magnificent new seminary, give us a paper view of the total. If to this we could add a visit to some of the outstanding colleges, hospitals, churches and academies, we would begin to comprehend the magnitude and the beauty of those years.

The cardinal was a worker and always had been. In getting so much done, he ran his diocese according to strict rules. Because of his own hard life as a youth and later as a missionary, he sometimes was impatient with the lack of results. He considered young priests inclined to be pampered; the strict rules he made for them in regard to cars and other creature comforts were in their eyes old-fashioned and out of tune with a large diocese and the demands of the age. Yet they all took pride in his Eminence's accomplishments and the fact that he remained one of the most learned men of his time.

It was with complete enthusiasm that they threw themselves into the celebration of his golden jubilee on May 30, 1940, an occasion that brought out one of the most notable gatherings of Church and state leaders that Philadelphia had ever seen and sparked effusive tributes, from the Pope to the humblest citizen.

At seventy-five, the cardinal looked young for his age and went through the tiring celebrations with zest, verve and flashes of notable wit.

Few priests live to see their golden jubilee, and if they do, are of an age to accomplish little after it. The cardinal was more blessed in that he kept his drive and complete faculties for over ten years more. Quietly he went on planning and building. In his fine new home at 5700 City Avenue, fifteen minutes from the chancery, he was able to return to the pleasure of his books and the casual entertainment of his wide circle of friends and notable visitors.

Death came on May 31, 1951, the day after he had celebrated his sixtieth anniversary as a priest; he had been a bishop for forty-eight years and a cardinal for almost thirty.

Most of his contemporaries were dead, but the cardinal's standing and fame were as bright as ever for the thousands who came to do him honor in a last great burst of solemn pageantry.

From earliest youth, he had been an outstanding intellectual, and to this he added the laurels of a great missionary and a courageous and wide-visioned administrator. The parable of the wise use of the talents had been beautifully exemplified in him. For his Lord, he had multiplied his gifts a thousandfold.

George Cardinal Mundelein

IT may or may not be prophetic that George William Mundelein, first cardinal of Chicago, and one of the greatest builders in the history of the Church in the United States, should have been born just about a year after the "great fire" that almost completely destroyed the city. George's father Francis Mundelein and his mother Mary were of solid German stock.

The scene of his birth on July 2, 1872, was a tenement on the lower east side of Manhattan in a section occupied largely by Germans who had fled the militaristic atmosphere of their homeland. The section within a half-mile radius of Mundelein's birthplace was noted for its crime rate. But the rain falls on the just and unjust, and the same circle was the nursery of many famous New Yorkers such as a Cardinal Hayes, Al Smith and many appealing figures of the American theatre.

The Mundelein family was poor but respectable, with an intense German regard for cleanliness and hard work. They were quiet, deeply religious and fiercely patriotic, though part of their poverty stemmed from the fact that their grandfather had left his moderately successful business to enlist in the Union Army at Lincoln's intitial call for volunteers. Mundelein was the first man killed at the battle of Fort Sumter. The large family he left behind him was two generations recovering from the blow.

President Grant's election to a second term of office coincided with the birth of the cardinal. One of the wonders of the world, the Brooklyn Bridge, was being built within earshot of the Mundelein home.

George began his education early at St. Nicholas' Parochial School which was staffed by the Sisters of St. Dominic. The boy was avid for learning and fairly raced through his tasks. Though he looked "amiable as an angel" in his altar boy's regalia, his muscular solidity enabled him to take good care of himself in the rough-and-tumble life of the district in which "micks, wops, kikes and polacks" fought each other and occasionally united against the nativism of patronizing Protestants.

Through family sacrifice and his own initiative in finding odd jobs, George was able to enter De La Salle Academy on Second Street. The young man applied himself to his studies with genuine German determination and completed his course in record time.

His notable sharpness and the interest of political friends led President Grover Cleveland to offer George a commission to Annapolis. It was a signal opportunity, but after contemplating himself as a noted admiral in a cocked hat, George smiled wryly and refused the offer. Another calling had come to dominate his mind.

Looking inward at himself and his heart-lifting religious orientation, and outward at the opportunities for distinguished service, George came to the conclusion that his talents and idealistic desire to serve his people could best be achieved in the priesthood. All through his childhood, at Mass and Vespers, he definitely had heard the call to the higher life.

It was this decision, aided by the advice and example of the devoted nuns and priests he had known, that took him on to Manhattan College from which he graduated in 1889 at the youthful age of seventeen.

George had already been "adopted" as a candidate for the priesthood by Bishop McDonnell of Brooklyn. Because of the boy's brilliant accomplishments, frank and engaging manners, and devotion to study, the amiable bishop came to take a personal and special interest in him.

As a result, George was sent on to St. Vincent's Archabbey near Beatty, Pennsylvania, for further study. Here in the idyllic calm and bracing air of the mountains, George kindled his appreciation of Benedictine scholarship and love of the liturgy for three years. His long walks through the winter forest and quiet hours in the great abbey church, listening to the monks singing the divine office in the moving melody of plain chant, intensified his love of the great artistic and philosophical heritage of the Church.

In 1892, Bishop McDonnell placed his protégé in the Urban College of Propaganda in Rome. The Mundelein clan thrilled at the appointment; George was the most thrilled of all. It seemed almost impossible that the innumerable exciting places he had read about would now become part of his daily life.

It was with nervous excitement that he arrived at the North American College after a fascinating trip through France. His cell proved to be a large almost bare room, some twenty feet square, paved with worn and chipped bricks. A desk-bookcase of the most rudimentary sort, a rush-bottomed chair, a narrow iron bed with a straw-and-husk-filled mattress clothed in coarse white linen, and a rusty iron washstand completed its furnishings. There was no heat.

His initial disappointment over these Spartan surroundings was swept away when he followed the line of cassock-clad students into the college chapel. Here all was exquisite perfection. The wealth of antique marbles glittering everywhere in the walls and pilasters was caught up in the baroque glory of the porphyry altar with its unforgettable madonna smiling down at the students on their walnut kneeling benches.

The tiny courtyard flanked by generous cloisters was also a delightful spot; songbirds loved its massed greenery. The pebbled paths led to a graceful column topped by a statue of Our Lady of Wisdom at its center, like a small geometric exercise.

At the base of the column, a tiny fountain sent up its pure jet with continual music.

The hour of rising was 5:30. Morning prayers in the chapel were from 6 to 6:30, followed by a half-hour meditation, Mass and thanksgiving. After breakfast, which consisted of coffee and hard rolls, George helped clean his room and made the bed. At 8:30 he joined his group of ten for the march through the narrow streets to the College of the Propaganda.

Classes were from 9 to 11, followed by an hour of study and a light lunch. There was a short visit to the Blessed Sacrament after lunch, then mail hour in the little garden, a time of excited babble until the big bell jangled for the brief siesta. There were two more classes at the Propaganda late in the afternoon. For many students, the most interesting part of the day was the long two-hour walk to the most celebrated buildings and gardens in Rome. This was augmented by longer sightseeing excursions on Thursdays, Sundays and holidays.

Having grown accustomed to the heavy German meals of St. Vincent's Abbey, the light fare provided by the North American College bothered George in the beginning, but he got used to it. The first lean years under Monsignor Denis O'Connell were followed by better ones when Father William O'Connell of Boston arrived to direct the college. Under his thoughtful care, the food was considerably augmented and some small semblance of creature comforts were gradually introduced.

Every day was a delight for the young man. Though he missed his family and friends, the challenge of studying under superb teachers and the living wealth of art, architecture and history spread out before him gave George a new concept of the Church.

At home, everything was built to be replaced or thrown away; in Rome, the Church seemed to build for eternity. Churches and public buildings there displayed magnificence; no costs had been considered too great in achieving this perfection. It was a lesson Mundelein never forgot and one that was to influence him profoundly in his important roles as bishop and cardinal.

There were other important social lessons to be learned as well. At the Propaganda, his fellow students were of every race and nation: black skinned, yellow, brown, white, and every shade in between, yet they all got along together in peace and respected each other's culture in the complete democracy of the Church. They learned, played and prayed together. Without respect for the fatherhood of God, George saw, democracy was merely a name without genuine reality.

The students at the college often joked about their uniform; the blue piping on the cassock, the red sash and gleaming white clerical collar were daily reminders of the red, white and blue of the national flag. They could joke about it, but the national colors they wore stimulated in them a pride in their appearance and conduct as they sauntered about the Eternal City.

George's years in Rome were significant ones for the Church. Leo XIII had already issued his great encyclicals and was at the very top of his fame. Crowds of pilgrims came to receive a blessing from the great pope. When they first saw him, he seemed almost too fragile to be alive, but when his wide mouth smiled and his large, dark eyes flashed, it was easy to appreciate the warmth and depth of his personality.

Leo had brought the philosophy of Aquinas back into vogue. Contemplating the perennial youth of the "angelic doctor" in his studies, Mundelein came to realize how necessary wisdom was in formulating any program that was to achieve success.

Much was also to be learned from the celebrated visitors who came to the college on important occasions. The students were particularly attracted to Monsignor Merry del Val in whom they found brilliant inspiration. Though as impressive as the most handsome Renaissance prince, he had retained the easy informality of his English school days; not even the humblest student feared to approach him. They delighted in his perfect English, and it was whispered that his skill with a rifle was equal to that of Buffalo Bill.

Normally, students at the college remained in Rome for three years and then were ordained by the cardinal vicar. At the end of his three years, George was ready for his ordination. He had attracted general attention because of his brilliant record, but the canonical age for ordination was twenty-four and George was only twenty-three. As a result, he had almost an extra year in Rome, during which he applied himself diligently.

About a month before his twenty-fourth birthday, Bishop McDonnell arrived in Rome. A dispensation was granted permitting George to be ordained in advance of the required age. What was still more extraordinary was the fact that Bishop McDonnell had secured a further dispensation to ordain his protégé instead of the cardinal vicar.

The ceremony took place in the seclusion of the chapel of the Holy Cross Sisters. A few days after the young priest's first Mass, offered again by special dispensation, the bishop and Father George began their voyage back to the United States. After a triumphal and restful summer with his family, George became assistant secretary to Bishop McDonnell and went to live in the bishop's house.

Responsibility and honor came to him within a few years. For a brief interval, Father George was in charge of the Lithuanian Church in the Williamsburg district. A short time later he was made rector of the cathedral chapel, Queen of all Saints. During his time as rector, Father Mundelein was responsible for building the widely admired Gothic chapel and school. He chose Gothic because it was a pure style little known in America, but entirely in keeping with tradition and the magnificence he had come to appreciate in France.

Two years after his ordination, at the age of twenty-six, Father Mundelein was appointed chancellor of the huge Brooklyn diocese. A great many of its parishes were Italian, and their problems were many and acute. The young priest, with his subtle understanding of the Italian language and mentality, was able to settle many of the outstanding difficulties. His work proved valuable in providing a bridge between Italian folkways and American citizenship.

Rome watched his rapid rise and shrewd judgment. In 1903, Mundelein became censor of the Liturgical Academy; in 1906, a domestic prelate of the Pope's household, with the title of Right Reverend Monsignor; and in 1907, a member of the ancient academy of Arcadia because of his sparkling defense of Pius X's encyclical condemning Modernism.

The busy monsignor was already a noted personage when, as the personal representative of the aged bishop, he arrived in Rome for the sacerdotal jubilee of Pope Pius X in 1908. Old Roman friends and acquaintances remarked on the monsignor's air of command and openhanded generosity. Merry del Val, who had become a cardinal and the all-powerful Secretary of State, was pleased to observe the vindication of his favorable first impression of the brilliant student. What the authorities were all saying privately was made public knowledge when the College of Propaganda honored the visitor with the degree of doctor of divinity.

A year later, Monsignor Mundelein became Auxiliary Bishop of Brooklyn. Bishop McDonnell consecrated him on September 21, 1909, and in the same year made him rector of the new preparatory seminary, Cathedral College of the Immaculate Conception, at the age of thirty-seven.

In the six years between his consecration and his translation to Chicago as archbishop in 1915, Mundelein endeared himself to everyone in the Diocese of Brooklyn. There was much regret and consternation at his departure. Admirers consoled themselves with the thought of his rapid promotion to the higher office.

George might well have trembled at the promotion. He was succeeding Archbishop Quigley, one of the most forceful bishops in the American hierarchy. The problems arising in the melting-pot atmosphere of Brooklyn were slight compared to the social problems and the national rivalries in Chicago. But George loved problems; they challenged him, brought out the best in him. On previous visits, the breezy character of the people of the Windy City had charmed and impressed the young bishop. Their self-reliance, outspoken manners, and love of progress with no thought of the cost, were entirely in keeping with what he had seen of the Church in Europe, particularly in Rome.

Headlines in all the papers and phalanxes of pictures marked the new archbishop's arrival. It was a case of love at first sight. Chicago was thrilled when the fair-haired young archbishop said: "I think Chicago is the greatest city in the world. The blood of New York flows in my veins, but it is no disloyalty that prompts me to voice my admiration for this my new city. It is such a mistake to say that New York is typical of the new world simply because it has so many nationalities represented there. The foreigners in New York have not become accustomed to their new country. They are Poles, Germans or Italians. They are not Americans. Chicago is a typical American city. We have as many nationalities here as in New York, but they are Americans all. They have lost their hyphens. I have great faith in Chicago and expect to see it grow and prosper every year."

These words expressed perfectly the city's mood at the time. Great plans were in the air. Already the long reach of the Outer Drive, reclaimed from the waters of Lake Michigan and studded with beautiful parks, showed faint signs of the splendor which makes it one of the most beautiful avenues in the world today.

Chicago had arrived. A group of Midwestern poets and writers, sparked by Harriet Monroe's magazine *Poetry* and including Carl Sandburg, Ezra Pound and Vachel Lindsay, were challenging New York. A man by the name of Frank Lloyd Wright was astonishing the world with "crankish" new concepts in architecture. North Shore millionaires were importing art by the carload. Despite the frenetic headlines reporting the inspiring words of Woodrow Wilson and the drift toward war, the talk was all of art and culture.

However, the archbishop soon discovered that the beautiful face lifting of the Outer Drive and "Mich Boul" was a mask for fetid alleys and dark streets in which terrible social problems cried for reform along the lines of the work already begun by Jane Addams at Hull House.

At the civic dinner tendered the new archbishop, a hint of Chicago's sinister side emerged in the action of a deranged anti-clerical chef who seasoned the soup with a liberal dash of arsenic. Fortunately, though many notable guests were made severely ill, no one died.

Archbishop Mundelein threw himself into the reorganization of his diocese. Within a year, his plans had begun to take shape and direction. A board of school supervisors was appointed to coordinate work in the diocese and schools. In November 1961, the archbishop turned the first shovel of earth for the new preparatory seminary named in honor of Archbishop Quigley. Once again Mundelein chose Gothic as the style for the new chapel and school buildings.

Education had been his first concern, but it was no nearer to his heart than his interest in social problems. The archbishop prompted the Knights of Columbus to sponser an institution for delinquent boys, and then prevailed upon important groups of women to establish clubs for working girls trooping into Chicago from all over the Middlewest. They came for many reasons, but what they often found was loneliness, boredom and a host of dishonest and greedy people who took advantage of their ignorance. The clubs offered them companionship, advice and the chance to meet better people.

The archbishop displayed the same hard-headed realism in dealing with the girl delinquents sent by court order to the houses of the Good Shepherd. A scale of wages was set up for the various kinds of work, and most of the girls soon had sufficient savings to insure them a chance to begin a new life after their release from the protectory. Big-brother and big-sister movements were also encouraged. The accent of the first year was strictly upon youth, a lesson the archbishop had learned the hard way in the neighborhood in which he was born.

In the second year of his reign, Archbishop Mundelein began the work of reorganizing the Catholic charities and strengthening the already existing St. Vincent de Paul societies at the parish level. Over the years he gradually unified and financed all charitable and social agencies under a single command. One of the splendid steps in the program was the establishment of the beautiful Misericordia Hospital for the relief and care of young mothers who could not afford the high fees charged by many of the big institutions of the county.

The archbishop found a lack of opportunity for the higher education of girls in the diocese. At his invitation, Dominican Nuns from Sinsinawa, Wisconsin, founded Rosary College in River Forest; and nearer the city, where it would be convenient for all, Mundelein College, under the direction of the Sisters of Charity of the Blessed Virgin Mary. None of this was achieved in a vacuum. The work of the chancery kept the archbishop busy at his desk for many hours each day. There were endless meetings with important religious and civil committees and endless confirmations throughout the diocese.

With the onset of war, Mundelein plunged into the Liberty Bond drives with a passion reminiscent of his grandfather's rush to the colors at Lincoln's call. In the third bond drive, the archbishop was largely instrumental in selling $6,000,000 worth of bonds. The Secretary of the Treasury made it a point to stop off in Chicago in order to congratulate him.

The archbishop worked on many levels including politics. Like Pius X in Mantua and Venice, Mundelein made his influence felt at city hall and in Cook and Lake counties, both by declaration and act. Politics had always been a "dirty business" in Chicago, but it was a dirty business the people tolerated.

By sheer charm and forthright action in word and deed, Mundelein worked for better government, yet his relations with the all-powerful Mayor Thompson and political bigwigs were usually good-humored, and on their side deferential. To the archbishop, politics was just another means to forward the work of the Church. Good relations with civil powers were often advantageous in expediting transfers in building new parishes and in securing permissions of all kinds. The archbishop was a realist, and he played the game to the hilt.

Among prestigious people like Samuel Insull and Potter Palmer, Mundelein's name had a special force and meaning. When the archbishop was on the bandwagon, the wagon rolled. The millionaires of the Gold Coast were quick to see the point. They found the archbishop useful; in turn, he found them valuable. In a city that admired optimism and big thinking, Mundelein charmed his gilded audience with grandiose plans that made them gasp and give.

Preparations for celebrating the diamond jubilee of the archdiocese took shape in 1920. No one was surprised when the archbishop announced that the chief work of the jubilee would be the building of a major seminary at Libertyville on the shores of Lake Area. Mundelein's plans called for one of the largest and most comfortable seminaries in the world. There was wide rumor that it was to be built in Early American instead of in such traditional Continental styles as Romanesque or Gothic.

The truth was that Mundelein's attitude toward architecture had changed. Summer vacations in New England had led him to admire the serene, pure style of the old churches he saw there, particularly the church at Lyme, Connecticut. It was this church the archbishop chose as his model for the seminary chapel. All the other buildings conformed with it.

Mundelein was equally original in staffing his seminary. The administrative offices were held by diocesan priests; the faculty was composed entirely of Jesuits. The arrangement worked well, so superbly well in fact that Rome eventually granted the seminary the unusual privilege of conferring on special students the doctorate of sacred theology. And the town of Libertyville changed its name to Mundelein, a well-merited accolade.

In March 1924, Mundelein received notice of his elevation to the cardinalate, which he kept from the public until he could draft a pastoral letter to his priests announcing the honor. Chicago was widely excited at the news. Gifts and congratulations poured in, and the cardinal-elect departed for Rome in a cloud of newsmen. He was especially pleased that his bishop friend of long standing, Patrick Hayes, was to receive the red hat at the same time.

In this strictly American consistory, Pius XI went out of his way to declare that he was elevating the two archbishops to the Sacred College because of their own merit and his gratitude to America for her world-wide charities.

In the ensuing ceremonies, Cardinal Mundelein, well qualified by long Roman training and observation, took the lead. His reply to the Pope was gracefully complimentary without overstating the many golden links that bound the United States to Rome and the See of Peter.

Chicagoans followed every step of the proceedings in long front-page articles in their newspapers. By the time the cardinal arrived home on May 11, 1924, welcoming committees had worked themselves to a fever pitch. All the careful plans were nearly swept away in the shouting mobs of people who greeted their cardinal. Everyone wanted to see him, to touch him, to congratulate him. Police lines were broken, horns, whistles and clackers sounded in complete pandemonium. The cardinal accepted the uproarious welcome and endless congratulations in a robust and delighted fashion that further endeared him to Midwestern hearts. There was no pretense about him; he obviously enjoyed the new honor and all the rowdy fuss.

Just how much they loved him was concretely demonstrated two days after the cardinal's return at the conclusion of the Pontifical Mass of thanksgiving in the Holy Name Cathedral when his priests and people presented him with a check for $1,000,000 for his new seminary.

The new honor enhanced and solidified his status in the city and the entire Midwest. On notable occasions when he made a dramatic appearance in his brilliant moire silk with the grand cross of the Knights of Malta glittering at his throat, people were thrilled at the sight of the boy from poor circumstances who had risen to such eminence. The millionaires along the North Shore, many of whom had bought in England a portrait or two of some bogus distinguished ancestor to hang on their walls, were equally enthralled at the sight of the real prince in their midst.

The cardinal's love of drama displayed itself in other ways. He was often late in starting out for important affairs. In fact some people referred to him (without malice) as the "late Archbishop of Chicago." When he finally left his house, three of the police department's best motorcycle cops preceded his big black limousine. With sirens blaring, they whisked the cardinal through every red light on the way to his destination.

He had arrived home with a fabulous plan in mind. His grand designs for his people had been chiefly concentrated upon youth. Now he wished to provide an unforgettable inspiration for the young and all those who loved God. The cardinal's plan called for an international Eucharistic Congress to be held in Chicago in June 1926. It was going to be the most fervent and picturesque pageant in the history of the city. The cardinal talked of the plan with such vividness that everyone could already see it coming to pass, but he left nothing to chance. Committees were formed carefully, funds were raised, enthusiastic advance publicity was sent out over the entire world. Hotel space was carefully surveyed and reserved in advance.

With the dawn of the summer of 1926, 1,000,000 Catholics had arrived in Chicago from almost every country in the world. Cardinal Bonzano, the Pope's legate *a latere,* was received in state, followed by the reception of eleven other cardinals by the time the week of devotion had come to its inspiring close. Three hundred and seventy-three bishops and archbishops added their brilliance to the occasion. Five hundred monsignori, 8,000 priests and tens of thousands of Sisters in varying and picturesque garb engrossed the interest of Chicago.

The congress was opened at a monumental altar in Soldier's Field. For days, pageant after pageant unfolded as the devoted delegates poured out their love of Christ in Eucharist hymns of praise. Ten thousand children sang the *Missa de angelis* with spine-chilling perfection on children's day. To the chagrin of some disturbed Protestants, Catholic news took over the front pages of all the newspapers. Reporters wore their adjectives thin in purple descriptions.

The grounds of the seminary had been chosen for the final procession and pontifical benediction. Everyone trooped out to Mundelein to witness the event. The dense crowds massed on the bright expanses of grass watched the seemingly endless lines of lights and color as the procession moved along the flower-bordered paths and over the gently curving bridges. A great flame of massed cardinals preceded the legate carrying the monstrance under a splendid jeweled canopy of gold. A sudden drenching rainstorm marred the close, but failed to dampen the enthusiasm of those who marched and those who watched them.

The resounding success of the Congress impressed Chicago with the cardinal's ability to do things in the biggest possible way. He was pleased with the tremendous devotion of his people and the cooperation of all those Catholics and non-Catholics who had aided him in achieving his goal. Best of all, he had proved to the timid and the doubters that there was a tremendous store of goodwill which the presence of Christ in the Eucharist could bring out in the open for all the world to see and admire. Communism had done much to kindle the enthusiasm of its followers by staging public spectacles of all kinds. The innate shabbiness and brute force of materialism, with its miles of muscles and cannon, was shown up in the mounting waves of love for Christ which were at the very heart of the vivid pageantry in Chicago.

On the cardinal's various trips to Rome, he always behaved in princely style. Honest need of any kind evoked from him an immediate and generous response. The restoration and refurbishing of his titular church, his open-handed response to every papal charity, the financial aid he offered to indigent German bishops and many others after the First World War, gave Cardinal Mundelein a special stature in the eyes of Rome. The rapidity with which he had built so many churches and schools at home and the splendor of the eucharistic congress led to the belief in the Eternal City that Mundelein was a genuine financial wizard. It was this combination of magnificence, *expertise* and responsive affability which led Pius XI to ask him to finance the building of the new Urban College, one of the Pope's pet projects.

The cardinal enthusiastically fell in with the Holy Father's plan. A commercial loan for the project was easily floated in Chicago, and the work began. Mundelein was distinctly *persona grata* at the papal court, and everyone commented on how much at home he was there. Pius XI selected him to take his place at the Solemn Pontifical Mass on the day the superb new building was dedicated. The tribute was deepened during the ceremonies when the Pope suddenly appeared to congratulate Mundelein on the great part he had played in the joy of this "consoling day." It was the Holy Father's second appearance outside Vatican City since the settlement of the Roman question in February of 1929.

The wearing business of directing his huge diocese did not distract the cardinal from his ability to look into the future. In 1928, he chose Father Bernard Sheil as his auxiliary bishop. In the beginning of his priestly career, Sheil was rated as something of a maverick. Actually he was a dedicated reformer who was consumed with rage at the many social ills confronting him. With his consecration, great things were accomplished. Notable among them was the establishment of the Catholic Youth Organization in which Sheil gave the youth of Chicago and eventually of the entire country a rallying cry and virile outlet for their energy and frustration. The magazine *Today* was founded, and young people began to reveal their talents for leadership. The cardinal warmly supported Sheil. When men of all faiths combined to praise his auxiliary, Mundelein gracefully stepped aside to allow the bishop to accept the limelight and the richly merited praise.

In forwarding the work of Mother Cabrini, the cardinal immensely aided another social reformer of top rank. He had been a friend of the saint in both Brooklyn and Chicago. When she died, the cardinal enthusiastically supported her cause, and it was with both joy and pride that he accepted the Pope's request to officiate at the glittering ceremonies of Mother Cabrini's beatification in 1938.

The cardinal's vision, like his charity, was world wide. Chicago was his diocese, but this did not prevent him from directing his discerning vision elsewhere. This outlook led him to shore up the extension society founded by Bishop Francis Clement Kelly for helping the mission diocese and churches of the United States. The society was assured of solid growth and continuing influence with the consecration of Auxiliary Bishop William O'Brien in April 1934. Under his direction, *Extension* magazine began to speak to an ever-growing popular audience and the magnificent work of aiding the missions began to reach a new peak of efficiency.

The cardinal was fearless in his public attitudes which showed none of the fussy caution that usually goes under the name of prudence. Mundelein admired Franklin Roosevelt, and when the President came to Chicago to dedicate a bridge in 1937, the cardinal entertained him at a formal luncheon. The two men joked about politics and discussed social legislation and the international scene, particularly the rise of Hitler in Germany. Earlier in the year, Mundelein had denounced Hitler's attempt to interfere with Catholic education in Germany—a denunciation Pius XI viewed with distinct approval as an assist in the battle he was fighting against the "crooked cross."

The following year, in January, in an address before a massive Holy Name rally, Mundelein spoke out against employers who defrauded laborers of their just wages. He also spoke of Hitler's regime with scorn, and referred to him as a paperhanger and "a poor paperhanger at that." The characterization evoked a great bubble of laughter around the world except in Germany. There the publicity machine of Goebbels, which had long specialized in the technique of the "big lie," directed its fulminations against Cardinal Mundelein. The cardinal shrugged them off with a jest; the very fury of the outcry against him informed him more surely than words that his thrust against the insane regime had gone home.

A new sign of the Pope's continuing favor was seen in the

appointment of Cardinal Mundelein as the Pope's legate to the eucharistic congress in New Orleans in October 1938. While en route to Rome to make his report after the congress, Mundelein was invited to be President Roosevelt's overnight guest in the White House. The evening was spent in discussing the international situation and the possibility of diplomatic relations between the Vatican and the United States Government. The talks eventually led to the appointment of a Chicago banker, Myron C. Taylor, as official observer at the papal court.

On September 20, 1939, the cardinal celebrated the thirtieth anniversary of his consecration as bishop. Twelve nights later he was stricken with a massive thrombosis and died before the members of his household could be called. A hush of genuine sadness fell on the great city when the news was broadcast. Everyone lamented his death at the age of sixty-seven at the very zenith of his power and influence.

As if to heighten the drama, Bishop Sheil went on the air in the evening. Laboring under the stress of shock so that his voice broke occasionally, he read the cardinal's message for the national convention of the Catholic Youth Organization, written a few days before:

> Let there be no mistake about it. The supreme battle of the modern world is the battle for God and the moral law. There are powerful, well-organized forces in the world today which are aggressively and fanatically anti-God. The vast resources of many governments themselves are being employed to uproot from the minds and the hearts of people the sacred ideas of God, religion, and morality.
>
> We must mobilize a vast army of young women and young men who have an abiding faith in the highest, an endearing love for the best, who are willing to sacrifice all they hold dearest in life, and lay down life itself for the cause of God. They must be drilled and disciplined in the knowledge and love of God. They must see clearly that the highest, noblest, holiest service is the service of God. They must have the blazing conviction that the supremely imperative loyalty is loyalty to God and to His cause without which no other loyalty can long endure.

From the time long ago when he had dedicated himself to the priesthood and the service of leadership of his people, George Mundelein had never once looked back. He had spent himself completely in God's service, with no count of the cost. Not since the time of Cardinal Gibbons and Archbishop Ireland had any prelate so thoroughly understood, long in advance, the direction of events and the necessity of molding them.

Chicagoans mourned him because they loved him. Time has put the stamp of greatness on his creation of the spiritual bulwarks that will enable our nation to endure.

Patrick Cardinal Hayes

ATRICK J. HAYES was born in Manhattan on November 20, 1867. It was a time of turmoil for the United States. The reconstruction of the Union was underway, accompanied by bitterness, hatred and violence. The Ku Klux Klan rode through the southern states, and crosses flamed at night. In Washington, D.C. the unloved Andrew Johnson feuded with the Congress as he struggled to carry out the healing policies of Lincoln.

New York City was going through acute growing pains. The stream of immigrants, slowed by the war, was again in full spate. Irish, Germans and Italians arrived in ever-increasing numbers. The reality they found in the city of their desire and dreams was shocking. Tenements were their homes; working hours, wages and conditions were inhumanly demanding; crime and vice flourished in the welter of alleys and saloons.

The Civil War had created countless new fortunes and relaxed morality. City and state governments were honeycombed with graft and corruption. The new magnates struggled with each other like robber barons fighting over enormous booty. Display and magnificence were their symbols. While the immigrants huddled in their shacks and shanties in lower New York and along the East River, the new rich flaunted their affluence.

In 1867, the year in which Hayes was born in a bleak tenement within the shadow of the city hall, there were 600 *more or less* public balls. "The cost of these balls were estimated at $7,000,000, and the average cost of a gown was computed to be $1,000, not including jewelry."

Observing this outer façade, one could hardly look forward to a glittering future for anyone born on the wrong side of the tracks. But life is not a mere mechanism in which superb human qualities are deformed by circumstances. Human character is able to rise above adversity, even above the corruption of wealth or power. Quality reveals itself for what it is. So it was with Lincoln; so it was with many outstanding figures in the history of the United States; so it was with Patrick J. Hayes.

He was born lucky in many ways. His parents were of solid Irish peasant stock to whom adversity and struggle were commonplace. Their great buttress was their religion. The day after his birth, Patrick was baptized in St. Andrew's Church. It was the Feast of the Presentation of Christ in the Temple, and the boy was named Patrick Joseph in a protest against the violently anti-Catholic and anti-Irish spirit prevailing in New York at the time.

He was less than three years old when his mother died. Gradually over the following years Patrick became the charge of his mother's sister Ellen Egan, who lived nearby with her husband.

Jim and Ellen Egan were childless. They had loved and fondled Patrick as a beautiful fair-haired baby. With the death of Daniel Hayes, when Patrick was about nine, the Egans grew closer still to their orphaned ward. After a time of sorrowing, it must have seemed to them and the boy as well that he had always been their own son.

The Egan home was a tenement, but Ellen kept it shining and spotless. She loved to tell the boy stories of Ireland and its saints and scholars. She imbued him with admiration and love of his religion, taught him his first prayers, and answered his questions about the truths of the faith with vivid fervor.

There were good public schools available, but Ellen Egan, with considerable sacrifice, enrolled her boy in the Transfigura-

tion Parochial School. It pleased her to see how rapidly he fell
into its disciplines of mind and spirit. She sent him off to
Mass each morning, a labor well repaid when she caught her
first glimpse of Patrick as an altar boy. Above the cassock and
snowy surplice, his young face and shining hair seemed of an
angelic purity that promised great things.

Life, however securely anchored in religion, is not a fancy
valentine. Coming and going to school, at play in his dirty
neighborhood, around the spouting hydrants or along the river
in summer and in the littered lamplit streets of winter, there
were innumerable shadows of evil. Foul words and suggestions,
drunkenness, theft, dishonesty, cruelty, filth—these were as constant as the sun rising each day over Brooklyn. But many
children normally move through evil circumstances with the
ease of Jack the Giant Killer. They exist in a world of their own
which can make them singularly unconscious of the evil about
them and singularly immune to the rotten impulses that dog
humanity.

Looking back from his eminence as cardinal, Hayes could
say to the boys of his old neighborhood: "I can see it now as I did
forty years ago. To you and to me it was then the top of the
earth. The great city we have today is, after all, but an expansion of what we found on the dear old highway. There was
the Board of Education at one end, typical of New York's care
of children; at the other end the old ferry which so often carried
across the river to God's acre our sacred dead; transportation
was then a problem as it is today; the various lines of streetcars converged to, and radiated from the old street; the impressive foundry and printing press establishment; the merchants
and shopkeepers then marking the beginning of departmental
stores—all this and much more gave to the old street and neighborhood a grandeur all its own."

Whatever the neighborhood lacked, whatever its evils, there
were things of compelling interest that a childish imagination
could manipulate into wonder: watching the presses, window-
shopping—less with envy than the possession of beauty that
comes with its contemplation—watching the whirling carriages

and clanging streetcars. Life was here—throbbing and absorbing life.

Patrick was a perfectly normal boy of his time and neighborhood, but his ideals and dreams lifted him above most of his fellows. He played their games, swam with them, spoke their language, followed them on exciting excursions, but when the day was over and most of them went to filthy and disordered homes, he returned to Aunt Ellen's ascetic cleanliness and the evening Rosary. In the midst of evil and disorder, he lived in a cleanliness and religious joy that promised glory after the crucifixion of life. Other boys wanted to be firemen, ward heelers or steamboat captains, or to operate beyond the law. Patrick's ambitions were centered on the priesthood. A priest wasn't merely a man who had to do great things; first of all he had to be something, a terrifying something—another Christ.

It was this sobering thought that kept Pat Hayes from swearing like the other boys and brought him to tears in the confessional over his minor lies, evasions and dishonesties. The boy wasn't angelic, but he was steady and good and knew the difficult steps to the goal he had in mind.

There was, as the future events of his life were to show, an abounding pity in his heart for those less fortunate than he. There was so much good wasted because of disordered homes, so much talent lost for lack of proper direction and a little monetary help.

Aunt Ellen and Uncle Jim saved and economized so that their wiry little Pat could enter the Christian Brothers' School on Second Avenue in 1883. They expected no more thanks than they received in the irreproachable conduct of their adopted son.

Grover Cleveland was the forceful new Governor of New York, and there were Democratic rumors of his running for President. New York was building and rebuilding furiously. There was a note of optimism everywhere.

De La Salle Institute was more than a high school; it served to prepare talented boys for college in the shortest time possible. Pat Hayes was talented and readily took to his accelerated schedule. The uncomfortable and shabby old classrooms offered little of the gracious atmosphere that is supposed to go with learning. Discipline was of the rough-and-ready type, but like Eton or Harrow at the time, the excellence of the school depended on intellectual competition and attainment. Competitive sports were also strongly encouraged. Young Hayes did not excel on these, but his enthusiasm and leadership brought him the post of cheer leader, in which he forcefully demonstrated his comradeship with the boys of his class. The quickness of Pat's wit, his ready laughter and love of a joke, were other characteristics that endeared him to the other students.

Among these was George Mundelein, a quick, strong boy of good German-American stock and a brilliant student and fine athlete.

Within two years, Patrick Hayes was ready for Manhattan College. By this time, everyone accepted the idea that the lively and humorous young man was destined for the priesthood. Though his ideals differed from those of the other students, he was one of them in the demanding and sometimes rowdy life of the school. It was only at Mass and in the sanctuary that the other boys witnessed the difference in Pat's solemn poise and the precise correctness of his genuflections and gestures. Two years after his entry into Manhattan, Uncle Jim and Aunt Ellen sat in the heat-saturated auditorium of the college and watched with pride as their boy received his beribboned diploma.

The past winter had been a terrible one for them and all their friends. The climax of the cold had come in a furious blizzard which raged for thirty-six hours and literally buried New York, isolating it from the rest of the world; messages to Boston had to be relayed via England. About 400 people died as a result of the storm, most of them in the rickety tenements along the east side.

After the graduation exercises, the family returned to Madison Street for a celebration in the modest apartment. They and their friends drank tea and ate Aunt Ellen's rich cake, while the twenty-year-old boy recounted the drama of the day, with a young man's wit and spontaneity. With the pink rose in his lapel and his boyish innocence, he reminded Aunt Ellen of the morning of his First Communion when, even as now, he had sat in the place of honor at the head of the lace-covered table.

The following September the Egans, with smiles and tears, watched the dark-clad form of Patrick as he mounted the steps of the train which was taking him to St. Joseph's Seminary in Troy, New York. They all dreaded this first separation, foreseeing how lonely they would be in the coming months, but they were brave in the knowledge that it was a great step forward toward the boy's goal.

During his first retreat at St. Joseph's, Patrick Hayes realized the full meaning of his call to the priesthood. Seen in the golden haze of a child's dreams, a priest was a luminous figure out of a fairy tale. Now the words *alter Christes* could be grasped in their full reality. To try to be as perfect as Christ, called for complete dedication to the rules of the seminary and an ever-deepening love of the Saviour.

Pat did well in his studies, but it was his iron devotion to the Christ life that brought him the admiration of his fellow students and the professors who watched him with eagle eyes. There was a touch of self-deprecating humor in all he did and said, but there was a stern gravity in his poise and in the meticulous devotion he brought to every step of his ascent through minor orders to the irrevocable subdiaconate.

The glowing reports of his progress led Archbishop Corrigan to ordain Patrick several months in advance of his classmates. It was a great day for the Egans. All their sacrifices seemed as nothing in comparison with the joy in their hearts in receiving their first blessing from their priest son.

There was added honor to and intense excitement among them and their friends because Archbishop Corrigan had given the young priest his choice of further study in Rome, or at the newly established Catholic University in Washington, D.C.

His worldly wise priest friends advised him to go to Rome;

he would know foreign travel, the outstanding professors in the Christian world, the most famous cardinals of the all-powerful Curia—and perhaps the Pope himself. Compared with these, what had a poverty-stricken university to offer?

The young priest listened to all the sage advice with his habitual grave and charming smile. All the ambitious and intellectual reasons were on the side of Roman studies, but it was one of Hayes' great qualities that all his life he treasured Pascal's phrase: "The heart has its reasons . . ." and followed it in dealing with men.

The grave smile was still there when Father Hayes announced to one of his close friends in the priesthood: "I'm going to Washington. I have others to consider. My aunt and my uncle have sacrificed much to see me a priest. I cannot leave them now that they are old."

In the two profitable years of study that followed, there were Christmas and summer vacations to be shared with the two who loved him best, and tranquil hours as they sat enthralled while the young priest related his experiences, well salted with the humor which they all enjoyed.

The licentiate in theology awarded Father Hayes seemed to the Egans as much theirs as his. They were equally delighted with the post given him at St. Gabriel's Church on East 37th Street, where Monsignor Farley—already vicar-general of the diocese—was making a great name for himself. And now Aunt Ellen could attend Father Pat's Mass every day.

It is always something of a shock to established pastors when they must receive a talented new priest into their homes. It was well known that Monsignor Farley was demanding in what he expected of his assistants.

Father Hayes was at once a surprise and a delight. He always made a careful meditation before Mass and a slow thanksgiving after. Watching him offer the Mass was a pleasure. He was totally absorbed in what he was doing, and his gestures and genuflexions were precisely correct without losing any of their grace. In the rectory he was unobtrusive, thoughtfully polite, deferential, orderly in his work and sympathetic with the people he consoled and advised.

Before long, Monsignor Farley found himself discussing things with Father Hayes. He was not quick in advancing opinions, but if asked for them gave crisp and objective answers that were prudent and original—a combination not too often found among clerical idealists fresh from seminary training.

Mutual respect between the two men grew into an enduring friendship. When Monsignor Farley became Auxiliary Bishop of New York in 1902, he chose Father Hayes as his secretary.

With his elevation to the direction of the diocese in the same year, Archbishop Farley took his able assistant with him. In 1903, Hayes became chancellor—a task that brought him into cordial and intimate relations with the diocese, its problems, its priests and people. With quiet vigor, Hayes at once proceeded on a businesslike reorganization of the chancery that facilitated the immediate handling of diocesan business.

His success was so brilliant and instant that Farley, in the same year, made Hayes the rector of the newly established Cathedral College, the minor seminary for aspirants to the priesthood.

The young people of St. Gabriel's Parish had been particularly fond of Father Pat. There was a childlike streak in his nature that seemed to make him one of themselves. As he listened and joked with them or told them stories from the life of Christ they were charmed with the sincerity of love that illuminated his phrases.

This talent in handling the young was of tremendous value at Cathedral College. The aspirants for the priesthood had no fear of consulting their rector about any of their problems, moral or physical. His solutions, advanced always with a tinge of light humor, were readily acceptable. Many of the boys came from poor families; in times of stress it was well known that Father Pat was the first one to put his hand in his pocket.

In his comings and goings in the sanctuary and out of it, the young rector was measured by the pitilessly idealistic yardstick of youth, and they all admitted that he measured up to their demands and expectations without any tinge of priggishness.

Those who worked with Father Hayes in the organization of Cathedral College were constantly amazed at his jovial urbanity on every occasion and his quick solution of the many vexing problems of the young institution. They marveled, too, at his serene handling of the chancery and his demanding duties as the bishop's secretary. His affectionate kindliness toward the priests of the diocese endeared him in every parish.

In 1903, Rome gave Father Hayes the doctor of divinity degree. Three years later, Cardinal Farley was pleased to reward his busy assistant with the rank of domestic prelate. We can imagine the joy in the Egan household when they first beheld their handsome son clothed in the purple of the Church.

Monsignor Hayes labored away on his triple assignment for eleven years. His graying hair was the only sign that his age and burdens were beginning to tell upon him. Many were quick to point out his resemblance to the reigning Pope Pius X and the same inner serenity which communicated to the planes of his face an air of boyish thoughtfulness.

The life had its higher moments. Weekly visits with Aunt Ellen and Uncle Jim and participation in the anniversary celebrations of the priests of the diocese displayed Monsignor Hayes as a man of warmth and ready wit. "After all, he's one of us," they said, watching his erect figure swinging down the lamplit street as he departed.

When Archbishop Farley was elevated to the candinalate, it was Monsignor Hayes' duty to see that everything was carried out with dignity and dispatch. Like all good executives, he readily delegated responsibility, and if praise was forthcoming, he gracefully stepped aside to allow his co-workers their just share.

To one of his romantic nature, it must have greatly pleased Monsignor Hayes that Archbishop Farley took him along to Rome for the great event in 1911. Pius X was already something of a legend, and it was with mounting excitement that the monsignor looked forward to the several meetings with the great pope. Added to this, he was to see at first hand the most beautiful shrines in Christendom. They had been names on his tongue for so long; now he would savor them by intimate acquaintance. His observations are set down for posterity in the vivid little booklet he wrote and published soon after his return to the United States.

Three years later, in 1914, Monsignor Hayes returned to Rome with Cardinal Farley. The papers of the world screamed war; the armies and navies of the two great alliances were already in motion. Cardinal Farley asked the Pope to appoint Monsignor Hayes Auxiliary Bishop of New York. The Holy Father, bowed down with grief over the impending struggle, readily granted the request. The young prelate, so like his younger self, must have brought him a brief feeling of joy. The briefs for the appointment were issued on July 3. Five weeks later Pius X was dead.

Cardinal Farley and Bishop-Elect Hayes lingered on in Rome for the conclave which elected Benedict XV to rule the Church during the terrible war that followed. Despite the submarine menace, the cardinal and his suite returned safely to New York.

On October 28, 1914, Hayes was consecrated bishop in St. Patrick's Cathedral in the presence of a brilliant throng. Everyone noticed the large number of the elderly and the crowds of children who came to watch the pageantry. Among them, Uncle Jim and Aunt Ellen thrilled to the vibrant voice of the new bishop as he gave his first aspostolic blessing.

There was little time for rejoicing. The United States drifted nearer to war daily. Woodrow Wilson's stern notes on the sinking of the *Lusitania*, German arrogance, brutality and failure to comply with international law, soon assured that American arms would aid the Allies.

The danger was amply apparent, but Americans went along at their driving pace. The first jazz bands emerged; Prohibition was just around the corner; village orators all over the land were declaiming Joyce Kilmer's "Trees"; United States troops were chasing Pancho Villa in Mexico.

With the declaration of war in 1917, American Catholics enlisted in great numbers. The duty of looking after the spiritual needs of the men in the armed forces, most of whom embarked for France from ports in and around New York, fell on New York's cardinal. He took the problem to the Holy See. The response was almost immediate. Benedict XV appointed Bishop Hayes ordinary of the armed forces of the United States on November 29, 1917.

The bishop already had burdens enough, especially since the cardinal's health was not good and most of the tremendous business of the diocese already rested on his capable shoulders. With astonishing organizing genius within a year of setting up the machinery of the ordinate, Hayes somehow found time to secure the services of 900 chaplains to serve the armed forces. This achievement gives us an idea of his capability as an organizer and his cordial relationship with all the bishops of the United States who responded so quickly in making priests available for service. The correspondence involved, the endless conferences, visits to camps and bishops, all these Bishop Hayes took in his seemingly leisurely stride. Lights burned late in the chancery, but the bishop found time to intensify his prayers and lengthen his visits to the Blessed Sacrament. Many a soldier en route to France observed the erect figure kneeling in St. Patrick's, oblivious to the parading thousands and the bands outside blaring "Over There."

Perhaps it was fortunate that the war was of short duration for the United States, since Liberty Bond rallies, the Catholic War Council and allied activities, made demands on the work-haunted bishop that might well have broken a man of stronger constitution.

The death of Cardinal Farley was a great personal blow to Hayes. They had worked together for twenty-four years, during which there had been no dimming of their mutual respect and affection. Hayes listened to the final absolution for his friend with tears in his eyes, and then, with realistic courage, turned to assume the full burden of the diocese.

His experience, training and proven capabilities were of such high order that it astonished no one when Benedict XV appointed Hayes to succeed Farley as Archbishop of New York on March 10, 1919.

On the day of his installation, March 19, 1919, St. Patrick's was far too small to hold the huge crowds. Those who could not get inside after marching in the procession waited patiently in the cold until many noted prelates including Archbishop Bonzano, the apostolic delegate, emerged for their return to the rectory.

It was in keeping with the new archbishop's innate piety and modesty that he had asked that all the festivity be kept at a minimum because it was Lent. The program he had announced was modestly simple—to be "a Shepherd of his people."

The new archbishop wasted no time in revealing the high quality of his shepherding. In June 1919, at the annual retreat, he gave the assembled priests of the diocese an outline of his plan for the complete reorganization and consolidation of Catholic charities in the diocese. Cardinal Farley had already begun the labor in 1913 with the establishment of the United Catholic Works. On this somewhat meager foundation, Hayes began to build.

The first step was a meeting of all existing Catholic charities of the diocese. Some 400 persons attended the first meeting. They were instructed to make a survey of their particular charity and its further possibilities and demands.

The entire survey was completed in about six months. Then the work of consolidation and coordination began, thoroughly covering every aspect of social life under the single title of the Catholic Charities of the Archdiocese of New York. There were six main divisions: families, children, health, protective care, social action and finance. Under these main headings were hundreds of great and small groups providing necessary aid for Catholics from the cradle to the grave. What had been a wastefully unorganized effort was forged into a massively effective instrument in the service of the people, in complete accord with the most modern sociological discoveries.

The wide-open heart of Archbishop Hayes must have taken justifiable pride in the statement issued by the state board of charities. It characterized the organization of the Catholic Charities in 1920 as "the most significant and important event of the year in the field of charitable work."

In the first four years of the organization, more than $3,500,-000 was raised for the modernization and support of the various clubs and institutions. The result gave great comfort to the archbishop. Long ago in his childhood he had sorrowed with a child's poignant sadness over the waste of talented and likely people who had been lost to the Church and a happy life through want of a helping hand in times of trouble or crisis. The reorganized charities were severely tested during the Depression. There is scarcely a like institution in the country which met the challenge with such boldly conceived magnificence.

As a corollary to his reorganization of the charities of the archdiocese in 1920, Archbishop Hayes gave cordial and sympathetic encouragement to Julia Teresa Tallon in the formation of a new religious community, the Parish Visitors of Mary Immaculate. Through its assistance, social work in many parishes was speeded up in various ways, particularly through the visitation of the poor and sick in their homes. People soon grew to realize that these magnificent women came primarily neither to pry nor to pray. They went into homes as friends, rolled up their sleeves and went to work, restoring cleanliness, order and some semblance of comfort. Their influence was incalculable.

Less than five years after his installation as Archbishop of New York, Pius XI signified his intention of elevating Archbishop Hayes to the cardinalate in March 1924. It was a strictly American consistory in that Archbishop Mundelein of Chicago received the red hat at the same time.

Both prelates and the American people were given the warmest commendation from the Holy Father, who did not ordinarily pay gracious compliments without solid reasons. Yet it must be said that Hayes, like Pius X, had dreaded the honor and had prayed that he would not receive it. When it came, the gentle and obedient archbishop bowed his head in graceful acquiescence. Like Cardinal Farley, he chose to think of the cardinalate less as a personal honor than a justified reward for all that New York had accomplished in the field of national and international charity.

Santa Maria in Via was assigned to Cardinal Hayes as his titular church. It is worthy to note that Santa Maria in Via had once been the titular church of St. Robert Bellarmine, whose democratic principles had strongly influenced the founding fathers of our country.

The new cardinal took possession of his church with the proscribed pomp and responded in English to the cordial welcome tendered him. After all the pressing obligations of the multiple ceremonies were over, the cardinal found time to send a message upon embarking for home. "God bless little old New York," he said.

His ardent love for this city was amply demonstrated in the ecstatic reception he received. Religious boundaries were forgotten in a veritable Niagara of praise. Aunt Ellen was no longer living, but Uncle Jim, bent and frail, had been waiting on the pier in the midst of the assembled dignitaries. The cardinal hurried forward and folded the old man in a warm embrace.

During the following fifteen years of his rein, Cardinal Hayes continued his major work of modernizing Catholic charity. Though his health was not of the best, he refused to spare himself: graduation exercises, endless board meetings, confirmations, receptions for distinguished guests (including Cardinal Pacelli the papal Secretary of State), saw him erect, gracious and smiling, with no hint of the fatigue that was his constant companion.

He was particularly appreciative of the splendid work done by the religious women of the diocese, and continually praised them in public. To observe him in his visits at important women's schools was a memorable experience; his kindness, sympathy and lavish praise were in keeping with those of the most perfect gentle knight. The radiance and courage he left behind him—in groups too often forgotten by the public—was one of the true measures of his simplicity and greatness.

One of the important efforts of his last years was the organization of the Cardinal Hayes Literature Committee. The board was composed of noted writers and editors under the leadership of the much loved Monsignor Lavelle, Rector of St. Patrick's Cathedral. Lists of good books were published in a monthly pamphlet, "The Book Survey." It was a positive attempt to sort the sheep from the goats in the enormous flood of trash pouring from the presses.

The last years of the cardinal's life were immeasurably saddened by the political scandals in which prominent Irish-Americans were heavily involved. If the cardinal had one fault, it was accepting people at their face value. He forgave transgressions again and again; he refused to listen to rumors. But he was cut to the quick by irresponsibility and crooked dealing. His forgiving attitude, above all, marked him as the true "cardinal of charity." The hurt he kept to himself; it was part of his cross that he quietly accepted, with many added prayers for the sinner.

Cardinal Hayes died of a heart attack while saying his night prayers on September 4, 1938. The members of his household found him in his bedroom at St. Joseph's Villa, Monticello, in the morning, with the crucifix clasped in his cold fingers. More than 200,000 people filed past his coffin as he lay in state. In death, his face was serene and young looking, with a hint of the grave smile at the corners of his expressive mouth. Many cried unashamed tears as they passed the coffin. It was not his eminence they remembered, but his charity—which is only the Latin term for love.

John Cardinal Glennon

———◆———

WITH the coming of the railroads to the West in the sixties and seventies, Kansas City leaped from the status of a frontier town to that of a large, bustling city. Of equal swiftness was the growth of the Church in those years. Kansas City, which had long played second fiddle to St. Joseph, became a new diocese in 1880, and John Hogan, Bishop of St. Joseph, was moved to the newly erected see.

Priests were needed, badly needed, so the bishop turned to his friends in Ireland who could put him in touch with young clerics of promise suitable for missionary work on the frontier. Among those who elected to come to Kansas City was a tall, raw-boned student by the name of John Glennon, a fresh-faced, clear-eyed country boy from the Clonard Kinnegad section of West Meath. He had been born there on June 14, 1862, and was the eldest son of Matthew and Catherine Glennon. He had made a brilliant record in the classics at St. Finian's College in Mulligar, at the head of the lovely blue lake of Ennell.

Glennon had prepared for the priesthood at All Hallows College near Dublin. Once again, as he had at St. Finian's, he had distinguished himself in his studies and was ready for ordination at twenty-two.

Bishop Hogan was so pleased with his subject that he at once sent funds for his passage to the United States, with the assur-

ance that he himself would undertake the further training of
the young man.

Glennon arrived in Kansas City in 1883, in what must have
seemed to him a strange rough atmosphere after the calm beauty
of his native land. Bishop Hogan was impressed with what he
saw and heard. This tall, dignified stripling was more than
learned; his personality was completely outgoing, his manners
were charming, his speech elegantly graceful.

Scarcely a year later, after a thorough course in pastoral theology given by Bishop Hogan, John Glennon was ordained on
December 20, 1844. It was a day of bitter cold. Because the infant diocese couldn't afford to waste heat except on Sundays
and holy days, the ordination took place in the sacristy where
weekday Masses were normally offered for the small congregation.

St. Patrick's Church was Father Glennon's first assignment.
Soon he was the talk of the town because of his beautiful sermons filled with deep piety and liberally seasoned with the
spice of wit. So winning were his ways, so outstanding his learning and practical sense, that Bishop Hogan—after three years
of close observation—permitted Father Glennon the luxury of
a visit to his people in Ireland as a prelude to a time of further
studies. Upon his return to the United States, Father Glennon
became rector of the cathedral. Soon the bishop was consulting
him on important questions and decisions. Although Father
Glennon was only in his late twenties, no one thought it strange
that he should be appointed vicar-general of the diocese, a job
usually given to much older and more seasoned men.

As the bishop's alter ego, Father Glennon soon met the other
bishops of the province, along with Archbishop Kain of St.
Louis. All were impressed with the force of Glennon's personality and judgment.

Between the heavy duties of the busy cathedral parish and
the tragic problems growing out of gambling halls and saloons,
the brawny young priest helped Bishop Hogan with the paperwork. In the process, he learned what a difficult thing it was
to be a bishop—doubly difficult to be a frontier bishop.

When the long winter ended and the prairies became a flame of living green, there were endless confirmations. Father Glennon went with the bishop. It was his job to see that the vestments were packed in the big valise and that everything was at hand once the church was reached. Sometimes, if it was possible, they went on jolting trains; usually they set off in a buggy along country roads that were little more than cowtracks, with Father Glennon holding the reins. Often they were drenched with sudden rainstorms, arriving at their destination soaked and much the worse for wear from clods thrown up against the leather lapboard by the heels of the trotting horses.

When they had freshened themselves a little with the primitive means at hand, the two men would don their cassocks and take their places in the procession from the rectory to the church. Father Glennon invariably brought order out of chaos, counseling the awkward altar boys with a merry wit that set them at ease.

When the long ceremony was over and the last echoes of "Holy God We Praise Thy Name" had died against the tin or plaster ceiling, the procession re-formed for a return to the house through a cloud of white-veiled children to the inevitable reception and collation. Much of the talk was bound to be centered about the cardinal down in Baltimore who was fighting the battles of the century, and the great Pope Leo with his well-reasoned encyclicals and towering scholarship.

Sometimes the succession of confirmations lasted for days or weeks. When they were over, there was the long trip back, with the horses stretching out to a gallop as they felt themselves nearing home. All along the way, the strong young priest protected his superior—when he could—from the bores, the difficult, and the constant repetitions that could exhaust a man.

Father Glennon pursued his busy way for twelve years. Nobody doubted that he would be a bishop, and when at last the papers said that Pope Leo had named him Coadjutor Bishop of Kansas City, everyone rallied around to felicitate him and to plan for the ceremony of consecration and the banquet after it with its presentation of purses and florid oratory.

Bishop Glennon was consecrated on the Feast of Sts. Peter and Paul on June 29, 1896. Archbishop Kain had come from St. Louis as chief consecrator; Bishop Louis Mary Fink, O.S.B., of Kansas City, and Bishop Maurice Francis Burke of St. Joseph were his assistants. There was a moving moment when the handsome young bishop, in full episcopal panoply, turned from the altar to intone his first blessing.

A cheer went up for him as the procession moved through the throngs outside and they saw his graceful hand raised in constant blessing. The new bishop was thirty-four years old, a fact that led many among the doting Irish to speculate that he had a great future in store for him.

Seven years later, on April 27, 1903, at the age of forty-three, with the joyous concurrence of the bishops and priests of the province, Glennon became Coadjutor Bishop of St. Louis, with the right of succession. Archbishop Kain died on October 13 of the same year, and Bishop Glennon succeeded him.

The day of his installation revealed to Archbishop Glennon what his first task must be—the building of a new and more spacious cathedral. Though the old cathedral was an architectural gem in the classic style, the diocese had been growing like prairie corn in the heat of July, and as a result, the cathedral could no longer accommodate even a part of the crowds that came out on great occasions. The sanctuary was totally inadequate to hold a throng of bishops and still permit the liturgy to be carried out with fitting pomp.

In the four years during which the drive for funds went on, the archbishop kept the subject alive with graphic phrases that spurred people to give and give again. "We want a million-dollar structure," he said on one occasion, "that should not be Classic, Gothic or Renaissance. We hope to have a large and very beautiful structure. Its seating capacity is estimated between four thousand and five thousand. We do not expect to go into debt. It is a bad thing to have a mortgage between you and the Almighty."

The cornerstone was laid on October 18, 1908. As the fabric of the cathedral grew and people gasped at its splendid and imposing proportions, they were amazed at the archbishop's vision and shrewd financial ability. Everyone knew what the building meant to Glennon, for if you passed by on Lindell Boulevard you could see a majestic figure crowned with a tall silk hat inspecting every step of the work and making jests with the workmen.

True to the archbishop's promise, everything was paid for on the day the cathedral was opened for worship, October 9, 1914. He mentioned that fact with pride in his sermon; he also justified his selection of the Byzantine style in poetic phrases that were a model of elegant persuasion and an indication of the source of his popularity as a preacher on great occasions.

> The Gothic spire [he said] like the prayer offered, goes upward to the skies; the Byzantine, like unto a prayer answered, brings the dome of heaven down to earth. One is a prayer asked, the other a prayer answered. The Gothic tells of northern forests where the stately pines go upward unchallenged until pine is joined to pine near the summit, and as you look through the vista as in a Gothic church, the vertical pine tree multiplies itself in every pillar, while up in the roof the branches unite as sure protection against the inclement sky. The Byzantine, on the other hand, takes its first line from the desert where the Baptist preached and the Saviour prayed, and brings to it no other covering save the sky above, under which the Saviour's life was lived and beneath which He agonized and died . . .

> The Gothic is best when the gray monotone of the north rests upon her every arching line and stately column, but the Byzantine will not be complete until it has set on its walls the luster of every jewel, the bright plumage of every bird, the glow and glory of every metal, the iridescent gleam of every glass. If the diction of the Gothic be more stately, the working of the Byzantine is more varied.

> Its argument is that Christ came to men here on earth in His temple to dwell, and therefore the flowers of the field with fragrance, the birds of the air with their songs, and the children of men with their prayers, shall unite in making His home, in so far as they may, acceptable to Him. Hence the decoration of the Byzantine with its involved capitals, its delicate arabesques, with its blending of the iris, acanthus and the fleur-de-lis with

all the flowers that bloom in the valley or on the hillside, with all the blossoms of May and all the fruits of autumn, with the antlered stag and fabled pelican, with the dove that proclaims innocence, and the peacock, bird of immortality, will call them into being and set them into splendor of mosaic unity, beckoning them to chant, with the servants of God, His praises and to live in His service, and in so far as possible, speak in their myriad tongues of the earth's subjection to its Lord and Creator.

By the time the cathedral was consecrated on June 24, 1926, St. Louis and the Catholics of the United States took justifiable pride in the imposing building which, without and within, was a tribute to the archbishop's taste and exuberant fancy. What started out to be a $1,000,000 structure has grown into one of the outstanding cathedrals in the United States. Costs, quite naturally, multiplied with the years; modest estimates are in the neighborhood of $8,000,000 to $10,000,000, but St. Louisans, who like things to be big, say with complaining pride that the cathedral has cost over $20,000,000 and will never be finished.

It has become a place of pilgrimage for visitors; at almost any hour of the day, in winter's cold or summer's heat, one can see lines of cars parked along the boulevard, an indication of the groups inside, walking about, pausing for prayer in the various chapels, staring up at the walls and domes. Pairs of nuns whisper discreetly to each other as they discuss its art and architectural splendor; groups of farmers from the prairies are impressed with so much magnificence; the old and lonely of the city, blue-veined hands sifting their beads, find consolation in its beauty and the monumental silence that begets resignation and tranquility.

Archbishop Glennon was a remarkably healthy man during his forty-three years as Archbishop of St. Louis. Perhaps his radiant health and consciousness of longevity had much to do with his perennially happy and optimistic outlook and easy manner of working. While he was building his fine cathedral, he was also thinking and planning for the future and growth of the priesthood in his diocese. The first fruits of his thoughts were seen in Kenrick Seminary for the study of philosophy and theology and the St. Louis Prepartory Seminary on Shrewsbury Avenue, both under the competent direction of the Vincentian Fathers.

Archbishop Glennon was not merely content to provide beautiful and comfortable buildings for the education of his priests. Often, like a father with his sons, he could be found at either institution, learning at first hand just what the boys were doing as he talked *to* them in conferences and *with* them in a great burst of laughter at recreation time.

There also arose a network of homes and protectories, making the Archdiocese of St. Louis one of the most modern social centers in the United States.

In the field of education, Archbishop Glennon was outstanding because he loved learning and followed it all the days of his life. His lights burned late at night as he pursued his wide reading in history, biography, philosophy and theology. Poetry was an old love that revealed itself in the rhythm of his every utterance, in the glowing colors of his figures and comparisons. When one reviews the significant growth of St. Louis University and the other splendid schools of the diocese during the archbishop's long reign, it should be obvious to all how ardently he encouraged every effort in the field of education. The careful planning went on into his vigorous old age, and plans for eight new high schools were on his desk at the time of his death.

It was his high regard for the wider aspects of education and Catholic literature that led Archbishop Glennon to encourage Sister Mary Joseph of the Sisters of Loreto in founding her gallery of Living Catholic Authors in 1932 at Webster Groves, outside St. Louis. It has grown into a noted repository of manuscripts and pictures of famous Catholic authors from all over the world and is an inspiration to young writers, an accolade for authors of professional skill and international eminence.

Hardly a bishop went through the city without stopping off to visit, not merely for the font of wisdom they found in the archbishop, but for his wit and joy of life. From the big rambling house of gray stone, they were taken out to see how the cathedral was progressing, regaled meanwhile with his inimitable comments on life; he was like an exuberant boy as he showed them around and explained his dream.

Few went away from his home without feeling refreshed. His reputation inevitably led to speaking engagements. Audiences were enthralled with the mellow cadence of his voice and the word pictures he painted with such vivid phrases.

He was particularly welcome on any and all occasions, and he served longer on the Catholic University's board of trustees than any other bishop in its history, not merely lending his name, but attending lengthy and sometimes acrimonius meetings. Bishops Keane and Shahan leaned on him heavily for his advice and help in the difficult early days of the school when politics between factions almost wrecked its growth. But they depended on him even more for a sense of hope—an incorrigible optimism which saw beyond the hurdles of the time to the glittering future that is now being realized.

Some indication of his talent and human importance can be gleaned from the fact that he was chosen to preach the panegyric at the funeral of Cardinal Gibbons. With oratorical power, he summed up the tremendous achievements of the great cardinal; the eyes of all his hearers misted as he pleaded in emotional tones that in the presence of his mortal remains we pledge ourselves that "we shall not break faith with him" and the great enterprises he set in motion such as the Catholic University.

The esteem at home was still more obvious. Funds for Glennon's imperial projects were usually oversubscribed, the rumor of his presence at any church or civic affair could insure a record turnout, and he could always sweep his listeners up into a mood between laughter and tears.

A delightful story has come down to us from one of the earliest occasions on which a child indicated his admiration by choosing the name of Glennon at confirmation time.

The pastor of the parish, as is customary, read off the names selected by each child as he presented himself at the communion rail to be confirmed. When the name of Glennon was announced, the archbishop started briefly, then—instantly—in a stage whisper audible throughout the church, he said, "Tell him to take the name of a *dead* saint!"

In time the archbishop was pleased and touched with this name compliment. As the years went on, he assembled a card index of all the boys named for him from 1938-1942, and gave a New Year's reception for them in his home at which he and his housekeeper, Miss Flynn, regaled the boys with soft drinks, cake and ice cream. During the sessions, he circulated among the boys, cracking jokes, quizzing them about their ambitions and studies, giving them good advice. It was hard to say whether the children or the archbishop got more fun out of these affairs.

Women adored him for his delicate courtesy, good humor, sympathetic quickness and sterling good looks; in their eyes he was a father image completely without flaws. They came to him with their troubles, asked his advice, enthusiastically supported him in his drives and invited him to speak at their conventions and celebrations. In return, the archbishop treated them all with an old-fashioned courtliness which showed a quick flare-up toward anything that might tarnish or mar his image of womanhood.

It was with regret that he saw women competing with men in the world of business and finance. "Take the women today," he observed from the pulpit. "They are in the race. Some of the women go downtown in the race and race beside the men— working very honorably and very properly, that is, if they have to do so. It is regrettable that men have to let them, are compelled to let them. Time was when the father of the house, the husband, cared for the home and sustained it in all its splendid unity, in all the homeliness of a home."

Not one of those who boasted "my country right or wrong," Glennon had a solid patriotism based on justice and sober idealism. At the outbreak of the First World War, he was one of the signers of the Gibbons' patriotic manifesto which so thoroughly pleased President Wilson. But as Archbishop Glennon saw the second great holocaust approaching he deplored

John Cardinal McCloskey

James Cardinal Gibbons

John Cardinal Farley

William Cardinal O'Connell

Denis Cardinal Dougherty

George Cardinal Mundelein

Patrick Cardinal Hayes

John Cardinal Glennon

Edward Cardinal Mooney

Samuel Cardinal Stritch

Francis Cardinal Spellman

James Francis Cardinal McIntyre

Richard Cardinal Cushing

John Cardinal O'Hara

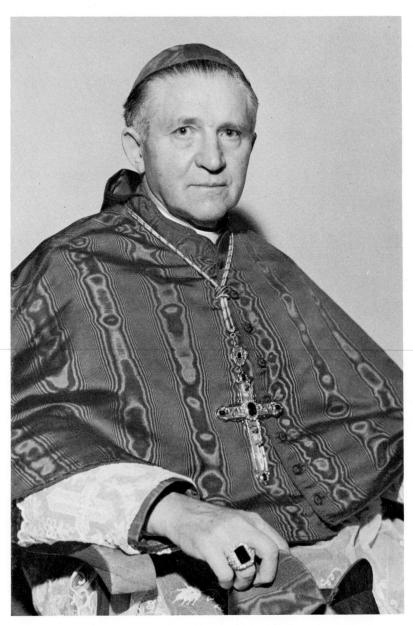

Aloisius Cardinal Muench

Albert Cardinal Meyer

Joseph Cardinal Ritter

it and stressed the ideas of peace so dear to the great modern popes beginning with Pius X.

Yet after the infamy of Pearl Harbor, Glennon said: "We are not a military nation. But we are at war. We are not a nation prepared to go to war—no democracy is—and yet we are at war. In a democracy, there has to be so much discussion, an opportunity given to every citizen—for that is the essence of democracy, to express his opinion and we cannot obtain the unity of purpose until the cogent reasons therefore are known. So, when a democracy declares war, it is only the end of much discussion and agitation."

Then he continued, with a Christian warning: "Churches have a duty in time of war not to promote hatred, racial or otherwise. Churches should give their moral aid and their physical support to the nation. I am glad to say yes, to rejoice that the Catholic Church has been doing its full duty. It stands in the nation at perhaps twenty percent or a little less of the entire population, but in the ranks of the Army, its ratio is thirty percent of these brave young men who are facing the fortunes of war."

He loved the land of his birth and gave practical and monetary encouragement to make Irish independence possible.

"That mystic light," said the archbishop, speaking on a St. Patrick's Day in Kansas City, "it comes from the wild sea that washes the Irish coasts; from the heather that covers its hills; from the moaning winds that crowd its woods; from the woods themselves with their silent life and mystic gloom; from the open meadows and the summer night; from the banshee's cry and the fairy's companionship; from out of all the scenery and association and that life that becomes a part of the Irish character, there comes a strange yearning, that great desire, that unwillingness to be part of the commonplace; that restlessness, energy and fire which, as a dissolvent set here in American life, makes crass materialism impossible and sets across the face of our land a rainbow of light and hope."

It was the privilege of St. Louis to have had the same outstanding bishop at the helm during all the years it was growing from a small town to a great metropolis. Archbishop Glennon was particularly keen in forecasting population trends, so expert in fact that real-estate agents were careful to watch where he was building new parishes. Almost a hundred new parishes were founded; universities and colleges grew from primitive plants into magnificent centers of culture and scholarship.

Wherever the archbishop went, he took with him the joy of life—to the four international Eucharistic Congresses where he was one of the chief speakers, on his *ad limina* visits to Rome, or on his frequent trips to Ireland. Part of this joy came from his apt sense of humor and childlike gaiety. There are so many sterling examples of his wit that the mere recounting of them would be tedious, but a few examples can give us an insight into his verve and quickness.

Though he enjoyed baseball and sometimes threw out the opening ball for the Cardinals, it was remarked by one of his friends that people found it odd he didn't play some game. "Glory be to God," the archbishop replied. "I once tried golf, but I so disfigured the scenery that I never played again, in fear of public indignation and reprisal."

Someone wondered why he wasn't a cardinal, and the swift reply came: "And sure the Holy Father wouldn't want me in competition with the home team." In public, his reply to the Mayor of St. Louis on the same subject was more elaborate. "Our mayor would like me to wear the red robes," said the archbishop. "But when the great Cardinal [Gibbons] conferred on me the pallium, he appointed me the Pope of the West and this would put me in white robes. I have to wear something," he continued in comic confusion. "I'll wear anything as long as it is all wool and a yard wide."

On his visit to St. Louis in 1936, Cardinal Pacelli was tremendously impressed with the cathedral and its majestic archbishop. He would probably have shown his appreciation by raising the archbishop to the cardinalate if the war had not intervened. Glennon already was dean of the American hierarchy, and his accomplishments richly deserved the highest honors.

Yet when Jim Farley called from New York on Christmas Eve, 1945, with the announcement of his elevation—almost ten years after Pacelli's visit—everyone was jubilant. Hierarchy and laity fairly deluged Archbishop Glennon with messages of congratulation. At the advanced age of eighty-four, he had fancied himself indifferent to such recognition, but he was cheered and made happy by it as an honor for his people.

Cardinal Spellman, who had been delighted to learn that the Archbishop of St. Louis was one of the four Americans to be honored, warmly invited Archbishop Glennon and his suite to join the Spellman party in New York. The archbishop was pleased with the invitation, and it was in the best possible humor that he took off in a large plane with Cardinals-Elect Spellman and Tien, along with twenty-five newsmen.

Originally it had been planned that the entire party would stop in Ireland for two days. The first day was to be devoted to sightseeing, the second to the conferring of governmental honors on Cardinal Glennon at a state dinner in the President's palace in Dublin.

After conferring with Prime Minister De Valera, who met his distinguished guests at Shannon and escorted them on a tour of Killarney's lakes, it was decided that a better arrangement would be for Cardinal Glennon to receive his Irish honors on the return voyage when he would be able to appear in the blazing splendor of the Roman purple.

After a brief stop in war-weary and dejected Paris, they flew over the mountains to Rome. The wartime iron gratings were still down on Ciampino Airport on February 14 as the planes taxied in for a landing. The Holy City was occupied by English and United States soldiers.

The cardinals-elect settled in at the Grand Hotel. Its grandeur was somewhat shabby and tarnished, its heat less than would suffice to keep out the damp cold. Many guests soon had colds, among them Archbishop Glennon. It was a nuisance, of course, but he made light of the cautionary advice of his brilliant young secretary Monsignor Cody and the remedies of Commodore MacMahon, his personal physician.

On Monday morning, February 18, the four distinguished Americans waited in the Hall of the Hundred Days in the beautiful old Roman chancery building. They were surrounded by members of their families and hundreds of distinguished friends, both lay and clerical.

There was drama in the presentation of the *biglietti* of nomination as the Pope's messengers arrived from the Vatican after the secret conclave. The first letter of nomination came to Archbishop Glennon, who sat in the armchair on the right, befitting his dignity as dean of the American hierarchy and his forty-three years as an archbishop. His next in seniority, Archbishop Mooney of Detroit, had been a bishop for a mere seventeen years.

A great storm of applause burst against the ceiling as the Pope's messenger congratulated the new cardinal. In all the magnificent pageantry that took place during the following four days, correspondents and friends noted the joyous verve with which Cardinal Glennon went through the most complex ceremonies. In going up to receive his red hat, he made the three genuflections of ceremony with the graceful ease of a man half his age. In visiting the curial cardinals and in taking possession of his titular church, he conquered everyone with his erect carriage and Celtic charm. Yet his cold lingered on, deep-seated and stubborn, in the chilly rooms he found everywhere in war-torn Rome.

It was with a sense of near relief that Cardinal Glennon and his party took the plane for Ireland with its creature comforts and blazing peat fires. Arriving at Shannon on March 4, the cardinal was met by Prime Minister De Valera and other officials. After a warm welcome to the new prince of the Church, the entire party flew on to Dublin and went by car to the presidential palace in Phoenix Park where Glennon was the guest of President Séan Thomas O'Kelly.

It was after they reached Dublin that Monsignor Cody and Dr. MacMahon noted a lassitude in the cardinal that alarmed them. They tried to persuade him to remain seated while speaking at the state dinner that evening, and when he jocosely put them off, they prevailed upon President Kelly to enforce the rule.

After the glowing citation and the gift of honors, the President said, "As President of Eire I insist that His Eminence remain seated while he talks to us." It was a smiling Glennon who obeyed the order, but in his few remarks he carried the distinguished audience along with him in gales of laughter.

He made fun of the war to end dictators that had spawned a new crop, like those of his entourage who made him sit down when he wished to stand up. He referred to his cold, amid a volley of laughter, "as deep rooted, like the Roman faith." Then he introduced Monsignor Cody, calling him "an expert in protocol." "I will say," the cardinal added, "that so far he has kept me out of trouble and perhaps can tell you, if he wishes, how he has done it." Of Commodore MacMahon, the cardinal said, "He is my personal physician. Perhaps in that official and informed capacity he can tell you how he succeeded in making this cold last so long."

Amid ringing applause and cheers, the cardinal was given a standing ovation as he rose and majestically left the room with Monsignor Cody, who shortly returned for a brief speech of thanks for all the kindness they had shown his revered cardinal —sentiments which were echoed in the bluff words of Commodore MacMahon.

After much discussion, Cardinal Glennon was prevailed upon to take a five-day rest before returning to St. Louis. He radiated such sparkling humor from his sickbed that everyone hoped he would soon be up and as vigorous as ever. But Commodore MacMahon discovered that uremic poisoning had set in. Monsignor Cody anointed his beloved superior, and Cardinal Glennon died as he had lived, in an atmosphere of humor and deep piety.

His Irish farewell took place at Pontifical Mass in the Cathedral of Christ the King, in Mullingar, where he had preached its dedication sermon in 1939. Country people of the district rubbed shoulders with the bigwigs of Dublin and the Irish Government. The sanctuary was ablaze with Irish purple and the thrones of three princes of the Church: James Cardinal MacGuigan of Toronto, Norman Cardinal Gilroy of Sydney, and Bernard Cardinal Griffith of London.

The people of St. Louis were almost incredulous at the news of the cardinal's death. A large percentage of the city's population and most of the hierarchy of the United States came to honor him during his lying-in-state and at the Pontifical Mass of Requiem at which the new-minted cardinals of Detroit, Chicago and New York said their farewells in the bronzelike accents of the final absolution.

St. Louis had grown used to him; it would miss his fatherly counsel and witty remarks, as well as his superb aplomb. Those more thoughtful than others pointed out that Cardinal Glennon was the last of the Church's links with the Baltimore councils and the last intimate friend of the great Gibbons and all the giants of his time.

It has been said that a man is not a hero to his valet. If so, Glennon was a grand exception. For thirty-eight years, his housekeeper Catherine Flynn had looked after the archbishop. No one among his close friends knew him as well as she did. In an interview granted to Thomas Morgan after the funeral, Miss Flynn spoke of the cardinal's love of reading and study. She told of his outgoing ways and the joy of life which masked a monastic spirit and childlike love of God.

"God created him perfect," she said, with a deep sigh. "Only once in five hundred years do we see a perfect man. Archbishop Glennon was the one of our time."

It was a lovely epitaph that few princes of the Church could match.

Edward Cardinal Mooney

E DWARD MOONEY was born in Mount Savage, Maryland, on May 9, 1882, the seventh child of Thomas Mooney and his wife Sarah Heneghan Mooney. The child was baptized in St. Patrick's Church on the following Sunday.

Grover Cleveland was in the second year of his first term as President, and the United States was in a period of tremendous expansion. Among the steel cities, Youngstown, Ohio, had a phenomenal growth. Within a generation it had jumped from a quiet village to a bustling city of smoking chimneys sprawling on both sides of the Mahoning River. Growth spells opportunity for the immigrant, and Tom Mooney was fiercely determined that his children would not be condemned to the obscurity that had been his lot. After talking things over with his wife, he moved his family north and joined the Irish colony in Youngstown—on the wrong side of the tracks. Edward was five at the time.

Tom Mooney was a vigorous man and he took his strong muscles and alert mentality to the tube mill. Before long he was an expert in wrestling the big white-hot steel plates which he fed through the bender that turned them into pipes. Wages were good enough to maintain the Mooney family in a drab frame house like those of their neighbors in the Irish section. Good schools were available, and there was competent religious instruction at St. Columba's Parish nearby.

Things looked grim for the Mooney family with the death of their father when Edward was in his early teens. But Sarah Mooney, who was praised in the community for her cooking, quietly established a small bakery business. Each afternoon after school Eddie and his brothers delivered the crusty sweet-smelling loaves to her customers. It was hard enough work in the heat of summer, but when winter came, the self-reliant children suffered from snow and the biting north winds blowing down from Lake Michigan as they made their rounds through the soot-darkened streets.

The Irish neighborhood, known as Kilkenny, was hard-boiled. Ed Mooney held his own with the best of the lads, and though he was a good student at St. Columba's School and a devoted altar boy, he spoke the language of his neighborhood and shared the robust and rowdy games of his companions.

Edward felt that he had a vocation to the priesthood, and Monsignor Mears, the pastor at St. Columba's, was consulted. It was arranged that the boy would go to St. Charles College in Maryland for his classics, and later to St. Mary's Seminary in Baltimore for philosophy and theology. Bishop Horstmann of Cleveland would pay the expenses.

Edward's progress was so swift and his record so excellent that when he received his A.B. at St. Mary's in 1905, Bishop Horstmann sent him to Rome for further study. The young man's devotion to learning, his excellent showing in examinations, and deep but practical piety gave him stature among the students and brought him the rewards of two doctor's degrees in philosophy and theology.

Edward was ordained by Cardinal Respighi in St. John Lateran on April 10, 1909, and offered his first Mass in the pillared splendor of St. Paul's Outside the Walls, his favorite church in Rome. The young priest returned to Youngstown for his first Solemn Mass and a happy reunion with his family.

Bishop John P. Farrelly, who had succeeded Bishop Horstmann as Bishop of Cleveland, was pleased with the attainments of his cultured young priest and assigned him at once to the professorship of dogmatic theology at St. Mary's Seminary in Cleveland.

For seven years, Father Mooney gave his polished lectures to the seminarians. His talks were spiced with amusing insights and vignettes culled from the Roman years, but though he could make the students laugh with his genial summations and looked mild as milk, there was a quality about him that demanded respect. They were all rather proud of his growing fame as a retreat master for both religious and lay retreats.

With the foundation of Cathedral Latin School, Father Mooney became its first president, a position he held for five years while it grew from a small school to an enrollment of 1,200 students.

Administrative duties, the wise use of never-sufficient funds, the governance of the faculty composed of diocesan priests and the Brothers of Mary—all these Father Mooney fulfilled with alacrity and informed common sense. What he wanted was not just another school; he desired scholastic excellence of the highest order. That was why he warned that any student with thirty demerits would be dismissed. Above all, he wished this to be a school for gentlemen, not "seventy-five percent gentlemen," as he said ironically.

Cathedral Latin School served an even more important function in recruiting and training boys for entry into the senior seminary. Father Mooney was especially successful in this endeavor; his attractive spirituality and manly ways gave boys an insight into the magnificence of the priesthood.

In 1921, Bishop Schrembs became Bishop of Cleveland. The new bishop saw that many new parishes would have to be built, and decided he would need every available priest for the work. With this in mind, he persuaded the Brothers of Mary to bring in more men and take over the complete operation of the Cathedral Latin School.

Father Mooney was appointed Pastor of St. Patrick's Church in Youngstown in 1922. The welcome given him was cordial, and his family was delighted to have him so near after the long years of intermittent separation.

A story has come down to us from Father Mooney's brief reign as Pastor of St. Patrick's at the time when the Ku Klux Klan was active. Father Mooney, the story says, was having an outdoor ice-cream social for the purpose of raising funds for his church. The Klan hired the next empty lot, assembled in its white gowns, and as Father Mooney was appealing for funds burned a huge cross that lit up the entire area. Some $12,000 was pledged as Irish and German tempers began to boil in the Catholic group. Father Mooney calmed them and walked over to the Klan platform where, in the astounded silence, he thanked the Klansmen for so beautifully lighting up his fiesta and invited them to partake of ice cream and cake at his expense. According to the tale, a great many of them accepted and some even pledged money to the funds being raised. Whether true or not, it is the sort of legend that sums up the kind of situation in which Father Mooney excelled and conquered.

After barely a year as pastor, the news came that Father Mooney had been called back to Rome as spiritual director of the North American College. The change was a welcome one; it offered full scope for his spiritual discernment, love of study, and a near genius in guiding young men toward the complete realization of themselves in the priesthood.

No light can hide under a bushel in Rome. Such distinguished curial visitors to the college as Monsignor Marchetti Selvagianni and Cardinals Gasparri and Van Rossum discovered in Doctor Mooney a subtle approach to ecclesiastical affairs and a theological wisdom of the first order. Cardinal Van Rossum, the Cardinal Prefect of the Sacred Congregation of Propaganda, was particularly impressed. Soon it was said that Father Mooney was destined for high things. The rumor was borne out with his appointment to Gasparri's commission for the revision of the Roman Catechism and later as apostolic delegate to India in 1926. Mooney himself protested to Van Rossum that he did not have the qualities for the position.

"I'm afraid I shall not live up to expectations," he said.

"Don't worry," Cardinal Van Rossum answered. "I'm sure you will."

The consecration of Father Mooney as Archbishop of Irenopolis took place on January 31, 1926. Soon after, the apostolic delegate sailed to take up his new responsibilities.

En route to India, he stopped in the United States for an affecting reunion with his aged mother, who had played such a large part in directing his steps toward the priesthood. The priests of the diocese, who prized Archbishop Mooney, gave him a magnificent banquet at which they spoke of their admiration in unmeasured terms and presented him with a generous purse to further his mission work.

The voyage was long and there was ample time to mull over the complexities of the tasks he faced. There were conflicting privileges and loyalties between the Portuguese enclaves and the native bishops; there were problems with the native princes and the British Raj. Most important of all, it was necessary to make all the parties involved see the wisdom of building up a strong native priesthood, as Pius XI so ardently desired. All of this would have to be done in a strange climate on a strange diet by varied and often primitive modes of travel. As he walked the decks of the ship Archbishop Mooney must have smiled a little, comparing his new problems with the old days when he and his brothers delivered bread in the heat and cold of Youngstown.

The apostolic delegation at Bangalore, in the province of Mysore, largest province in South India, surprised the archbishop; the climate at 3,000 feet above sea level was pleasant most of the year. The white buildings of the city of some 600,000 people made a pleasant contrast with the lush green of the trees and exotic flowering shrubs. There was advantage in the fact that Bangalore was an important railway center and the seat of a university.

Archbishop Mooney found the Indians both subtle and shyly reserved. Conversation with them proved to be delightful; often they could see a point quite invisible to the Anglo-Saxon mentality, and there was usually warm friendliness behind the shy façades.

The archbishop was not content to be a mere paper delegate.

He moved about in official society with sure charm, and starting out on the convenient and excellently organized railway, proceeded on a personal visitation of his vast territory by car, carriage and bullock cart.

Father John A. Killian, S.J., who observed the work of the delegate at close range, offers us an inspiring summary of those years:

> In four short years in India, he won the undying affection of every missionary priest and bishop and the laity. He scoured the vast country from east to west and from north to south. He visited every mission field.
>
> He saw all the missionaries. He was one with them in food and travel. There was no place too remote for him to visit, no abode too wretched, no food too poor. He welcomed all with delight and contagious amiability.
>
> Fifteen new missionary territories were erected under his supervision; three existing diocese were transferred to native bishops.
>
> The crowning achievement of all was the reconciliation with the Church of about sixty thousand Christians of the Malabar Rite who had been in schism for centuries.

The strangeness wore off after awhile or was consumed in the delegate's intense zeal which saw beyond the present moment to the fields white with the harvest of souls. As an American, he was above and beyond the political battles and narrow national interests. This gave him enormous advantage in settling rivalries and disputes objectively, and his pleasant manner and long experience in handling perplexed or maverick youngsters proved to be of great value.

In the almost five years of his mission, he had fulfilled Van Rossum's optimistic prophecy to the hilt in settling outstanding problems among bishops and princes and in immeasurably forwarding the movement for the native priests and sisterhoods.

There had been sticky moments in trying to settle difficulties between the Portuguese and Indian bishops, but through the employment of patience and endless reasoning in pointing up loyalty and duty, Archbishop Mooney was able to solve the

most vexing problems in a fashion that established good prece-
dents for a peaceful future. In doing so, he had completely
charmed officialdom, particularly Lord Halifax, Viceroy of
India, who became his lifelong friend.

The reward for good work is usually more of it. Archbishop
Mooney realized this in 1931 when he was transferred to the
apostolic delegation in Tokyo. It was quite a change to go from
a country in which facility in careless living is almost genius to
a land in which the mannered mode of life is nearly a mania.

The intense neatness of the land and people delighted the
archbishop. Scarcely less interesting was the compartmental
character of the Japanese mind, which could maintain op-
posites with serene aplomb. Their good taste, love of art and
stark drama, conspired to make life among them something of a
charming game. Yet Archbishop Mooney could see that behind
their outmoded religio-patriotic fervor was an uneasy search for
philosophical and religious certitude.

One of his first endeavors was to act as a bridge between the
government and the educational and social groups of the Catholic Church in Japan. Authoritarian education, symbolized by
the Catholic University and the religious schools, appealed to
all that was best in the Japanese character—it took little
energy to explain that to the great princely and commercial
families. Even many of those who were not Catholics came to
see the wisdom of sending their daughters to the schools governed by the nuns, in which discipline and graceful conduct
were the norms.

When Archbishop Mooney arrived in Japan, the outstanding
issue between Catholics and the government was the question
of the Shinto shrines or national cemeteries which all Japanese
were required by law to visit and pay homage to. Japanese Catholics had quietly stayed away, maintaining that they could not in
conscience take part in Shinto worship. Were such visits merely
patriotic or were they also religious?

Archbishop Mooney found a way out by insisting that the government must make a public declaration to the effect that visits
to the shrines were merely patriotic and not religious. The

declaration did not come until after his departure, but when it came, Japanese Catholics gradually frequented the shrines and became less suspect to their compatriots.

Another outstanding achievement of the Japanese days was the calling of a plenary council of the bishops of Korea. All the sessions of the council were conducted in Latin, because of the diverse languages of the bishops participating. Archbishop Mooney presided genially, and under his direction a uniform discipline was established for the territory and measures were taken for increasing missionary zeal and effectiveness.

Pius XI was pleased with Archbishop Mooney's achievements. His usefulness in Japan, however, had run its course. That country's aggressive colonialism had aroused the anger of the United States Government, and the American prelate was no longer *persona grata* at the Japanese Foreign Office. With this in mind, Pius XI appointed Archbishop Mooney Bishop of Rochester, in upstate New York. It seemed a modest reward for tremendous achievement, but it was to be of short duration and a genuine steppingstone to ecclesiastical preferment.

The Depression was at its height. Bishop Mooney suffered acutely with his people in Rochester, since he knew from his childhood what it meant to be poor and insecure. He multiplied himself in public service, in lectures at the seminary, in conferences in all the parishes—especially among the many foreign groups that were often forgotten and seldom encouraged.

Though Bishop Mooney's body had been out of the United States, his mind had been shrewdly concerned with the progress of papal social teaching and its progress in America. These he proceeded to emphasize in speeches throughout the diocese and—as a crown to his efforts—arranged a conference on industrial problems in the fall of 1936 in which the ideas of Church and Labor were shown to be in complete accord.

The Bishop of Rochester may seem a minor figure in the national conference of bishops, in which ruling archbishops and cardinals usually have the chief say. Such was not the case with Archbishop Mooney. In a sense, he was a bishop's bishop. The hierarchy knew his reputation intimately and admired his success and tremendous ability. These were the main reasons which led them to elect him to the chairmanship of the National Catholic Welfare Conference's administrative board from 1934 to 1939 and again from 1941 to 1945—periods in which some of the most important decisions for the future of the entire Church in America were made. It may further be said that the N.C.W.C., as we know it today, is largely his creation.

Detroit became an archdiocese in 1937, with Edward Mooney as its first archbishop. Priests and everyone else received him with a great demonstration of loyalty and affection. There were several bands at the Michigan Central Station when his car arrived at 7 P.M. on Ausust 2. A large group led by Governor Murphy welcomed their archbishop with noisy enthusiasm. Tens of thousands of people, carrying flags and banners, were massed in Roosevelt Park.

In a brief speech to the throng, Archbishop Mooney said that he came among them to fulfill the law of Moses, confirmed by Christ: "Thou shalt love the Lord thy God . . . and thy neighbor as thyself." He stressed the beauties of peace, the horror of hate. A glowing tribute was paid to his predecessor Bishop Gallagher, and then everyone—regardless of creed or race—was urged to cooperate in the public service.

On the following morning, Archbishop Mooney was enthroned in the beautiful Church of the Most Blessed Sacrament. Over half the hierarchy of the United States had come to pay him honor at the ceremony over which Archbishop Cicognani presided.

It had been foreseen, well in advance, that the old Cathedral of SS. Peter and Paul would be much too small for the occasion, so the spacious Gothic Church of the Most Blessed Sacrament had been selected. (It later became the new cathedral, after Rome granted the archbishop's petition for the change.)

When the apostolic delegate had returned to his throne on the Epistle side of the altar, Archbishop Mooney, in full regalia, addressed his new flock. A dead silence fell in the crowded church as bishops and laymen listened to one of the most clear and ringing declarations of purpose they had ever heard. He said: "I carry the Gospel of Christ. This is the Gospel of brotherly love and peace—not peace at any price, but peace at the price of doing justice, of practicing charity, of exercising the discipline of conciliation and restraint, of pursuing the way of mutual understanding, of using methods of calm discussion and responsible agreement, of standing faithful to the given word."

Detroiters liked their new archbishop instantly—his geniality, his trenchant summaries, his deeply religious orientation, his subtle explanations of doctrine, his width of view.

But when the celebrations were over, the actual situation proved more serious than Mooney had expected. The huge Detroit diocese had been drastically reduced in area. The era of boom in the twenties, which brought thousands of Catholics streaming into Detroit, had been followed by the depression of the thirties, with its astounding tragedies and misery. Capital and Labor were locked in a struggle with few or no holds barred; racial hatreds were at a peak. In addition, Archbishop Mooney was succeeding Bishop Gallagher, a good and kindly man who had ruled the diocese for nineteen years, but who had become overwhelmed and confused toward the end by the mounting issues crowding upon him. The diocese was in debt to the tune of $20,000,000.

Then there was the problem of Father Coughlin. A fabulously successful pastor, publicist and speaker, his name was a power in the land. Some said he had courage, others that he lacked prudence. All admitted that he disliked our much-adulated President. Though Bishop Gallagher had usually supported Father Coughlin's efforts in public, the considered opinion among United States Catholics was that the Detroit priest had grown too big for his diocese.

If Archbishop Mooney shuddered a little at the problems to be solved, he must have smiled a little too at his motto: "We serving the Lord." He seemed to be doing that with a vengeance.

The first thing to be tackled was the debt. Archbishop Mooney discussed the entire problem with noted lawyers and financial experts, after which he met with the heads of banks, in order to reduce the interest rates and widen the base on which the debts rested.

With his talent for convincing people, the archbishop was able to secure the enthusiastic interest of more than 200 pastors who pledged the full resources and credit of their parishes. They agreed to devote a definite minimum of their annual incomes to the reduction of the entire debt. Even parishes out of debt offered the same help. As a result of the guarantees, the archbishop was able to provide banks and insurance companies the security they demanded on their loans.

While this plan was being worked out most parishes were also working to reduce their own debts to some degree. Consequently, when it came time to put the new loan agreement into effect in February of 1941, the total debt of the diocese had shrunk to $18,000,000. Insurance companies took $10,000,000 of this total on 12-year notes secured by mortgages. Banks of the Detroit area, Chicago and New York, assumed the balance of $8,000,000 on an 8-year loan covered by serial notes. This refinancing project was accomplished without any compromise of principal.

On loans from parishes out of debt, the archbishop agreed to pay a just interest rate. He also agreed to return the principal when it was needed for parish expansion. By the time the third anniversary of this refinancing program dawned, the diocese had reduced its total debt to the banks and insurance companies by nearly $12,000,000.

Imitation is the sincerest flattery. The cardinal's successful annual drive has moved many bishops in the United States to institute an annual development fund campaign in their own dioceses. They even use Cardinal Mooney's title for this fund-raising effort.

Archbishop Mooney had genuine financial vision which enabled him to see that the mere payment of the diocesan debt was not his real goal. He must build if the diocese was to excel in the service of God and his people. That meant churches, schools, hospitals and centers for social service.

Out of his own fertile mind came the Archdiocesan Development Fund in 1943, which even in the midst of war looked forward to the future after victory had been won. In May, an army of enthusiastic volunteers set out to gather funds which, beginning with a new seminary, embraced every future contingency and included sections of the diocese that had only begun to develop.

When Archbishop Mooney came to Detroit, his diocese embraced nearly 603,000 souls. At the time of his death the Catholic population had risen to nearly 1,400,000, all adequately served with churches, schools, hospitals and social centers of the most completely diverse kind—all as a result of his development fund.

It is possible to single out of these accomplishments the projects which were nearest to his heart. The first of these was St. John's Provincial Seminary which, with its soaring bell tower and flowing façade, delights the eye and contains every modern facility for the formation and training of young men for the priesthood. The priesthood is an elite corps of the Church, and upon its piety, zeal and learning depend the stability and progress in bringing Christ to the people.

St. John's Seminary is the only true canonical provincial seminary in the United States enjoying the approval of the Holy See's Congregation of Universities and Seminaries. It is governed by a board of all bishops of the province, and each bishop has an equal vote. The tuition is set by vote, and any deficit is met by all the dioceses, which are assessed sums in keeping with their size and the number of students enrolled.

In staffing the major seminary, the archbishop turned to his old mentors, the Sulpician Fathers, who had so beautifully fostered his own gifts and spiritual life.

Hardly less dear to the archbishop's heart than the good boy with a vocation were the orphaned, retarded and troubled children. For these, he provided pleasant homes where they could be cared for and educated according to modern ideas. The most notable achievement in this field was Boysville at Macon, Michigan, which helps troubled young men to find themselves and guides them toward self-reliance and useful lives.

Last but not least was the archbishop's completion of his cathedral in the best tradition of late Gothic splendor. Its beautiful twin towers are one of the outstanding landmarks on Woodward Avenue.

In addition to these important items, there were large sums loaned for the purchase of parish sites and for pioneering religious efforts. Among these was the firm establishment of the Catechetical League under trained leadership. Quarters were found near all the great public school centers, and 60,000 Catholic children were thus enabled to learn the truths of their religion with a minimum of inconvenience.

Unique is the fact that the seminary and Boysville were built and financed by the combined efforts of all the bishops of the province. This was not merely an indication of the cordial good feeling that prevailed under Archbishop Mooney; it reflected a talent for getting cooperation that went back to his early college days when he was head of the Students' Mission Crusade and later coached and directed a lively debating society. The art of convincing minds was his, and he had a near genius for showing people how necessary it is to cooperate in the achievement of important goals.

The problem of Father Coughlin was solved with a minimum of fuss. In *Speaking of Cardinals,* Thomas Morgan says that the solution came through a new synodal law making it obligatory for all priests of the archdiocese to secure the archbishop's approval on anything to be printed or broadcast. Whatever transpired is a secret between Archbishop Mooney and Father Coughlin. It is to the everlasting priestly credit of both men that they said nothing and went on to new successes: Father Coughlin to become a devoted pastor of his beautiful shrine church of the Little Flower with its active grade and high schools; Archbishop Mooney to the Sacred College of Cardinals.

The news of his elevation to the senate of the Church came by a telephone call from the apostolic delegate on Christmas morning 1945. During the war, the Holy Father, as a sign of mourning, had made no cardinals. Now that peace had come, Pius XII signalized the Church's joy in elevating thirty-two distinguished prelates chosen from all over the world. The United States had the distinction of four new cardinals: Glennon of St. Louis, Mooney of Detroit, Stritch of Chicago, and Spellman of New York.

The archbishop did not intend to publish the news immediately, but Heinie Hoch, veteran reporter of Catholic affairs for the Detroit *News,* who had the archbishop's private telephone number and had been tipped off from New York, called the archbishop for confirmation of the story.

The archbishop readily confirmed the news, and when asked for a statement, told Hoch to meet him at the Mother of Consolation Chapel on Mackey Avenue, which he was going to bless that morning. Archbishop Mooney then added something characteristic of his diplomatic alertness and even-handed justice; "Call the other papers, will you, Heinie? I'm sort of busy this morning."

Cameramen and newsmen in packs converged on the chapel long in advance of the designated hour. Archbishop Mooney greeted them with a broad grin and publicly confirmed the rumor. Then he said swiftly what was in his heart:

"Naturally I am deeply moved by this supreme token of confidence on the part of the Holy Father. I am profoundly grateful to him. The sobering thought of the responsibility this honor carries induces a mood of deep-felt humility in the recipient. But there is unalloyed joy in the thought of the compliment it implies to the clergy and the people of this archdiocese, whose cooperation through the years has been so heartening and so inspiring."

The two old friends, Archbishops Stritch and Mooney, made joint plans for the journey. When they departed for Rome with their friends, it was significant that no newsmen were on the plane. Both prelates were one in wishing to preserve intact the religious aspects of their elevation.

Cardinal Mooney stayed in a villa on the outskirts of Rome, and resolutely refused all the blandishments of reporters and cameramen. Yet after he received his red *galero* from the hands of Pius XII in the splendid Solemn Consistory of February 21, 1946, the new cardinal graciously made one concession to his favorite newsman in consenting to broadcast a question-and-answer interview from the Vatican radio direct to WWJ in Detroit. Hoch was all the more surprised and grateful because Cardinal Mooney had refused the same concession to all the major networks.

The plane trip home was a bumpy one. The weather was so bad in Detroit that the cardinal was forced to land in Chicago, proceeding to Detroit by train. Despite the weather, there was a tremendous crowd waiting at Detroit's airport. Monsignor Hickey, who was directing the reception, got in touch with the cardinal by phone, asking what time he expected to arrive. According to Thomas Morgan, the cardinal told Monsignor Hickey to send the people home. "Do not let them wait around in the cold. Why make them wait for me anyway? After all, I'm no mannequin."

It was in this mood of consideration for others and genuine manly gratitude that the cardinal went through the round of dinners and receptions in his honor. During his entire life he had shown striking consideration for the little man, a quality that remained unchanged with his new eminence.

Edgar Guest, an old friend and golfing partner, was the master of ceremonies at the civic banquet in the cardinal's honor. The high point of the dinner was the presentation of two cars by General Motors and Ford; the first was a Cadillac, then came Ford's gift of a Lincoln that could be turned in for a new car every year. After the applause had died down, Guest returned to the mike. "Now it is my turn to give the cardinal something I know he *can* drive." The poet held his gift high for all to see. It was a shiny new golf ball.

In his first public speech after his return from Rome, the cardinal urged his listeners to "join themselves ever more closely with the Holy Father by the study and practice of papal directives concerned with social problems and community and international cooperation."

During his first eight years as archbishop he had not hesitated to speak out bluntly in defense of the C.I.O. and U.A.W. when they were under attack or misrepresented. Phil Murray always dropped in for a visit when he was passing through Detroit. Walter Reuther and many others in the U.A.W. were on friendly terms with the archbishop, as were the titans of industry: Knudson and Coyle of General Motors, Keller and Hutchinson of Chrysler, and Henry Ford II and Bugas of Ford Motor.

In 1947, Cardinal Mooney accepted active membership on Detroit's Labor-Management-Public Committee, along with Reuther, Charles E. Wilson, President of General Motors, Henry Ford II and other noted community leaders.

Two years later, at the solemn dedication of St. John's Seminary, the cardinal bluntly reminded his distinguished audience of priests and prelates that he and most of the American priests and bishops had come from working-class families, that they must cherish their kinship with working men, and that they must profess and prove their active interest in workers' problems and welfare.

The cardinal spoke in much the same fashion in defense of the United Nations by reminding its critics that although it was an imperfect instrument, like all human instruments, it was a long step in the right direction, warmly approved by Pope Pius XII.

November 1951 was a significant month for Detroit Catholics, who were celebrating three events: Cardinal Mooney's silver jubilee as bishop, the completion of Blessed Sacrament Cathedral, and the 250th anniversary of the Church in Detroit. Four cardinals came for the solemn day of triumph: Stritch of Chicago, Tien of Peiping, China, Spellman of New York, and McGuigan of Toronto. Thirteen archbishops and eighty-eight bishops—a dazzling demonstration of Catholic solidarity and even more of a personal tribute to Cardinal Mooney.

In 1952, during the national convention of Holy Name men, there were tremendous public demonstrations of love for the Blessed Sacrament; in a fervid holy hour, massed thousands in Briggs Stadium poured out their love of Christ in prayer and song and marched down Woodward Avenue the following morning with bands and flying banners.

The cardinal had a right to be proud of his archdiocese as the fifties were coming to a close. Every aspect of Catholic life showed remarkable vigor; bishops, priests and people were in harmonious accord; a crusade against indecent publications and movies was successful; colleges and schools were growing fabulously.

The death of Cardinal Stritch in Rome on May 27, 1958, was a terrible blow to Cardinal Mooney. They had been close friends since their student days in the North American College. Cardinal Stritch had always been the "little brother," and it was this loving title with which Cardinal Mooney hailed his friend as he lay in state on the day of the funeral.

The news from Rome in early October of the same year was that Pius XII was ill. This great pontiff had been a true father for suffering people everywhere, and men of all faiths admired and loved him. He died on October 8, 1958, and was buried with universal mourning. The cardinals of the world began to convene for the election of a new pope.

Cardinal Mooney had not been well for some time, and had the occasion been of less importance, he might well have followed the advice of his doctors to rest as much as possible. But he who had preached duty to others all his life was not one to spare himself in the solemn duty of electing a new Holy Father.

At the conclusion of the Mass of the Holy Spirit on the morning of the day the conclave was to open, Saturday, October 25, Cardinal Mooney felt tired. Yet he returned to the North American College after Mass and was his old jovial self at luncheon with Cardinals Spellman and McIntyre.

Near the close of the meal he asked Cardinal Spellman if there would be time for a brief rest. The cardinal didn't think so, but when Cardinal Mooney reminded him of the old adage, "When in Rome do as the Romans do," which certainly enjoined a siesta, New York's cardinal laughingly acquiesced.

At 2:15 P.M. Cardinal Mooney retired, instructing his secretary Monsignor Breitenbeck to call him promptly at 2:45. When the monsignor knocked on the door at the appointed time, he got no answer. Entering the room, he found the cardinal dying of a massive heart attack. After calling the doctor, he gave Cardinal Mooney extreme unction. Cardinals Spellman and McIntyre, hurriedly summoned along with the rector, Bishop Martin J. O'Connor, arrived for the last absolutions.

The two cardinals were overcome by the sudden tragedy, but as the opening hour of the conclave was near at hand, they had to hurry off despite their shock and grief. It was particularly sad to think that Cardinal Mooney, who had been an outstanding leader of men the world over, would never excercise his highest prerogative in helping select a new pope.

It was this duty, which now took precedence over all church business, that made the presence of a dead cardinal in Rome something of an embarrassment, in a sense. Everything was expedited for his departure for home on the following day. Fortunately, three who loved and admired him—Bishop O'Connor, Monsignor Breitenbeck and Father Arthur M. Karey, Assistant Chancellor of Detroit—were there to see that everything was carried out to the last degree of permissible splendor.

Special permission to offer a Requiem Mass was obtained for Bishop O'Connor, since it would be Sunday and the Feast of Christ the King on which Rome would say its final farewell to the dead cardinal in the superb chapel of the North American College.

After the Mass, the cardinal's body, accompanied by Monsignor Breitenbeck and Father Karey, was flown to Idlewild, and then to Detroit, where it was met by the cardinal's grief-stricken curia led by Bishops Zaleski, Donovan and Donnelly, followed by throngs of priests and people.

For two days the body of the cardinal lay in state in the beautiful home given to Bishop Gallagher by an admirer. It is notable that some 10,000 people made the long pilgrimage to the house in Palmer Woods to show their love and respect for this outstanding prince of democracy, impressive even in death. Later in the week the dead cardinal lay in state in his cathedral while thousands of his people waited patiently in long lines for a last look at his beloved countenance.

On Friday, October 31, the morning was heavy with the sad sound of tolling church bells all over the city of Detroit. The apostolic delegate offered the Solemn Mass of Requiem, and after four absolutions, the cardinal was borne away to his beloved seminary of St. John. There, after the final absolution by Bishop Zaleski, the cardinal's body was laid to rest in the crypt beneath the high altar.

Pope John XXIII sent a message of praise and condolence; others flowed in from faraway places all over the world. In his own city, the talk was all of the cardinal's achievements and the realization of how much the city and state would miss his force and vision. No one doubted his greatness as priest, nuncio, bishop and cardinal. Always Edward Mooney had been in the van of the struggle for the head and heart of the modern world. Priests and people had loved the man. They would sorely miss the inspired leadership that had enabled them to see and share his high destiny—"We serving the Lord."

Samuel Cardinal Stritch

———⟨●⟩———

THE WARM summer dusk was settling over Nashville, Tennessee, when Samuel Stritch was born August 17, 1887. Garrett Stritch, Samuel's father, had come from Dublin in the seventies. His first years in America were spent at the home of a cousin in Louisville, Kentucky. They were important years which brought the bright young man the friendship and interest of Colonel Lewis, one of the wealthy men of the district, and the acquaintance of Catherine Malley, an American-Irish girl of striking brunette charm. Acquaintance grew into love and marriage.

Colonel Lewis at first thought there was greater opportunity for his protégé and the growing family at Sycamore Mills in Tennessee. The nearest Catholic church was in Nashville, a long journey by boat or carriage, and Mrs. Stritch was acutely miserable when she was unable to attend Sunday Mass.

Garrett Stritch and his family returned to Louisville for six months. At the end of that time, Colonel Lewis offered his friend the managership of the Nashville office of Sycamore Mills. Garrett gladly accepted and found a comfortable frame house for his brood in North Nashville, at the corner of Madison and Fifth avenues. It was in this high-windowed house that Samuel Stritch was born.

Assumption Church, three blocks from home, was the scene of his baptism and early religious training. He received his introduction to learning at Assumption school, and his teachers found him unusually bright and lively. Though the second youngest of eight children, he cheerfully helped his older brothers in their daily chores of chopping and carrying wood for the capacious stoves and fireplaces of the day.

The reward for this labor came in summer with long excursions to the swimming hole in White's Creek. There the bursting joy in a boy's heart seemed almost too great to be borne as the sun-dappled hours sped by.

Sam's intellectual opportunities widened when he transferred to St. Mary's Cathedral School and came to the attention of Father John Morris, rector of the cathedral. Father Morris enjoyed his encounters with the lighthearted boy whose ready repartee and quick comprehension of the deepest thoughts seemed to mark him for a career in the Church.

When Samuel was in his ninth year, his talented father died. Fortunately Catherine Stritch had the complete self-reliance that enabled her to be both father and mother to her children. They all looked to her for direction and advice. The tender-hearted Sam was particularly attentive; the bond between them was close and affectionate.

Sam Stritch literally flew through high school, graduating at the age of fourteen. Boyishly shy and quite sure that he had a vocation, Sam made ready to go to St. Gregory's Minor Seminary in Cincinnati.

A picture taken at the time shows an alert wide-browed child with delicately chiseled features and large blue eyes.

The great battles within the American Church were over in 1901, but the issues were still discussed with more heat than light, even among the neophytes at St. Gregory's. The famous Cardinal Gibbons of Baltimore was a national figure, the admired friend of presidents and people alike.

Sam's fellow students at St. Gregory's soon learned respect for this small, determined scholar. The devotion he brought to his studies in the classics and philosophy was remarkable. He was an ardent reader, and the perfection of his conversation and phrasing added luster to the tasks of learning.

Within two years, the bright boy had earned his A.B. Father Morris was proud of his protégé. Bishop Byrne of Nashville echoed this encouragement by suggesting that the young student be sent to Rome.

Catherine Stritch was sad to see her son go, but managed to voice a blessing through her tears on the day of his departure.

During the trip to Naples, Sam thought about the world he was to enter. But the reality of color, charm and strangeness was even more exciting than he had imagined it. The ancient world lay before him like a glittering mosaic of some great master. All the way to Rome he peered through the train window at the little towns perched like eagles on the mountains. It was all so different; even the smells were new.

The first glimpses of Rome enthralled him. Everything he had read about was here, beckoning him on every side in golden walls, sun-lustered domes and soaring columns. It was a great treasure chest, and he would have six long years to savor the treasures.

At the North American College Sam felt that Bishop Kennedy was more than a little surprised at the sight of his small knickerbockered figure, and perhaps he wished that his mother had been less reluctant to see him grow up. But he could sense that the bishop was intrigued by his alert replies and boyish charm.

Things promised well. No knight donning armor for the first time was more thrilled than Sam as he put on his colorful uniform with its blue piping and red sash. In his imagination, he was one with the great churchmen of history.

The sense of excitement and perpetual newness lasted all through the six years of intensive study. Other boys found the climate and the cold house trying. To Sam it seemed much like the climate of Nashville, but here there was so much more to see, so much more to learn, and such fascinating visitors and events.

In summer it was even more charming up at the Villa Santa Caterina. The blue lake, the hikes through the pines, gardens and vineyards, the endless summer succession of famous churchmen, the tennis, the picnics. He bubbled endlessly of it all in letters to his mother, easing her loneliness by his romantic happiness and vivid descriptions.

On various feast days, Cardinal Merry del Val invited groups of students to his nearby villa. On these occasions he doffed his air of ecclesiastical grandeur and became one of them. They watched with amazement as he displayed his marksmanship with a rifle. He would set up a row of pennies on the garden wall and unerringly shoot them off at thirty paces. They tried to copy him, but they couldn't match him. In their minds he was a cross between John Barrymore and Buffalo Bill, with all the added glamor of being the Pope's Secretary of State.

Sam found his studies as exciting as the excursions into the countryside; St. Thomas or Blessed Albert opened up ever-increasing vistas of the mind and the power behind it. But for Sam, the lovely little chapel was a special place of solitude. There in the comforting warmth of his long cloak he could let his mind and heart soar away into the landscape of immortality. As sacristan, a post of great honor, he was careful not to let others know what hours of devotion went into the care and decoration of the altars.

By 1910, Sam had triumphantly passed the examinations for his two doctor's degrees, one in philosophy, one in Theology. As a sacristan and an officer of the college, he was ready for ordination. But canon law said he was too young to be ordained at twenty-two.

Bishop Kennedy, with fatherly solicitude, took Sam to an audience with the great pope-saint, Pius X. With a piercing intensity that recognized a dedicated soul, the Holy Father looked at the young man. Before the Pope lay the shining record of Sam's studies and conduct.

The pontiff smiled at Bishop Kennedy over the bent head of his charge, then laid his hand on Sam's shoulder. "He is young in years," Sam heard the silvery voice say, "but old in intelligence. Let him be ordained." The smile on the Pope's face lit an answering one on Sam's. He was ordained by Cardinal Resphigi on May 21, 1910.

After his homecoming Mass in the cathedral and the excitement of the parish reception, there were long hours spent in regaling the family with the stored-up excitement of six exciting years.

Father Sam was happy in his assignment as assistant to Father Morris. To be stationed so near to home, to have his old friend as adviser and companion, were gifts he had never expected. In fact he had often had romantic dreams of doing missionary work in the poorest Negro parish in the diocese.

After several happy years at Assumption, Father Sam was transferred to St. Patrick's Church in Memphis. Within a year he became pastor, and everyone in trouble was beating a path to his door. The small salary he received never had time to get warm in his pocket. Like Pius X in his youth, Sam's devotion to personal charity work and his good use of every minute of his time brought extra burdens; he became Bishop Byrne's secretary in 1916, and chancellor of the diocese in March 1917.

War came. Wilson was the idol of the South, which was sending its sons into the service by the thousands. The bishop's secretary burned his lights far into the night, yet he was never so busy that he couldn't find time to console or advise the mothers and wives who came to him with their sorrows and problems.

No one was surprised when the boyish priest became a monsignor in 1921. "He'd make an ideal bishop," people said. Rome seemed to feel the same way about it. Three months after he first donned the purple, Benedict XV named Monsignor Stritch Bishop of Toledo, Ohio.

The Church of St. Francis de Sales in Toledo was jammed to the doors for the consecration on November 3, 1921. The bishop looked small and frail from a distance, but his minute figure and cameolike profile were impressive at close range. More memorable still was the warm personal charm of the man who seemed almost shy as he listened and then made big decisions with a minimum of soft-spoken words.

His biggest adjustment concerned the northern climate, which did not agree with him. Of his first year in Toledo, he said, "I didn't get warm until August."

Grateful for his teaching, the boy bishop gave his attention to education which he called "our first charity." In 1924, he opened a Catholic teachers' college, the first of its kind in the United States; Mary Manse College had been started in 1922. The teachers' college opened the way for Catholics to acquire the necessary credits and degrees that would enable the Church to keep pace with nonreligious schools and colleges.

All the mission activities of the dioceses were put under centralized control in 1923. The charitable works were unified the following year and became Toledo Catholic Charities, Inc. The bishop himself still believed in personal charity. Known as a soft touch to everyone in the city, he seldom had a dime in his pocket.

A pilgrimage to Rome in 1925 seems to have given Bishop Stritch the incentive to build a cathedral in Toledo. Soon he was talking about his dream and incessantly working for its practical realization.

The cornerstone of the Cathedral of the Holy Rosary was laid by Cardinal Czernock of Hungary on June 26, 1926. Four years later, on August 26, 1930, before he could finish his cathedral, the bishop was elevated to the Archbishopric of Milwaukee, upon the death of Archbishop Messmer. The promotion was entirely unexpected and not entirely welcome. Bishop Stritch loved Toledo, and had even hoped to be buried there in the Visitation Convent. Doubtless his success in handling the various foreign groups in the diocese, his pastoral zeal and outstanding learning, had played a large part in the promotion. "To think with the Church," had long been one of the bishop's favorite slogans. Now that thinking demanded a simple act of obedience and the assumption of heavier burdens. The cold Toledo winters had been his greatest cross; they weren't likely to be less severe in Milwaukee. Besides, the United States was in the midst of the Depression, and the large groups of workers of foreign descent in Milwaukee suffered most as the wheels of industry practically ceased moving.

Yet why should the bishop feel discouraged? People were still people. Five thousand of them crowded into the civic auditorium in Toledo, to bid him farewell. So reluctant were they to lose him, that 400 went with him on a special train to see him installed in Milwaukee. Pondering it all in his daily holy hour in his chapel, the archbishop could see that love was the real treasure. Money was important, but without love it achieved nothing.

The real necessities of the times were "God and good fathers and mothers," the bishop said in his farewell speech in Toledo. Then his soft voice broke a little as he concluded; "I leave you, but I take you with me in my heart."

Milwaukee welcomed him with fervor. Cardinal Mundelein installed him in his new cathedral on November 19, with the gracious magnificence of which Mundelein was a past master. A few days later the governor and civic officials welcomed their new shepherd with warmth.

In response, the archbishop promised them his care, his love, and a "helping hand"; he wished chiefly to be a "useful citizen" among them, "doing his share toward the realization of those ideals which make life worthwhile."

The problems he found would have daunted a man less spiritual. Banks and financial houses failed or were in the grip of panic, and no relief was yet in sight. Many of his people saw their life savings and livelihoods swept away over night.

The archbishop agonized with his people for two terrible years. Sometimes he suffered days of depression. He always criticized himself first, and the sorrows and tragedies of his first Milwaukee years led him to blame himself. Could he have done more in any given circumstance? Could a more loving attitude have prevented sorrow or tragedy?

Fortunately he did not have to suffer alone. Early in his reign he had selected a brilliant young Polish priest, Father Roman Atkielski, as his secretary. Father Atkielski was treated like the archbishop's younger brother; he was at once a friend and a conscience. Though the archbishop had occasional days or periods of depression, Father Atkielski's presence provided him with a safety valve for his self-questioning. Behind the façade of the archbishop, Father Atkielski found the depth and simple warmth of a great soul.

Things in the diocese took a turn for the better after 1933. There was a new current of optimism and hope in Washington, and its electric impulse began to be felt in the farthest corners of the United States.

The archbishop was just as active as ever in gathering every penny he could for charity. This meant long and exhausting trips up and down the diocese and the organization of committees and dinners, but no amount of personal service was too much, as long as the money came in.

Among the movements nearest to his heart was the Catholic Youth Organization that crusading Bishop Shiel had organized. It had quickly caught the fancy of important people in and out of the Church and the fancy of the young as well. In place of do-nothingism, there were drives, goals, games and all sorts of opportunities and incentives for the young people of the area.

The great Pope Pius XI spoke with vigor and fire of Catholic Action, the Christian penetration of society under the leadership of the hierarchy. In season and out of season, the archbishop preached the doctrine he saw only too clearly—that mere activity was not enough; activity informed with the spirit of prayer, sacrifice and self-conquest was needed.

Cardinal Mundelein was quick to appreciate the knowledge, talent and cordial friendliness of the neighboring archbishop. By friendly persuasion, Stritch became vice-chancellor of the Extension Society. His first-hand knowledge of the crying mission needs of the South was of prime advantage in apportioning funds raised. The position also brought him into contact with Bishop O'Brien, who became his closest friend and adviser in later years.

In the beginning, the archbishop was not in favor of drives for building even such necessary things as high schools. The first goal was the elimination of human want and misery; after that there would be time for a long-range plan for diocesan schools.

The bishop's modest personality registered well with the national groups of the diocese. Even his name was a help. The Irish weren't quite sure there wasn't a hint of German lurking in its fringes; the Germans were quite sure there was, especially since the bishop could speak the language; the Poles and Slovaks found the name Stritch somehow akin to their own difficult names. He came among them to ask about their children and their businesses; his small empurpled figure was on hand for parades and Holy Name rallies.

Father Atkielski often had trouble keeping the archbishop looking like an archbishop: the busy small shoes would lose their shine, the black suit would be a mass of wrinkles, the thinning hair would be straggling over his collar. The young priest would call a halt until the physical luster was restored and he saw his beloved friend shining and well-groomed, hurrying off to the next meeting.

What the bishop meant to his people was amply demonstrated on his silver anniversary in 1935. Thousands gathered in the civic auditorium for the Pontifical Mass. The archbishop sat very erect on his throne. The smile he wore deepened when he leaned forward as his old friend and advisor, now Bishop Morris of Little Rock, ascended the pulpit for a homely sermon of congratulation that recalled old and fragrant memories. Before the year was over, he had been serenaded by the symphony orchestra and 1,500 Catholic school children and 30,000 Holy Name men had received communion from him.

These were the things the bishop prized, not for their personal meaning to him—though that touched him deeply—but as signs of the personal love he had tried to kindle among them in pastorals, sermons and lectures pointing up the glories of purity, kindness and self-conquest—to be deed Catholics not name Catholics.

Cardinal Mundelein's death on October 2, 1939, brought great sorrow to Archbishop Stritch. Mundelein had been a tremendous force in the Midwest. Though a natural born aristocrat who had a positive genius in using his talents to advantage, his heart had been like that of Cardinal Gibbons—completely wrapped up in the struggles of the common people.

Archbishop Stritch guessed which way the the winds were blowing. Though he briskly went on with the normal business of the chancery and the annual charity drive, a cold fear gripped him, and prayers multiplied in his mind and heart.

On Christmas eve a slip of yellow paper was delivered to him as he and Father Atkielski waited for the summons to Midnight Mass.

"I can't do it," the priest heard the archbishop mutter. That could only mean he was going to Chicago.

Christmas afternoon Archbishop Stritch went to the telegraph office and personally sent a cable to Rome, asking to be relieved of his burden. Father Atkielski could see how depressed he was. Though the secretary did his best to cheer him with his light banter, the gloom failed to lift and the answering cable ordering the archbishop to accept put an end to the tension, but failed to dispel the cloud of self-questioning humility.

The mood of quiet leave-taking in Milwaukee was completely shattered in the Windy City; 50,000 people jammed themselves in and around the Union Station to greet him. Twenty thousand of them were young people led by Bishop Sheil. The din of their shrill voices was augmented by twelve bands. It was the kind of welcome that always delighted Cardinal Mundelein. For a moment the small figure of the new shepherd stiffened, then the spontaneous and spine-tingling enthusiasm carried him away and he began to grin like a boy at a circus. It was this warm grin that had first conquered Chicago.

After the brilliant installation, the archbishop threw himself into the work of governing "the largest diocese in the world." Unlike Cardinal Mundelein, he preferred to remain in his town house instead of commuting to the more opulent villa at Mundelein.

In the first months of his reign the archbishop was busy finding out the complex details of the vast works Cardinal Mundelein had started. Next came the task of finding the proper people to direct the various activities and organizations. In this he proved to be a shrewd evaluator of men, ready to take advice from his auxiliary bishops Sheil and O'Brien. Everyone found him humorously approachable. They called him "the Boss," with affection, and he in turn often enough gave them a nickname; Bishop O'Brien, his junior auxiliary and closest collaborator, was "Juny."

All of those in authority discovered that the new archbishop readily delegated authority. The delegation was complete and he held those in command strictly responsible.

One of his first big projects was the strengthening and improvement of the diocesan newspaper, *The New World*. Diocesan newspapers had a reputation for being provincial and riddled with ecclesiasticism. The archbishop wanted to get as far away from this as possible. His own vision and interests had the width of the Universal Church. In time, *The New World* achieved the same informed and freshly expressed viewpoint. Through enthusiastic drives and publicity, the subscriptions—in a little over a decade—jumped from 10,000 to 210,000. It was a first-class achievement and a continuing one that merits the highest praise.

In the first seven years of his reign Archbishop Stritch made Catholic Action a living force in the diocese. "It is not enough," he said, "to go to the Sacraments and attend Sunday Mass. We must live and participate in the life of the Church. What we are trying to do is to educate people to understand what it means to be a Catholic."

Social studies, the liturgical movement, the use of correct church music, world-wide missionary activity, were all enormously encouraged in a fashion that attracted the favorable attention of the entire nation.

During the war years, the archbishop mourned the misery and death that plagued mankind. Even stronger than his private patriotism and love of country was his interest in the Pope's peace plan for the world, which put the emphasis on the love of God as the only sure guarantee of the love that should exist between all nations.

Chicago went into a frenzy in 1946 when the news of the archbishop's elevation to the cardinalate was released. The cardinal was excited rather than elated. To him the honor belonged to his priests and people, as much as to himself.

The monumental pomp of Rome, an old story to him, was a masterly frame for the spiritual splendor of Pius XII. The new cardinal was pleased with the titular church assigned him, St. Agnes Outside the Walls. In formally taking possession of his church, he stressed the symbolism he saw in St. Agnes. Her pure life and heroic death were a protest against the materialism of her times; in our own day, she is an inspiration to Catholic womanhood in the struggle against materialistic humanism.

While in Rome, the cardinal reopened St. Mary of the Lake, which Mundelein had bought as a residence for his young priests taking postgraduate work in Rome.

In a broadcast beamed to the United States over Vatican Radio, Cardinal Stritch gave a significant address on Christian unity as it exists in the democracy of the Church. At the close he stressed the duty of Americans to "make Christian truth shine forth in all our activities and undertakings" in tragic times.

On November 19, 1946, Cardinal Stritch celebrated his silver anniversary as a bishop. Three cardinals, the apostolic delegate and over a hundred other priests came for the occasion.

The Pope sent a personal message which praised the cardinal for "the power of his mind and the generosity of his heart," so amply demonstrated in his own diocese and the world at large. Pius XII particularly commended the cardinal's work as chairman of the board of the National Catholic Welfare Conference, in which post he had directed "monumental works of charity" that "channeled relief contributions gathered in the United States to the suffering peoples almost everywhere."

One of the cardinal's first acts was the mounting of a crusade against Communism through the powerful Holy Name Society. Education, a central lecture bureau, retreats and discussions, holy hours, the rosary crusade, all were used as weapons in fighting the monolithic conspiracy.

The cardinal himself was always available for big or small

occasions. Sometimes he wrote his sermons, pecking them out with two fingers on a typewriter while a mounting pile of cigarettes burned out in the big ashtray; at other times he spoke extemporaneously with the graceful ease born of his wide reading.

Some inkling of his courtesy comes down to us from his Good Friday custom of preaching the three-hour meditation on the Passion of Our Lord for the Franciscan Sisters of his household. He felt it was some slight return for the devoted attention they lavished on him, even remembering his numerous anniversaries with cards, in addition to cakes and special things they had baked in the hope of tempting his somewhat capricious appetite.

The twelve years after his elevation to the cardinalate brought Cardinal Stritch increasing burdens, but they also brought many consolations. The social work of his senior auxiliary Bishop Sheil received national recognition and became the pattern followed by many dioceses.

The growth in the Catholic high schools and colleges of the diocese was phenomenal. From New York to California, he was the inspired spokesman for the Pope's various peace plans. The grueling work of his great diocese kept him ever on the move, but did not dim his piety or warm regard for the humblest people.

On the many occasions of his trips to Rome—*ad limina* visits to report on his diocese, the dedication of the splendid new North American College on the Janiculum, and other occasions—Cardinal Stritch showed in word and deed a universal comprehension of the Church and its needs.

It was with complete astonishment and considerable dismay that on March 1, 1958, the cardinal received the news that he had been appointed sub-prefect of the Congregation for the Propagation of the Faith, which controls and finances the worldwide missionary activity of the Church. Never before had an American prelate been honored with such an important position in the government of the Church.

After some struggle, the cardinal knelt in his chapel and

found the strength to say, "Thy will be done." In his public expressions, he was careful to stress the fact that the great honor belonged to America and its people rather than to himself.

It was hard to leave Chicago and its warmhearted people. He had been their shepherd for nineteen years, and he was woven into the fabric of their lives with a thousand golden threads. But the voice of Peter was the voice of God, and Cardinal Stritch was ready to obey the call to wider responsibility in God's service. "Ambition is for young men" was his practical way of phrasing it.

Quietly he went on with his rule of the diocese. Yet he somehow found time for the affecting farewells, dinners, personal visits and speeches and activities already listed on his schedule.

On April 15, he and Archbishop O'Brien took a train to New York and were the guests of Cardinal Spellman. On April 17, accompanied by some of his family and dearest clerical friends, Stritch sailed for Rome on the liner *Independence*.

The last American picture, taken at the ship's railing as he waved to the distinguished group that had come to see him off, is touching. The friendly grace of a father is in every line of his face, but there are also hints of age, weariness and sorrow.

The first days of the voyage were happy. The cardinal was cheerful and philosophized on the difficulties of high position and the joys of being a pastor. In Chicago, he had had painful cramps in his hand and right arm, but had responded to treatment. Now as he was nearing Naples the pain returned. This time it was excruciating and nothing helped it.

With his customary courtesy, he insisted on receiving the bishops and priests who had come to welcome him in Naples. They saw that he was too ill to stand and that his right arm was tucked inside his cassock below a face wearied with pain. Somehow he was able to thank them; his soft southern voice had lost none of its charm. In Rome, an even more imposing group of 200 met him at the station and included prelates and heads of religious orders. A resplendent guard of *carabinieri* escorted the cardinal to his car.

By evening he was hospitalized at Clinica Sanatrix, under the care of Dr. Valdoni, who diagnosed the illness as an "occlusion of the main artery of the right arm." This was confirmed upon the arrival of the cardinal's Chicago doctors, who had flown to Rome.

Amputation of the arm slightly above the elbow seemed to be the only remedy. Cardinal Stritch faced the disagreeable necessity with cheerfulness, made jests with his Chicago clerical friends, and said in conclusion, "Fifty years ago here in Rome, in the subdiaconate, I gave my body to God; I shouldn't begrudge him an arm after all these years." He rallied strongly after the operation. Pius XII, who kept in constant touch with the clinic, expressed his joy at the cardinal's progress.

On May 18, he was well enough to offer Mass. "Now I feel like a priest again," he said at breakfast. That same night he had a severe stroke which paralyzed him. He died eight days later.

The age-old ritual of a Roman funeral fitting a curial cardinal's rank followed, with its notes of high pomp and prescribed form. Then the cardinal's body was flown to Chicago, and after lying in state while thousands came to show their love and sorrow, was buried in the bishop's vault at Mount Carmel Cemetery on June 3, 1958.

The flood of eulogies, even from the simplest people, clearly showed how strong a hold Cardinal Stritch had had on the hearts of his children all over the world. Everyone felt a sense of tragedy in his sudden death. Given years, he might have left as shining a record in Rome as he had in Toledo, Milwaukee and Chicago.

Francis Cardinal Spellman

———◆◇◆———

SHORTLY before the Civil War, Patrick Spellman, a master shoemaker from Clonmel, Ireland, settled in Abington, Massachusetts, about twenty miles south of Boston. Like many of the Irish of the era, Patrick was quiet and saving in his habits. He was soon attracted to Honora Hayes, a lovely girl whose family came from Limerick. Sometime after their marriage, Patrick formed a partnership with the owner of a general store; in his spare time he worked at his trade of bootmaker in the loft above. Within a few years he was able to buy a house on Glen Street. His son William Spellman was born there in 1858.

William grew up to be much like his father, provident and with an ironic Yankee turn of phrase. He went to work at Jones and Reed shoe factory and at the age of twenty-two was able to open a grocery store of his own on South Avenue.

The young man was equally careful in selecting his bride Ellen Conway; they met in 1886 and were married two years later. William settled her in a rented house on Temple Street. There on May 4, 1889, their first child was born, a boy for whom his mother selected the name of Francis.

The grocery store prospered. About the time young Frank Spellman was eight years old, his father bought a lovely Georgian house with five acres of land, a pleasant orchard and a large carriage house at 96 Beulah Street.

The family had now grown to five children: Francis, Martin,

Marian, Helene and John. As the eldest of the family, Frank took the lead in all their games and play. It was a happy home in which the strong religious conviction of their mother made them all conscious of their responsibility to God and their neighbors.

At the age of ten, Francis learned to serve Mass in the Holy Ghost Church, but though he was a good reliable altar boy, no other early signs of his vocation manifested themselves.

Frank dutifully helped his father about the store, but it was soon apparent that his interests were in people, not in canned goods or coffee. Outside the store and public grade school, in which he was an undistinguished pupil, Frank's interests were centered mainly on baseball and photography. He was a good first baseman during his first year in high school, but a hand injury forced him to stop playing, and in 1906 he became manager of the school team.

It was during his high school years that he revealed a talent for writing essays. On his graduation, Fordham University was chosen as his college. His aunts in the metropolitan area could be expected to keep an eye on him.

In 1907, Fordham was still a small school and its teachers and pupils were on a familiar footing. Francis was a good student, but no more than that. Tennis, drama and oratory offered the boy a release for his energies, and in the college magazine, *The Fordham Monthly,* the young student published criticisms and amiable essays.

He was a normally religious boy with little about him to indicate a religious vocation. But the inclination was there. He had confided to his mother, at the end of his high school course, that he might like to become a priest. Except in her prayers, Ellen Spellman did not try to press the issue. Yet on the day of his graduation when Frank announced his decision to study for the priesthood, his mother's heart must have overflowed with gratitude.

After some family discussion, Frank was allowed to point his course toward the North American College in Rome. Through Bishop Anderson, the Auxiliary Bishop of Boston, the final permission was obtained from Archbishop O'Connell, and official arrangements were made.

Spellman sailed on the liner *Franconia* on September 26, 1911. The excitement of the voyage to Liverpool was followed by a leisurely tour of London, Paris, Cologne, the Rhine country, Heidelberg, Lucerne, Milan, Venice and Florence. With mounting excitement, Francis finally reached Rome.

The cold spartan atmosphere of the dark cell to which he was assigned in the North American College was an anticlimax. Donning his black cassock with its pale blue piping and red sash, the somewhat disappointed student went to his first interview with the rector, Bishop Thomas Francis Kennedy.

The bishop was old-fashioned and punctilious. The casual easy manner of young Spellman, who had never experienced anything but friendly informality in his dealings with hometown priests and the noted Jesuit scholars with whom he had rubbed elbows at Fordham, seemed lacking in respect, to the rector. Bishop Kennedy's attitude did not alter during Spellman's years in the college and was shared by Vice-Rector Monsignor O'Hearn. It insured that Francis Spellman would hold no position of honor in the governance of the house.

The young cleric accepted his lot with equanimity. He was popular among the students and was usually at the center of their sports and excursions. Like his father, Frank had a dry, ironic sense of humor that could cut through the core of things. A telling quip enunciated with the baby-faced innocence Frank was always able to command could dissolve the students into gales of helpless laughter.

Among those nearest to Spellman was Louis F. Kelleher. They had met earlier when Kelleher had been an outstanding member of the Boston College debating team. Kelleher was one year ahead of Frank, he knew the ropes at the college, and was able to advise him on customs and strategy.

Their daily schedule began at 5:30 in the morning with a jangle of bells; it ended at 10 at night with the final bell and lights out. The first year, with a review of philosophy, offered Frank no special challenge. Coached by Kelleher, he made the acquaintance of the superb corps of teachers: Dante, Lepecier, Tardini and Corti. They were obviously destined for great things, but Spellman was especially intrigued by Borgogini Duca, a brilliant and fascinating young teacher.

The consistory which elevated Archbishop O'Connell to the cardinalate came two months after Spellman's entry into the college in the autumn of 1911. Cardinal Farley, elevated at the same time, had conferred the A.B. on Francis the year before, and the boy could brag a bit—as boys will—about knowing two cardinals, one of them his own bishop.

With the coming of the summer heat, the students went to their summer home, the Villa Santa Caterina in the Alban Hills, not far from Castel Gondolfo. There life was much easier and far healthier, with many long excursions into the beautiful countryside, though the boys also studied history and foreign languages, wrote sermons, meditated and prayed.

Wherever Frank Spellman went he carried his camera, and, never one to be shy unless the occasion demanded it, this paved the way for a visit to Cardinal Bisleti's villa at Veroli. The cardinal was pleased to be photographed in many poses. With a slight hint from the youthful photographer himself, Bisleti invited Frank to present the finished picture in person after his return to Rome—a first step into the charmed circle of influential cardinals.

During his second year, Spellman attracted the special attention of Borgogini Duca. It was the beginning of a life-long friendship which profoundly influenced Frank Spellman's entire career.

The remaining years of Spellman's attendance at the North American College were dogged by illness and mischance; pneumonia laid him low and he spent several months in Italian hospitals and fell behind in his studies. The unsympathetic rector proposed to send him home, but his many friends among the students rallied to his assistance, and by dint of great personal effort and courage, Spellman triumphantly achieved his doctorate.

On May 14, 1916, came the crown of his student years when he was ordained a priest in the eighth-century Church of Appolinare. The exaltation of those moments is the secret of Cardinal Spellman's own heart; he was never one to wear his religion on his sleeve, but his faith in God and love of Him ran deep, like his own emotions.

The family could not come for the great occasion of his ordination and the offering of his first Mass at the tomb of St. Peter, but the young priest felt a sense of destiny and a compelling unity with the first apostles.

The journey home and his first Mass, offered in Whitman on July 23, 1916, added to his joy. All that he had suffered seemed slight compared to the radiance of his mother's face on that great day.

A much needed vacation was followed by undistinguished assignments, first as a chaplain to an old ladies' home, and then as a curate at All Saints Church in Roxbury. Father Spellman mastered the killing routine of parish life with a zeal and interest that the people were quick to appreciate.

With America's entry into the First World War, Father Spellman was eager to enter the chaplain service. Hope of entering the Navy ended with his spirited response to the arrogant examining officer. Then, at the very last minute when he expected to go into the Army, Cardinal O'Connell abruptly appointed him to drum up subscriptions for the *Pilot,* the diocesan paper. Father Spellman's success in that work led to his appointment to the chancery, where his knowledgeable efficiency earned him the envy of some of his co-workers and descent into the basement of the chancery as archivist. The great cardinal did not seem to appreciate his bright young Roman student.

In the Holy Year of 1925, Father Spellman went to Europe with a diocesan pilgrimage under the leadership of Bishop Anderson. The cruise began inconspicuously for the young priest. Though he had been appointed the bishop's secretary for the pilgrimage, it was obvious to all that the bishop resented the arrangement. Once in Italy, however, Spellman's services as interpreter and his quick way of making important decisions forced the bishop to change his mind about the value of his assistant. The bishop was not uninfluenced by the fact that Borgogini Duca and a distinguished delegation of Roman prelates had greeted Father Spellman warmly upon his arrival in Rome.

Monsignor Borgogini Duca, who was now a person of great importance in the Secretariat of State, had for some time been having difficulty in running the new playground projects sponsored by the Knights of Columbus, under the direction of Mr. Edward Hearn. Spellman's talents seemed to promise the answer to the difficulties. The Pope, prompted by Borgogini Duca, requested Cardinal O'Connell to release the young priest for the work. Such a request was in the nature of a command, and Spellman's Roman friends found it hard to understand his wise decision to return home for the purpose of securing the cardinal's consent.

In the course of the interview, Cardinal O'Connell asked Father Spellman what he wanted to do about the offer from Rome.

"Whatever my Ordinary wishes me to do," was the quick answer.

"You have answered correctly," the cardinal said, with a glacial twinkle in his eye.

Perhaps His Eminence of Boston recalled that it was a similar request from Italy that had been his first step to the cardinalate. In any event, he gave his permission and graciously allowed Spellman to retain his diocesan stipend of $1,000 a year.

Father Spellman, the first American priest to be attached to the Secretariat of State, began modestly by settling in at the Minerva Hotel. Each morning he offered Mass in the hotel chapel.

The task of smoothing out the playground difficulties did not engross too much of the young cleric's time. Tennis kept him in good physical shape, and visiting Americans of note appreciated his services in securing audiences with the Pope and tickets to the various important galleries. Soon Father Spell-

man was a member of an intimate circle of people like John
J. Raskob and Mr. and Mrs. Nicholas Brady.

The Brady's were prodigal in their charities. They entertained cardinals and princes in the splendor of their Italian
home, Villa del Sole. Father Spellman became an intimate of
the household and offered his daily Mass in their private
chapel.

Through his friendship with Borgogini Duca, Spellman was
drawn directly into the orbit of Secretary of State Cardinal
Gasparri. He and his assistants soon discovered in Spellman a
mine of information concerning American conditions. They
discovered, too, that one of Father Spellman's great talents was
a rounded and imaginative grasp of affairs. In approaching a
problem, he did so from every possible angle and often enough
could suggest not one but several solutions.

The first rewards of the young priest's services soon followed.
In 1928, he was made a secret chamberlain, with the title of
monsignor, and a few years later a domestic prelate and a right
reverend monsignor. Mr. Hearn soon found himself overshad-
owed by his brilliant young assistant. When Spellman secured
a gift of $45,000 from John J. Raskob for a publishing project
of Pius XI, Hearn was piqued. Spellman now received a new
title from the Pope, who called him, "his precious monsignor."

The precious monsignor's influence grew after Hearn's resignation. Some of Monsignor Spellman's ideas were incorpo-
rated in the settlement of the Roman Question in 1929. He
became the confidant of such future cardinals as Pizzardo, Ottaviani, and Tardini. Still more important for his future was his
acquaintance with Francesco Pacelli and Enrico Galeazzi.

While on vacation in 1927, Monsignor Spellman met Archbishop Pacelli in Berlin. The good things the archbishop's
brother had said of the American priest and Galeazzi's high
opinion of him led to a cordial friendship that was to grow
more intimate through the years.

When Pacelli became cardinal and the successor to Gasparri
as Secretary of State, Monsignor Spellman's role took on
greater importance. He became the favorite translator of the

Holy Father's speeches and the favorite consultant on American affairs. In the Pope's first broadcast on the newly built Vatican Radio on February 12, 1931, Spellman was selected to give
the English summary of the Pope's speech—an honor that
brought him national prominence in the United States.

It was Pacelli who selected Spellman for the exciting and
dangerous task of smuggling out of Rome the Pope's encyclical,
Non Abbiamo Bisogno, which contained a vehement denunciation of Mussolini's attempt to crush the Catholic Action
Groups in Italy. En route to Paris, Monsignor Spellman translated the document and gave it to the world press in the French
capital. The encyclical caused a tremendous stir and served to
moderate the Black Shirt tyranny. For a time after his return
to Rome, Spellman was often threatened by Fascist bullies. He
stood his ground with tranquil confidence, and in time the nui-
sances abated.

Vatican approval of Monsignor Spellman's worth and work
soon appeared in his appointment as secretary to Cardinal
Lauri, papal legate to the eucharistic congress in Dublin
in June 1932. Days of fervid splendor marked the congress,
and Monsignor Spellman's indefatigable labors were commended in the highest quarters.

There had been persistent rumors in Boston that Spellman
would soon be a bishop. It was also whispered that his post
would be Auxiliary Bishop of Boston. As if to forestall this
eventuality, Cardinal O'Connell suggested Spellman's name
for the Bishopric of Portland, Maine, which had become vacant with the elevation of John Gregory Murray to the Archdiocese of St. Paul.

The official announcement from the Vatican finally came.
Monsignor Spellman was appointed Auxiliary Bishop of Boston. The new bishop's consecration was a clear indication of
his coming eminence. In offering him this post, Pius XI informed Monsignor Spellman that ultimately he expected him
to succeed Cardinal O'Connell.

The consecration took place on September 8, 1932, at the
altar of the chair below the Gloria of Bernini, in which the

chair of St. Peter is enshrined. Cardinal Pacelli was consecrator. His co-consecrators were Archbishops Borgogini Duca and Pizzardo. Bishop Spellman went through the complicated ceremony with ease under the eyes of a distinguished assemblage. It was significant that he wore a splendid chasuble of cloth of silver which had been worn by Cardinal Pacelli on March 13, 1917, when he was consecrated Archbishop of Sardes in preparation for his mission to Germany.

The reception after the ceremony was in the baroque splendor of the Borgia apartments—the first time an American bishop had been so honored. The bishop's father and sisters were unable to attend the great event due to Mrs. Spellman's illness, but his two physician brothers were in the glittering crowd, along with a small party of his oldest friends.

At the close of the dazzling day, Bishop Spellman retired to his plain room in the Hotel Minerva and took a crumpled cablegram from Whitman: "God bless and keep our boy. Keep him kind and humble. This is the prayer of father and mother."

Before departing for Boston, Bishop Spellman went on a final holiday with Cardinal Pacelli. A leisurely sea voyage brought the small party to Gibraltar, by boat to Cannes, and then overland to Chamonix. A few days in Rome, after vacation, were crowded with farewells from high and low: the children of his playgrounds entertained him at a touchingly emotional party; Pius XI warmly received him in a two-hour audience and presented him with expensive gifts among which were a pectoral cross and ring.

The ecstatic reception and Mass in Whitman, at which no picture-taking was allowed, were followed by endless confirmations throughout the big diocese. Bishop Spellman was assigned to the cardinal's suite at the seminary for the time being, since all the parishes of the diocese were filled. When he applied to the cardinal for the first good parish that became vacant, the request was denied and he was sent to Sacred Heart Church at Newton Center, a parish heavily in debt. After a dignified protest, the bishop accepted the new burden. In his usual practical fashion, he went on with the innumerable confirmations and chipped away lustily at the parish debt.

In the years that followed, the winds from the cardinal's palace blew hot and cold as occasion brought Bishop Spellman in and out of the spotlight. But the bishop was busy enough not to mind the sudden changes in the weather. His parish became a model one. The school particularly enlisted his keenest interest. Children and teachers loved to see him and responded completely to his gentleness and arch sense of humor.

The death of the bishop's mother on July 28, 1935, was a terrible blow. She had been ailing for several years, but her departure saddened the bishop beyond measure; she had been one of the greatest stabilizing instruments of his entire career. By a superhuman effort, he managed to sing the funeral Mass and impart the last absolution.

The visit of Cardinal Pacelli to the United States in 1936 electrified the whole nation. The trip had at first been envisaged by Mrs. Brady as a much-needed private vacation for the cardinal at her superb estate Inisfada at Manhasset, Long Island.

Bishop Spellman, one of the first to whom Mrs. Brady communicated the news from Paris, saw the impossibility of such an arrangement and the loss of an important publicity opportunity for the Church. Four letters written to Rome changed the Vatican point of view completely.

The cardinal arrived in October 1936. Newsmen were charmed with his wit, urbanity and complete discretion. The United States was on the eve of a presidential election. The bigots were on the alert for any possible indication of "Vatican interference," particularly because of Father Charles Coughlin's intemperate and bombastic denouncement of Roosevelt.

In the month he spent in the United States, Pacelli saw most of its great cities. Mrs. Brady herself assured this author that the expenses of the trip were paid by the Most Reverend John Gregory Murray, Archbishop of St. Paul. The ovations accorded the cardinal everywhere—from New York to San Francisco—were extraordinary.

The cardinal secretary looked to his capable young pupil for advice. All arrangements were in Bishop Spellman's hands, and the timing and organization of the trip were faultless. It was a great triumph for the cardinal secretary—greater still for the adroit bishop.

The final event of outstanding importance was Pacelli's visit to President Roosevelt the day after his second overwhelming election. Out of the private conversation between the two great men grew the President's conviction—first suggested by Cardinal Mundelein—that the United States ought to be represented at the Vatican. Bishop Spellman was the trusted intermediary between the two states, and though the intemperate uproar of bigots prevented the full implementation of the plan, Myron Taylor went to the Vatican as the President's personal envoy, and Spellman for a time became a trusted adviser of the President and the first priest ever to offer Mass in the White House.

With the election of Cardinal Pacelli to the papacy on March 2, 1939, Bishop Spellman once more came into the spotlight. The Diocese of New York had been vacant since the death of Cardinal Hayes on September 4, 1938, and Bishop Spellman's name was among those mentioned for the post. The news troubled the bishop; Pius XI had signified his desire that Spellman should succeed Cardinal O'Connell as Archbishop of Boston. Now, after six years of an active life in which he knew intimately every priest and problem of the diocese, the bishop felt that he could do a much better job in Boston.

Besides, he knew he wasn't wanted in New York, for very obvious reasons. In all the long years since the creation of the diocese, the men who came to the direction of affairs had come up through the ranks of the local clergy. McCloskey, Farley and Hayes were all home-town boys, and it seemed incredible to New Yorkers that an outsider should be chosen, however glittering his talents.

While the decision hung in the balance Spellman himself wrote to the Pope asking to have his name removed from consideration.

It was with a sense of almost surprised alarm that Bishop Spellman received a letter from Apostolic Delegate Archbishop Cicognani, indicating that the news of his appointment was imminent in Rome.

Once the news was public, Bishop Spellman, like a good soldier, prepared for the new tasks. His reception in New York on May 23, 1939, was tumultuous and cordial. When the fanfare was over, the new archbishop discovered the size of his burden and headaches.

The finances of the diocese were in anything but good shape; things had grown slack during the last six years of Cardinal Hayes' life during which he suffered from a heart ailment. There were $28,000,000 in mortgages on church property at 6 percent interest. Archbishop Spellman approached financial friends in New York and Boston and was able to refinance the tremendous burden at a very low rate. By selling certain valuable church properties, notably Cathedral College and the chancery office, at a very high price and buying other properties lower in price but much more suitable for their purpose, Archbishop Spellman displayed financial talents of the highest kind. With a considerable sum of ready cash at his disposal, the archbishop proceeded to put his entire house in order. A building commission and a buying commission were set up for the entire diocese. In future building and expansion, these bureaus were to save millions in time and money.

Amid a welter of pressing duties, the archbishop found time to rehabilitate Bishop Broderick, who through no fault of his own had got lost in a confused ecclesiastical shuffle and was living as a private person in Millbrook, New York.

It is impossible to give a complete survey of the archbishop's business accomplishments in a sketch of this length. They flowed out into innumerable schools, hospitals, colleges, homes for the aged, foundling homes, and protectories for the disturbed.

Outstanding examples are the tremendous progress made at Fordham University in buildings, faculty and students, and the transfer of Manhattanville College from its valuable but no longer suitable grounds on the rocky escarpment above Harlem to the spacious Whitelaw Reed estate at Purchase, New York. Condemnation proceedings brought in almost $9,000,-000. This sum provided the first buildings of a $14,000,000 development plan for the future of this fine school.

Equally important was the gradual reorganization of the diocesan seminary into three schools: Cathedral College for high school; St. Patrick's for four years of philosophy and the classics; St. Joseph's for theology. For this change and for other building plans, a drive for $35,000,000 was launched on October 7, 1960. By June of 1961, over $39,000,000 had been pledged.

That there was nothing provincial about the archbishop's vision is apparent in his achievements for the Catholic University of America. No other men in its history, except Cardinal Gibbons and Bishop John Lancaster Spalding, have done so much to forward its prestige and future, including a new edition of the *Catholic Encyclopedia* published by the McGraw-Hill Book Company under Cardinal Spellman's powerful patronage.

He has been a leader in all the struggles to achieve justice in apportioning government aid to schools. In Canada and England, it is evident that just government aid to all schools is a good thing. That Catholics who believe in religious education for their children should be penalized for their belief is something of a scandal in a country usually fair-minded about such things, especially in view of the fact that Catholics have contributed so much in the defense and service of the nation.

It was Cardinal Spellman's outspoken conviction that led him to write a letter to Mrs. Eleanor Roosevelt on July 21, 1949. On several occasions, her widely syndicated column "My Day" had seemed to accuse the archbishop of unnecessarily stirring up trouble about auxiliary benefits such as lunches and bus transportation to Catholic school children. Mrs. Roosevelt was against these practices, though the Supreme Court had decided that the individual states were free to include Catholic children in the benefits if they wished.

Finally the cardinal sent Mrs. Roosevelt and the daily papers a sharp letter of protest in which he pointed out her circumscribed and uninformed attitude toward the whole question. His blunt letter shocked many people including "Catholic liberals" and led to bad publicity and a whispering campaign against him. A truce was patched up gradually, and while en route to a church dedication, the cardinal called on Mrs. Roosevelt at Hyde Park.

Though the smoke of battle had settled, President Kennedy's 1961 proposal to subsidize public schools and pupils to the tune of $9,000,000 brought Cardinal Spellman back into the fray. It seemed to him and to the entire Catholic hierarchy that to levy a heavy tax against Catholic citizens and then leave them and their children out of consideration in spending such funds was actually a penalization of all religious education.

When he believes that he is right, Cardinal Spellman never hesitates to take an unpopular stand on all questions that concern moral and public welfare. He has spoken out plainly many times for the censorship of blasphemous or indecent films. He was equally clear in his stand on what he considered an unwarranted gravediggers' strike in 1948. Many, including Catholics, considered the cardinal to be antilabor, and he got a very bad press as a consequence, though he triumphed in the end. His victory, says Father Robert I. Gannon (his official biographer), did much to reveal Communist infiltration of the labor unions and was important in arousing the public indignation that forced a union clean-up.

But in 1939, other matters seemed more pressing; the United States was on the threshold of the Second World War. As America grew more and more involved Archbishop Spellman wisely prepared for the struggle by enlarging the military ordinariate and increasing its efficiency. Father John O'Hara, C.S.C., with his enormous knowledge of men and their problems, accumulated as spiritual director and then President of Notre Dame University, was brought in as military delegate to head the ordinariate. The recruiting of chaplains was pursued with vigor, and the auxiliary Catholic services were strengthened inestimably.

The military vicar guided and controlled every step of the reorganization. After Pearl Harbor, he proceeded to make his visitation to the far-flung battlefields of Africa and Europe. The cardinal's vision is world wide, but his patriotism is a white-hot flame. Completely unperturbed about his safety, he went by plane, train and jeep to every active front, saying Mass in the open, in all kinds of weather, visiting hospitals with an engaging thoroughness that impressed the patients and the entire world. How he found time to call on all the heads of state on his route, doing everything in his quiet power to ease the situation for prisoners of war and the unhampered functioning of the Church, is something of a miracle. His on-the-spot summation of situations everywhere was of great help to Pius XII in his titanic struggle for humanity and peace in the midst of a hating world, and it was largely through the military vicar's efforts that Rome remained an unbombed open city.

What the military vicar did for Europe was duplicated in 1945 by a thorough visitation of the camps and fighting fronts of the Orient. Once again the vicar endeared himself to United States fighting men around the world as he watched the war come to a close. Since that time his Christmas visits to our troops abroad has become an annual affair, dear to both the troops and the fatherly heart of the cardinal.

On the morning of December 23, 1945, the news came over the wires to the United States that four new American cardinals had been named: Glennon of St. Louis, Mooney of Detroit, Stritch of Milwaukee and Spellman of New York. The New York Chancery was inundated with messages of congratulation.

Imperturbable as usual, Cardinal Spellman spent the weeks in planning for the comfort of his family and friends who were to accompany him on the memorable journey to Rome. On February 11, 1946, two chartered planes with Cardinals Spellman, Glennon and Tien, their families and friends, and a cargo of ubiquitous newsmen, left La Guardia for Gander, Newfoundland.

A stop was made in Ireland. Its government and people

greeted their guests with frenzied enthusiasm. There was a trip to Killarney and the Gap of Dunloe, capped by a splendid banquet in Dublin. After a short visit in war-weary Paris, they took off for Rome.

For Cardinal Spellman, the "great consistory" in which thirty-two cardinals were elevated to the sacred purple was a homecoming to that Holy Father he revered as a saint. Spellman's return to New York was a triumph of affection and city-wide rejoicing marred only by the funeral of Cardinal Glennon, who had died in Ireland en route home.

The new cardinal settled down to the old tasks. The burdens of schools and social efforts grew greater each year; the Korean War once more brought him into the news of the world as the military vicar visited his embattled sons scattered throughout the Orient.

Despite his crushing burdens during the war years and their frenetic aftermath, the cardinal—by dint of rising early and going late to bed—wrote four outstanding books that reached millions of readers. In *Action This Day* and *The Road to Victory* he realistically demonstrated his enormous sympathy for the human cost of war, and a patriotism of the highest order. In *The Risen Soldier,* hope and inspiration rounded out the earlier themes. In 1951, with the publication of a well-plotted novel, *The Foundling,* Cardinal Spellman revealed his creative talents. This book reached an audience of over 500,000 and sparked a revival of interest in the cardinal's orphans and other charities. All of the royalties from his books were poured into the foundlings' home, which is very dear to his heart.

With the death of Pius XII in 1959, an era closed for New York's cardinal. Pacelli had been his nearest and dearest friend, and in the cardinal's eyes he was a genuine saint and world father of the highest rank.

Cardinal Spellman stayed on in Rome for the election and coronation of Pope John XXIII, and squared his shoulders for the ever-multiplying tasks of his diocese and his world-wide responsibilities as military vicar. Not one to live in the past, he moves in the main current of American affairs. His words and presence lend éclat to any gathering of notables, and though he can assume an air of hieratic grandeur, his lively eyes betray his intense interest in everything that goes on about him.

His Church and government have conferred upon him most of the high honors given their most distinguished sons. A current of praise has flowed in his direction for many years, but the cardinal has kept his simplicity, and he remains thoroughly approachable.

A displaced retina kept him in darkness for several weeks in 1961, but failed to slow him down or dim his world vision. Creative imagination, executive brilliance and deep and abiding faith have made him the man he is. Those gifts flow out to the world in an ever-deepening tide of charity and personal service.

James Francis Cardinal McIntyre

I N 1886, in the heat of a torrid day—June 25—James Francis
Aloysius McIntyre was born in mid-Manhattan. He was the
son of James Francis and Mary Pelley McIntyre. The future
cardinal's father was a native New Yorker, a member of the
mounted police. His mother came from Kiltorma, Country Gal-
way, Ireland.

Their home was a modest one and the boy grew up in comfortable circumstances. At the age of six he entered Public
School No. 70 because there was no room for him in the over-
crowded parochial school nearby. Despite a lack of the careful
religious instruction he might have had from the Sisters, James
Francis, who was of a deeply religious nature, became an altar
boy early and served with great devotion and constancy.

A run of bad luck hit the family when the father was thrown
from his horse in Central Park and sustained serious injuries.
Mary McIntyre, undaunted, established a small dressmaking
business which kept the family going. Their doctor recommended that Mr. McIntyre spend as much time as possible out
of doors, so he took a job as a trackwalker in upstate New York.
This proved ill advised, as the severe winter caused complica-
tions and McIntyre became a complete invalid.

When James was only ten years old, the greatest sorrow of
his life came to him in the death of his loving and self-reliant
mother. Fortunately a favorite cousin, Mrs. Robert Conley,

lived nearby and with great charity took into her home James Francis, his younger brother and their invalid father.

The Conley household was a comfortable one. Robert Conley, an attorney, specialized in real-estate law and was fairly successful in his profession. James Francis was a favorite of his and he enjoyed talking to the boy about his profession. James soaked up the talk like a ready blotter and with his fine mind and exceptionally good memory retained information that was to serve him well in his double career of broker and priest.

Young McIntyre was thirteen when he finished public school. With a kind of Horatio Alger determination, he decided to seek a career in business instead of going on to high school; he eventually wanted to be able to support himself and his father and perhaps help to reimburse the Conleys for their generosity.

On the morning of setting out to look for work in the exciting world of the stock market, young James was polished and neat. He wore a visored cap, short pants, a coat and black stockings—the normal dress of all well-bred boys of his time.

It was his intention to apply at all the Wall Street brokerage houses until he found a job. En route he ran into the old curb market at Broad Street and Exchange Place, which completely fascinated him. At that time the curb market was conducted in the street. The brokers milled about, trading with each other, signaling manually to men leaning out of the windows, telephones clutched in their hands. The atmosphere was both noisy and frenetic. It offered the kind of raw excitement bound to delight a boy of thirteen whose life had been on the rather quiet side.

By applying here and there, James Francis found a job as errand boy with David Pfeifer, a curb broker. The job demanded that he move swiftly through the jostling crowd, observe the prices posted on the blackboards, and then run to report major price changes to his employer. The workday was from 8 A. M. until dusk. The long hours of strenuous exertion called for strong legs and a clear and precise memory.

James usually walked to the market on good days, but when the weather was bad he rode to work on the Third Avenue El, which was run by steam locomotives. The fare was 5 cents each way; he carried his lunch to work.

Already, in those early teens, young McIntyre had determined to become a priest. At Mass and Benediction he prayed hard that he might remain constant in his direction toward the altar. Despite the anguish of having to wait for the realization of his "call," he had a sense of duty which—even then—was one of his strongest qualities; this made him conscious that he was doing God's will in looking after his father, and the awareness of this duty well done gave him both satisfaction and pleasure.

As a tall, straight-backed and handsome young man of sixteen, he moved from the curb market and took a job with H. L. Horton & Company, an old-line brokerage firm in Wall Street. Now he was a runner, with a salary of six dollars a week—twice what he had earned on the curb market. In addition, there were good chances for advancement.

Like other "self-made" men of his time, young McIntyre was not merely content to work. Ever since he had left grade school he had gone to night school; first in the public schools near at hand, and later at Columbia University and City College. In addition to his regular studies, he learned shorthand through the Munson System. This was "an all but extinct variant of the venerable Pitman System"; he has used it all his life to record telephone conversations, compose sermons, public addresses and his longer letters.

Steady advance with Horton brought him both money and influence. Though only in his mid-twenties, he had become office manager and found that older members of the firm deferred to his opinions. In 1914—when he was twenty-eight years old—he was offered a junior partnership in the firm, with a higher salary and a percentage of the profits. The offer held no attraction for him. His father had just died, his brother had a good job, and John Francis was free to realize the desire of his heart.

He entered Cathedral College under special circumstances. He was half a generation older than the young men in his class, and Cardinal Farley decided that the special courses he had taken in the city schools, plus his business knowledge and experience, had already advanced his education far beyond that of his classmates. There was one stumbling block—his Latin was poor.

James concentrated on the language with a fury, studying it in the daytime at the college and taking special night courses under an elderly Jesuit at St. Francis Xavier High School.

After only one year at Cathedral College, he moved on to St. Joseph's major seminary. Normally, six years are required to finish the course, but once again Archbishop Farley intervened and reduced McIntyre's required time to five years. As a student in the senior seminary, he was something of a legend because of his financial success, and something of an oddity because of his advanced age and serious outlook on life.

Father McIntyre was ordained by Archbishop Hayes in St. Patrick's Cathedral in 1921. His first assignment was assistant pastor of old St. Gabriel's Church on East 37th Street. This was the church where Cardinal Farley had laid the foundations of his eminence. It was also where Cardinal Hayes had been Farley's assistant. An assignment here meant a sure step to preferment.

None of this was in the mind of Father McIntyre. St. Gabriel's was dear to him because his father had attended school there in the early 1860's, and his one desire was to be a good parish priest.

Archbishop Hayes frequently came to St. Gabriel's and gradually got to know Father McIntyre. In 1923, Hayes invited him to become a member of his household and one of his assistant chancellors of the New York Archdiocese.

As Cardinal McIntyre himself says, "For the next twenty-five years I lived in the room that was assigned to me in the archbishop's official residence." During his stay in New York he occupied a desk in a corner of the big paneled chancery office— one of a twin row of desks which stretched the length of the high-ceilinged room. During all those years he took his regular turn in the services of the cathedral.

In 1934, after eleven years as assistant chancellor, he was promoted to the office of chancellor, with the title of Papal Chamberlain (Monsignor). Within two years he became a domestic prelate, with the title of Right Reverend Monsignor.

There were varying opinions regarding his personality and talents at this time: some said he was scrupulous; others that he was too great a stickler for protocol and hewed too closely to the letter of canon law; still others admired him for his financial acuteness and his complete information on the faults and virtues of the archdiocese and all its priests. One thing is certain, he was not a member of the inner circle that—along with the Archbishop of New York—made the policy of the great archdiocese.

All this changed when Bishop Spellman succeeded Cardinal Hayes as Archbishop of New York in 1939. As Spellman has said in his official biography, he knew he wasn't wanted in New York; we may believe that he found coolness and reluctant cooperation during his first days in his new archdiocese.

Monsignor McIntyre, however, responded with his customary punctilious sense of duty and respect for authority. As a consequence, the monsignor and the archbishop became good friends. Spellman was amazed to discover how completely McIntyre knew the archdiocese and what had to be done to improve it. The result was that Monsignor McIntyre was reappointed chancellor and elevated to the diocesan board of consulters.

From this point McIntyre's advance was rapid. As the United States moved closer and closer to the Second World War, Cardinal Spellman very early saw that it would be necessary to free his hands for the tremendous job of military vicar in which he would be required to travel all over the world, both as a courier and representative of Pius XII and chief bishop of the far-flung United States Chaplains' Corps.

In preparation for the future, Monsignor McIntyre was named Titular Bishop of Cyrene and Auxiliary of New York on January 8, 1940. He was consecrated the following January in St. Patrick's Cathedral with great splendor and a multitude of bishops in attendance.

Further honors and responsibilities came in 1945, when in

addition to his other duties, McIntyre was made vicar-general. And in May 1946 he received the Grand Cross of the Holy Sepulcher. Two months later Pope Pius XII named him Archbishop of the Titular See of Paltus and Coadjutor Archbishop of New York.

Just how much McIntyre had helped Cardinal Spellman and how much Spellman owed him in the great things he accomplished in his early days in New York may be seen in the tribute Cardinal Spellman paid Archbishop McIntyre on his 25th anniversary as a priest. Speaking from his throne in St. Patrick's Cathedral, Spellman said: "I have never undertaken any important matter without consulting him. In nothing have I gone contrary to his advice. He is outstanding as a man, as a priest and as a bishop."

During the war years, when Cardinal Spellman was busy with world affairs and the proper functioning of the military ordinate, practically the entire burden of the New York Archdiocese fell on Archbishop McIntyre. He played a tremendous part in reordering the financial picture in the diocese and pushed forward reforms of all kinds. Many of these were not too popular with pastors and others in authority. The archdiocese had always been run in an easygoing fashion. The tight rein of Archbishop McIntyre irked many, and Jack Alexander, in an article in the *Saturday Evening Post,* said that many of New York's priests called the railroad cars that eventually transported the archbishop to Los Angeles the "Freedom Train."

Archbishop McIntyre had never been easy with himself. In the long years of patient sitting at his desk in the old chancery, he had done his work with thoroughness and a passion for perfection that were admirable. No unasked advice had ever been offered by him.

In the early morning he made his meditation and said Mass, devoting the remainder of the day to his various tasks as vice-chancellor. The only time he showed obvious annoyance was when visitors did not observe proper protocol or when pastors and those in authority failed to finish projects on time. To most visiting prelates from all over the world, he was the very soul of cordial hospitality; his manners were courtly in the old-fashioned sense of the word.

Archbishop McIntyre is tremendously patriotic. He loves his country deeply and is indignant at any attempt to water down the principles of the Constitution and the Bill of Rights. An excellent example of this came in 1947 when an attempt was made to rush the Austin–Mahoney Bill, which innocently seemed to bar discrimination in education through the legislature.

After carefully reading the bill, the archbishop said publicly: "The bill states that education is a function of the state. Education is not the function of the state. It is the function of the parent. If the statement that education is the function of the state is written into the law, it will permit further encroachments on the parental function of education."

Following this attack, *The New York Times* said, on March 3, 1947: "Chances of adoption of the Austin-Mahoney antidiscrimination bill faded yesterday when Co-adjutor Archbishop McIntyre put the Roman Catholic Church of New York on record as flatly opposed to it. The Archbishop denounced the bill as after a Communistic pattern."

With the war over and the elevation of Archbishop Spellman to the Sacred College of Cardinals, McIntyre began to play a more important role in running the archdiocese. He was a resounding success as Coadjutor Archbishop of New York, but every assistant bishop, however great his power, yearns for a diocese of his own where he can shape things according to the desires of his own mind and heart.

Such an opportunity came to Archbishop McIntyre when on February 12, 1948, Pope Pius XII appointed him Second Archbishop of Los Angeles in succession to John J. Cantwell who had died on October 30, 1947 after a reign of thirty years. Everyone in the archdiocese had expected Bishop McGucken to succeed Archbishop Cantwell, but in spite of their disappointment, welcomed their new archbishop with native warmth and enthusiasm.

Cardinal Spellman installed Archbishop McIntyre in St. Vibiana's Cathedral, characterizing him as "a human idealist and a divine realist." It was the Feast of St. Joseph—March 19, 1948. Perhaps it was symbolic that the new archbishop was installed on that feast day, since the Archdiocese of Los Angeles had more problems than a porcupine has quills. Their solutions would require a shepherd of extreme devotion—one who could work endless hours and drive matters through to conclusion over every kind of opposition.

Archbishop McIntyre had never been in California before, and his installation-day speech attempted to strike a personal note that might appeal to the emotions of his audience. He said, in part: "I stand before you and knock—not at the city gate, not on the portals of this cathedral. I am knocking and continue to knock at the door of your hearts, now hallowed by comforting memories of my revered predecessor . . . The only force that will cause this mysterious door to open is the will, goodwill for the shepherd seeking admission. And the only power to loosen and open this door is love, the love that desires union and communion with the Shepherd, spirit with spirit."

Archbishop McIntyre was soon in close touch with his most vexing problems. His large archdiocese covered four counties. They had seemed easy and roomy enough until after the war when thousands upon thousands of ex-servicemen and their families who had had a taste of California and liked it came back there to live. Many of them were Catholics. In addition to this, there were the Mexican problem, the Negro problem and the migrant worker problem. It is perhaps significant that shabby old St. Vibiana's Cathedral is very near Skid Row.

Before plunging into his many tasks, Archbishop McIntyre strengthened his authority in the diocese by making it a corporation sole. This move put everything in the archdiocese in his sole charge and freed his hands for the work of diocesan discipline and endless fund-raising.

The first great project that engrossed his attention was the Youth Education Fund to build Catholic schools for his people, especially those in sub-slum districts.

In announcing the drive for the Youth Fund, the archbishop did so in his usual straightforward fashion, declaring: "To have public education supported by local government is a privilege of our American citizenship. But that does not take away for an instant the privilege of American parents to educate their children in religious public schools. This is the higher right than the right of the state to supply education. The exclusion of either right would be a violation of the freedom granted in our Bill of Rights."

It is also interesting to note that among the first schools to go up, 17 were in the poorer sections of the archdiocese. In all, something over $3,000,000 poured into the building fund, and in four years 26 new parishes, 64 parochial schools and 18 high schools were erected. Scores of other schools and churches were enlarged and renovated. The Cathedral was spruced up and beautified, but not replaced as many had expected. The enrollment of Catholic school children jumped from 52,000 to 90,000, but half the Catholic children of the diocese were still in public schools.

The total cost of the first four years' expansion was $15,000,-000, an extraordinary accomplishment for a diocese that had lived from hand to mouth and had occasionally been bailed out of its worst financial difficulties by gifts from a few multimillionaires.

It is interesting to note that in the terrible thirties, while McIntyre was chancellor, not a single parish in New York defaulted on its debts. The same is true of Los Angeles where Archbishop McIntyre is known as a tough financial bargainer with a businesslike approach to building costs. He and his council of pastor-consultants have worked out formulas for every type of diocesan structure, with such careful estimation of costs that the archbishop is able to evaluate construction bids down to the last nail.

For the Catholics of California, the greatest work of the archbishop was his successful campaign to do away with the tax on

Catholic schools. It had been in existence for many years and was obviously discriminatory; it had been sponsored and kept alive by narrow-minded bigots.

The first move to abolish the tax was made in the state legislature, which by an astounding vote of 108 to 3 exempted from tax all nonprofit, religious-sponsored elementary and secondary schools.

This law was soon challenged by the bigots, wearing the innocent mask of the "California Taxpayers Alliance." The archbishop played his hand with great shrewdness. A prominent committee was formed to uphold the legislature's action. It contained the names of important military men and noted film stars who were the darlings of the American public. It was a remarkable achievement, because many of the committee members were not Catholics at all. From this top group all the way down to the neighborhood level, other committees were carefully organized. Meetings were held, doorbells were rung, and friends and relatives were canvassed.

The result was a complete triumph. The archbishop's work stood out prominently, since Los Angeles contributed a plurality of 178,000.

Considering the archbishop's first five years in Los Angeles and his favor with Cardinal Spellman, few were surprised when on November 29, 1952, Archbishop McIntyre was nominated to the Sacred College in Rome.

At his press conference, he said humbly: "I have exalted the deep devotion to God and to the country of a wonderful people whose constant prayer is for peace and prosperity, which blessing can come only through walking with the Master."

On January 7, 1953, at an early hour, the cardinal-elect blessed the giant Constellation which was to fly him and his party to New York. Flash bulbs popped constantly as he greeted the crowds of reporters with his usual urbanity and said: "The distinction that takes me to Rome is a recognition of the important place the southland of California has taken in the affairs of the world . . . It is our hope and prayer that God's gracious providence will ever prevail over us and that we many be ever worthy of these favors."

The Constellation put down in Chicago in near-zero cold. A large group of priests, relatives and friends, led by Cardinal Stritch, greeted the cardinal-elect with enthusiasm and sent him off with cheers and good wishes.

The same scene was enacted at La Guardia. The auxiliary bishops of New York were there to escort their old friend into the city. The following morning, after a Mass celebrating the twelfth anniversary of his consecration, the cardinal-elect visited his many friends until 2 o'clock, departure time for the trip to Rome from Idlewild. By this time the party of distinguished prelates and laymen had grown to such proportions that two Constellations were needed to carry the group. Among the passengers was an aged nun, Sister Anacletus, who had been a friend of Archbishop McIntyre's family since the turn of the century.

Because of bad weather and heavy fog at Shannon and the other landing fields of western Europe, the planes were forced to return to Gander. When they finally landed at Ciampino Airport in Rome on January 9, a large and enthusiastic crowd awaited them. The official greeting was voiced by Bishop O'Connor, Rector of the North American College, who was to be the cardinal's host. The other members of the party were driven to the Grand Hotel.

The cardinal-elect spent most of the next day answering sheaves of telegrams and patiently submitting himself to being fitted for the elaborate costumes required by cardinals.

The reception of the *biglietto,* in the assembly room of the North American College, was a distinguished occasion. After the *biglietto* had been read aloud by Bishop O'Connor, the first to congratulate the new cardinal was Cardinal Spellman, who had flown in that morning after his Christmas visit to the Korean front. He himself received a tremendous ovation from the glittering audience.

In the remaining days of ceremony, Cardinal McIntyre con-

ducted himself with his usual grace and aplomb. Among the
gorgeous and grave occasions so beautifully captured in pictures
and writing in Monsignor North's booklet, "The Flight To
Rome," is a humorous and wonderful photograph that went
around the world. It was taken at the conferring of the biretta
on Cardinal McIntyre. According to Monsignor North, the official photographer's flash bulb failed to go off and the Pope
and cardinal obligingly re-enacted the ceremony, but they did
so with wide smiles. Even the usually grave and stately Monsignor Dante's face reflects the humor of the occasion.

Among the notable receptions given in the new cardinal's
honor was one by Ambassador Bunker at his magnificent home,
the Villa Taverna. Cardinal McIntyre was at his best in the
rounds of visits with the members of the Sacred College.

On Sunday, the cardinal took possession of his titular church,
the ancient basilica of St. Anastasia. "It is at the foot of the
Palatine Hill where a little valley opens out before the ascent
of the Aventine." It is one of the most ancient churches of
Rome, was greatly beloved by St. Jerome, and still contains the
small canopied altar at which the saint loved to say Mass. St.
Anastasia, an early martyr, is one of the few women saints whose
name is to be found in the Canon of the Mass.

After the entrance prayer and the sprinkling of Holy Water,
the gorgeous procession moved up the aisle to the chant of *Ecce
Sacerdos Magnus,* which had been set to new music by the choir-
master of St. John Lateran as a special tribute to Cardinal Mc-
Intyre. The pontifical decree assigning the ancient basilica to
the cardinal was read by the ninety-year-old Archbishop Carinci, and an address of welcome, warm in tone and historic in
flavor, was delivered by Monsignor Verzoroli, an honorary
canon of the basilica.

The cardinal made a short speech of appreciation in which
he paid warmest thanks to Archbishop Carinci and to Monsignor Verzoroli. He also summed up his happy impression of his
nine-day Roman stay and thanked Bishop O'Connor and all
those who had made his visit so memorable. When the final

prayer was said, the clergy of the basilica ceremoniously came forward to offer their homage. In conclusion the cardinal gave his solemn blessing.

The following day, after lunch at the airport with all the cardinal's Roman friends, Bishop O'Connor blessed the plane. A few moments later the big jet roared off into the sky. Once again weather and fog made it impossible to land at Shannon, where an elaborate welcome had been planned. Unusually high winds made it imperative to take the southern route, by way of the Azores. The plane put down in Boston, where Archbishop Cushing and Cardinal Spellman awaited Cardinal McIntyre and his party.

Archbishop Cushing offered a Mass of thanksgiving for the cardinal's safe return and after reading the Gospel, turned to praise Cardinal Spellman as the most "illustrious son of Boston." He also paid tribute to Cardinal McIntyre as "one whom I have reverenced for twenty-five years as a great and simple priest, humble still with the honor of the cardinalate."

The flight from Boston to New York was of short duration, and everyone took a much-needed rest before the formal dinner at the Waldorf given by the Knights of Malta in honor of the two cardinals.

Los Angeles went all out to welcome her famous son in a series of dazzling dinners and receptions. At one banquet in honor of the new cardinal, Bob Hope was one of the speakers. With mock seriousness, Hope looked warily at Cardinal McIntyre and began his speech with the following words: "Before I deliver my address, I should like to know if His Eminence has divested himself of his General Motors stock." This remark really broke up the crowd, and the cardinal laughed as heartily as anyone else. There had been much talk about members of President Eisenhower's cabinet getting rid of their stockholdings.

The cardinal accepted the enthusiastic homage of his city with humble grace. He was soon back at his desk, working for long hours, as he had all of his life.

A comparison between the *Catholic Directory* of 1948 and that of 1962 gives plain and telling evidence of Cardinal McIntyre's enormous accomplishments. To detail all of the vital statistics would almost take a book in itself, but a sampling of the most important will indicate how much was achieved.

When Cardinal McIntyre arrived in Los Angeles in 1948, he had 366 diocesan priests; the *Directory* of 1962 listed 580 clerics of the archdiocese. The number of parishes grew from 221 to 297. The religious orders of women increased from 1,965 to 3,735. The total of diocesan students in the seminary climbed from 312 to 536.

One of the most astonishing growths was in the increase in the number of high schools from 13 to 34. Formerly the students totaled 5,164; the 1962 total was 23,288. At the same time, the number of elementary schools leaped from 111 to 243.

In the social field, results were equally impressive. Among the most outstanding was the increase in the number of hospitals from 12 to 17; instead of treating 86,000 patients as in 1948, the hospitals treated 433,223 in 1962.

One major achievement of Cardinal McIntyre's reign was the building of the junior seminary of Our Lady Queen of the Angels in San Fernando. It was certain to increase and foster vocations. Another telling evidence of a spiritually alive diocese was the number of converts made: the 1962 *Catholic Directory* reported 4,555 for Los Angeles—an amazing indication of spiritual vigor.

Cardinal McIntyre played quite a prominent role at the Vatican Council in 1962, being particularly active in defense of the Latin Mass. Along with Cardinal Ottaviani and his group, McIntyre opposed any extension of privileges that might encourage Mass in the vernacular.

James Francis McIntyre, who had lived in a simple room and had never even had an office of his own in New York, had been amazed when he first arrived in California and saw the beautiful residence—originally bought and occupied by Archbishop Cantwell—which was to be his new home.

The house is a Spanish design, is large, roomy and quite luxurious, and stands in one of the most exclusive and wealthy neighborhoods in Los Angeles. The archbishop has converted some of its larger rooms into halls where meetings, small receptions and teas can be held. The house is staffed by an Irish housekeeper, a Filipino gardener and chauffeur, and a Chinese cook. The cook, it is said, finds the archbishop something of a trial because he eats whatever is placed before him and seems contented with any type of cooking.

Today, at the age of seventy-seven, the Cardinal still puts in a long day. Meditation is followed by Mass in his private chapel at 6:30 A.M. After breakfast he drives or is driven to the chancery. His hours are from 9 to 5 P.M., but he often stays longer if important affairs demand it. Usually he eats dinner at 6, goes through more work at home, reads his Breviary and pauses for half an hour's meditation at 9:30 P.M. At 10 o'clock he has a glass of milk and watches TV or chats with the priests of his household. He retires between 10:30 and 12. In agreement with his nostalgia for the past, he wears a clerical frock coat and a Homberg hat.

Cardinal McIntyre is widely read and his view of history, especially the history of the Church, is far ranging. It was this interest which led him to encourage Father Joseph Brusher, S.J. to compile his monumental and scholarly volume, *Popes Through the Ages*. The cardinal gave further encouragement to Father Brusher by graciously contributing a brief foreword which said, in part:

> The author . . . has drawn upon the best sources to present a brief but adequate picture of the enormous impact upon human history of the See of Peter. The vast drama of God's kingdom is, in its contact with the ever-changing face of human events in this brief work, vividly highlighted.
>
> The author has endeavored to present a completely objective account, seemingly realizing that the simple factual narrative is the greatest apologia for the spiritual, moral and cultural influence exerted by the successors of St. Peter in the shaping

of not only Western civilization, but in the most remote mission lands.

The cardinal is widely admired for his sterling patriotism and sound common sense. He does not hesitate to speak his mind on all the important issues of the day. He has a rigorous view of what becomes a bishop and a great "high priest," and he lives up to this conception with ideal simplicity.

Richard Cardinal Cushing

O N November 6, 1954, Archbishop Cushing of Boston
published the following message in his official archdiocesan newspaper, *The Pilot*:

MY DEARLY BELOVED CHILDREN IN CHRIST:

On November 8, 1944, the crozier of jurisdiction over the
Archdiocese of Boston was placed in my hand. Ten years have
since passed, years filled with work and responsibility, disappointment and satisfaction, sorrow and joy.

On this tenth anniversary and in this Special Supplement in
its honor, which Monsignor Lally, Father Grant and the entire
staff of *The Pilot* have prepared with great industry and affection to mark the occasion, I offer to you, my own dear people
and to all the people of the entire community, my fervent
prayers for your peace and happiness. May you ever be conscious of the loving guidance of your Heavenly Father, may you
love Him above all else and because of Him live in the love you
thus create between your neighbor and yourself.

To God we offer our thanks that He has given us this anniversary. To God's representative on earth, His Holiness, Pope Pius
XII, who appointed us your Archbishop, we give our love,
loyalty and prayers. To you, dear people, I give you my life and
service. The history of the past ten years is yours, not mine. To
you, after God, be all its glory.

We have done many things, as the pages of this Special Supplement show. Some of it is in new and shining construction, and

in properties acquired and dedicated to the service of God and mankind. All of this has cost a great deal of money, every cent of which came from your open purses and your yet more open hearts. It has represented a willingness to sacrifice your own desires, even your own necessities, in favor of the poor and needy. It has spoken of great faith and of extraordinary good will. It has paid me the compliment of your trust in my judgment and in my desire to live for others. I thank you.

Those of you who recall my words on the occasion of my installation as Archbishop know that I had no idea then of embarking on a great building program. No one was more astonished than I by the magnitude of the construction problems which were lurking around the corner, waiting for me to pull out the chair behind my desk. But since not one cent of the tremendous outlay involved could I have supplied myself, why then, should I think of the program as *mine?* It is *yours,* my dear people of the Archdiocese, especially the modestly paid working men and women among you; it is *yours,* also, my friends not of my own faith. It has been an honor to formulate the details of its expenditures, the manner of its implementation.

My own version of my apostolate was expressed in my motto: *Ut Cognoscant Te,* That they may know Thee, O Lord! It is the continuance of the mission that Christ gave to His Apostles: love one another as I have loved you. Unless we know God, we cannot love Him. This is a truism we all acknowledge. Through prayer, study, and an intensified Christian living of the commandment of love, we all grow in our desire for holiness, and in our earnestness to realize that desire.

I could not be complacent about the attention I have given to material needs had I not the assurance that through the cooperation, good will and hard work of pastors and their priestly assistants, of nuns and brothers, and of the men and women of the laity young and old, Our Lord is better loved, better served today than He was ten years ago. On the pages of this Special Supplement, you will find the story of a more fervent parish life, of more young people among the faithful dedicating themselves to the poor and the needy, giving of their time, their service, their money, their love, their example of holiness—giving, if not their very *all*, at least very nearly this, to God.

Herein are the sources of my joy, and I take this opportunity of thanking you all, lay, religious and clergy. As for myself, let me continue with work and prayer and sacrifice the labor of restoring all things in Christ. With my heart full of love and devotion to everyone, with a special measure for the poor, the shutins, the handicapped, I thank you for your prayers, your good-will, your generous support.

Let us go forward together, ever mindful that our sojourn here is but a pilgrimage, and our destiny the throne of God. Let us pray that in the time that remains to me, and to you, that we will do our utmost to make God better known, more loved and served.

Pray for me, as I pray for you. *Ut Cognoscant Te.*

And thank you for ten years of happy leadership. God reward you all.

This letter issued on the tenth anniversary of Archbishop Cushing's elevation to the See of Boston, has all the warmth, directness and virile grace which has marked Archbishop Cushing from the very days of his childhood.

The section of South Boston where he was born was anything but a privileged section. But those who lived there, though they lacked the luxuries of life, were self-respecting people who loved God and tried to get along with their neighbors.

Patrick Cushing and his wife Mary Dahill Cushing had brought with them from Ireland a love of God and virtue that made their marriage ideal and brought them sincere and deep rejoicing on the birth of their oldest son on August 24, 1895, just three years before the Spanish American War. The child was baptized Richard James Cushing.

The quick, open-faced boy entered the Oliver Hazard Perry Elementary School when he was six. A photograph taken sometime during the grade school years shows a young man of great seriousness, a good and deeply religious student.

At Boston High School there was already in his mind a partial conviction that he had a vocation to the priesthood; this became a certainty after two years of study at Boston College. At the completion of his sophomore year, Richard Cushing entered St. John's Ecclesiastical Seminary in Brighton, to begin his studies for the priesthood.

Cushing's fellow students soon grew to like his easy, open-hearted ways and broad sense of humor. He joined in their games, such as baseball, with the adeptness of one who was a natural athlete. Despite his good fellowship and easy ways, students were also quick to note his concentration at meditation time and the reverent gracefulness he displayed when assigned as one of the assistants for the liturgy.

It was not long before his classmates discovered his high qualities of zeal and leadership. Soon he was selected to be president of the Academia, a seminary organization that informed students on the needs of home and foreign missions and trained them in the best ways of satisfying those needs. Cushing devoured every book he could find on the subject, and so electric was his enthusiasm for the mission field that he left behind him a memorable record of fund-raising that was to have a profound effect on his future in the priesthood.

Richard Cushing became a priest on May 6, 1921. Both his father and mother followed the ceremonies in the sanctuary of the Holy Cross Cathedral, with tear-misted eyes as Cardinal O'Connell anointed the hands of their son. It was a day of honor and religious joy for the family, a happiness they had all looked forward to during the long years of sacrifice.

For about a year Father Cushing was a curate; first at St. Patrick's Church in Roxbury, and later at St. Benedict's Church in East Somerville. Then, to the surprise of no one, he was lifted out of parishwork and made assistant to the archdiocesan director of the Propagation of the Faith. Six years later he took over the office of director. It was an assignment that called for humility, fine preaching talent and a humorous charm that persuaded both pastors and people to love the missions and support them with magnificent generosity. Soon Father Cushing was known in every parish of the diocese; his style of preaching, direct and sincere, was widely admired.

Often enough he had to appear at several churches on Sunday mornings. After his own Mass and thanksgiving, he would dash off on his round of preaching. Yet in spite of the pressure, he somehow found time to greet the Sisters and altar boys. Frequently he would dash into the kitchen for a quick cup of coffee and a joke or two with the housekeepers. Everyone looked forward to his visits, including the pastors; for even though they realized that Father Cushing's sincere oratory was drawing goodly sums of money out of the parishes, they, too, were convinced that the missionary work of the Church depended upon his efforts.

Cushing was particularly adept in making people realize how much missionary Sisters and priests gave up in leaving home to labor in sections of the world where, often enough, they endured acute discomfort, perpetual hatred and discouraging ignorance.

The Sunday morning safaris in search of funds were but a small part of his job. The paperwork in the office of the Propagation called for endless hours of labor. Cushing also had to decide which of the thousands of appeals were most pressing and worthy of support.

Missionaries who came through Boston were sure to stop for a visit with the amiable director of the Propagation of the Faith. They were sure of a cordial reception and warm hospitality. They usually departed with a generous check for their missions.

How successful Father Cushing's efforts were may be seen in the thousands of mission stations that were furnished with chapels through his work among the wonderfully generous people of Boston. Almost as important was the organization of two missionary clubs; the Sen Fu Club for women, and the Father Jim Hennessey Club for men. The purpose of these two clubs had nothing to do with the actual raising of funds. They were media of instruction about the missionaries, their stations, their problems and their needs. For many people these clubs offered the first opportunity to learn that the missions are not something romantic and faraway, but as close and pressing as our own anguishing problems, and as near as our own hearts. Also among Cushing's most notable achievements was his insistence and aid in the establishment of seminaries to train a native clergy and hierarchy in the Orient and Africa.

The rewards for his work began to appear with the accession of Pius XII. In April 1939, the new pontiff elevated Father Cushing to the status of domestic prelate, with the title of Right Reverend Monsignor. Two months later, in June 1939, Monsignor Cushing received notice of his appointment as Auxiliary Bishop of Boston, in succession to Bishop Spellman, who had become Archbishop of New York.

Cardinal O'Connell consecrated his tall slim protégé on June 22, 1939. Bishop Cushing then assumed the pastorate of the beautiful Sacred Heart Church in Newton. In addition to his pastoral duties, he was still Director of the Propagation of the Faith.

Before America's entry into World War II, Bishop Cushing concentrated most of his assistance on the islands in the Pacific area. Later many servicemen had reason to be grateful to the bishop, because when shot out of the air or washed ashore on strange islands they found a friendly welcome from the natives who were grateful for the assistance and faith that had come to them through the efforts of Bishop Cushing.

All during the war Bishop Cushing spent a great deal of time trying to help and encourage the servicemen. He was prodigal in providing them with small religious kits, each of which contained a good rosary.

Cardinal O'Connell died of pneumonia on April 22, 1944, after a brief illness. He was in his 84th year. Archbishop Ameleto Cicognani, the apostolic delegate, celebrated the Solemn Requiem Mass in the Cathedral of the Holy Cross. The sermon was preached by Bishop Cushing, who spoke warmly of the cardinal, citing his achievements as patriot, priest and scholar. He emphasized the administrative brilliance of the dead prelate, who had established the diocese on such a strong basis that it had survived the worst depression in history without appreciable harm. "It was," he said, "the churches, schools and charitable organizations that were to be the cardinal's enduring monument."

Bishop Cushing was named administrator of the archdiocese, a position he held until September 25, 1944, when he received notice of his appointment as Archbishop of Boston.

The apostolic delegate installed Archbishop Cushing on November 8, 1944, with great pomp and ceremony. Crowds of bishops from all over the nation came for the occasion. The new archbishop had always been an active man of optimistic nature, but he must have been slightly perturbed when his first survey of the diocese roundly displayed the magnitude of the task before him.

In assuming the rule of the diocese, Archbishop Cushing realized that it would have to undergo a tremendous building program. He loved his people and admired them for their generosity, but he soon saw—as he had in the mission field—that there was a great deal to be done which would call for new enthusiasm and enlarged generosity.

One of his first acts was to provide funds to strengthen and refurbish the missions in the Pacific Islands. For this purpose, Bishop Feeney was consecrated and sent out to direct the work.

At home, Archbishop Cushing began an active campaign of fund-raising that was to channel $40,000,000 into diocesan improvements; these included chapels for workers in convenient parts of the city (including the airport and fishermen's wharf) the enlargement and modernization of older buildings and hospitals, and the creation of facilities for every type of social problem.

When he took over the rule of the archdiocese in 1944, there were 1,292 priests, 325 parishes, 225 brothers, 4,054 sisters, 6 hospitals, 3 colleges and universities, 2,552 students, 98,828 youths under instruction, and the Catholic population of the diocese was 1,133,075.

Within fifteen years, the number of priests had grown to

2,623, there were 390 parishes, 272 brothers, 5,370 sisters, 13 hospitals, 6 colleges and universities, 13,316 students, 364,093 youths under instruction, and the Catholic population had grown to 1,582,677.

This was accomplished because of the archbishop's subtle blending of intense spirituality and ceaseless activity. He rose early, as he had in the seminary. After Mass and thanksgiving, he ate a frugal breakfast, then quickly informed himself of the news of the day. After that he kept two secretaries busy with his huge correspondence and saw many people who came to him with their problems. It is symptomatic of his open heart that he saw people with or without appointments; and whether they were Joe Doe or Joe Kennedy, they all received the same courteous attention.

It was lucky that Archbishop Cushing had a strong constitution, because a glance at his schedule of meetings and ceremonies for a week make it hard to understand how he was able to keep up such a pace. This is all the more remarkable in that a second set of secretaries came on duty in the late afternoon when His Excellency might have been relaxing; the work sometimes went on as late as 10 o'clock at night. The archbishop's residence on Commonwealth Avenue, known as an exclusive place in the days of the old cardinal, was now a vibrant center of hospitality and charity.

In examining the life of this great prelate, it is hard to see which of his accomplishments is dearest to his heart. If ever a modern priest tried to be all things to all men—like St. Paul—Cardinal Cushing is that man. There are so many pictures of him in so many touching roles that the biographer is hard put to select his outstanding accomplishments. He worked well and lovingly in all he did, and as a result, there is near perfection in all his activities.

Among the things he worked hardest for was an increase in vocations. The results were astounding. An unimaginative bishop with an abundance of priests at his command might have called a halt to the drive for vocations. Instead, Archbishop Cushing, with the full consent of the men involved, leased scores of priests to dioceses that were poor and short of vocations.

Quite naturally, the seminary buildings had to be enlarged, including the chapel. A new research library was built, and the Cardinal O'Connell Junior College came into being. The archbishop loved his young aspirants to the priesthood, and took great pains to visit them often to gain an understanding of their problems and to increase their knowledge of the life they must lead in their zeal for souls.

Many of the candid-camera shots of the archbishop are unforgettable and utterly charming. We see him ladling the soup or carving the turkey for the aged on great feast days. His face wears a benign look above the capacious apron that covers his cassock, but the grins and complete hilarity of his guests show that he has been cracking many a joke with them. It is even said that sometimes on St. Patrick's Day the archbishop has danced an Irish jig or two, completely captivating his audience.

Equally touching is his appearance with the young or the handicapped. It is typical of him to call the handicapped or subnormal children his "exceptional children." He personally takes them on frequent excursions, and of late years has led them to Lourdes and Fatima, in the hope that some of them may be cured or at least consoled.

The archbishop is as much at home with workingmen and women, as he is with kings and presidents. That was why one of his first innovations as archbishop was the installation of a chapel on the wharf, the airport and the railway station. This was no mere gesture; he frequently appears at these centers, and one of the most joyous episodes of the springtime is his blessing of the fleet in the full pontificals of his office.

There is a danger for all bishops that they may become mere activists and expert businessmen. Such is not the case with Archbishop Cushing. As bishop, he chose for his motto *Ut Cognoscant Te* (That they may know Thee). The mainspring of all his active charity and all his endeavors springs from Christ and the liturgy. Courses on the Mass and the liturgy are given in schools and colleges; the dialogue Mass is firmly encouraged; evening Mass is a common occurrence. And by word and work the archbishop inspires interest and information in the Mass and the Sacraments. In carrying out the *motu proprio* of Pius X, young priests of musical ability are trained at the Pius X School of Liturgical Music and are instructing the children, and in some cases even the adults, to sing the Mass in Gregorian Chant.

How thoughtful the archbishop is for even the least of his children becomes beautifully clear when we discover that he has arranged televised Masses for shut-ins, normally forgotten in most dioceses.

From his earliest days, the archbishop had been truly devoted to the Mother of God. Whenever he is at home, he finds time in his busy schedule to lead the Rosary twice a day on television for his people. His sermons on Our Lady's feast days are filled with illumination and poetry that clearly indicate his reverence and love. One of the finest examples is to be found in the beautiful prayer which he wrote to Our Lady of Boston:

> Glorious Mother of God and powerful patron of all human endeavors, protect with thy favor this City of Boston and all who dwell in it. Intercede with thy Divine Son to bless its blue bay and rising hills, to bless its ancient streets and historic monuments, to bless its newest arteries and its everchanging face.
>
> Within its boundaries beg Him to sanctify those who live and labor here, cause their works to prosper and bring happiness to those whom they love. Ask Him to give guidance to all who are called to provide leadership in this community and grant them an honest intelligence and a far-seeing vision.
>
> For our City, O Holy Mary, be a Morning Star lighting the daybreak, a Tower of Ivory guiding those who wander, a House of God giving shelter to all who are troubled. As we pass through our fair city and elsewhere be for us all a Refuge of Sinners, a Comforter of the Afflicted and in our last hours, O Mary, be a Gate of Heaven through which we may pass to eternal life.
>
> Intercede with thy Son, our Redeemer, that His Providence may watch over Boston and its people; let His grace strengthen,

guide, defend and protect its every venture old and new; and finally in all our aspirations and actions "as he was with our fathers, so may God be with us." Amen.

In his writing, as in his preaching, Archbishop Cushing shows excellent talents; he is, in fact, so eminently quotable that one is hard pressed to know where to begin and where to end. The archbishop's sincere affection for men of all races and creeds is admirably shown in a speech given at the brotherhood dinner of the Lowell Hebrew Community on February 14, 1956, where he said in part:

> My friends, I have broken bread with you this night, and have talked with you, as a fellow American neighbor and friend. But in this matter I voice no mere personal opinion, but with the consecrated authority of my holy office, as a bishop of the Roman Catholic Church, and priest forever according to the order of Melchizedek, I can declare to you that no Catholic can despise a fellow man and remain a true follower of his Lord and Savior, Jesus Christ, and an obedient son of his Church.
>
> Any Catholic who reviles or wrongs a brother because of the color of his skin, because of race or religion, or who condemns any racial or religious group, ceases in that condemnation to be a Catholic and an American. He becomes a disobedient son of Mother Church and a disloyal citizen of the United States.

In a speech made to the C.I.O. on April 6, 1956, he said:

> Everyone has a right to a life-work, and to a life-work which is a congenial form of making something, of producing something. Such work is not just a job. It is life; the life of an artist painting a portrait on the canvas of time. I am not saying that we all ought to be poets or painters or authors or inventors. That is one of the weak things about society today; we think of makers as a very small group of painters, poets, musicians, and so on. But the artist is not a special kind of man; every man is a special kind of artist. And I am not insinuating that we all ought to be making pots and pans—things with our hands. If we can sail a ship well, if we can cook a good meal, if we can drive an engine, plough a field, be a lawyer, a doctor, a street-sweeper or a businessman—if we can do any of these things, we are makers.

In another speech on June 3, 1959, the archbishop, in a sense, rounded out the depth and complexity of his thought with this statement about the uncommon man, which fearlessly lashes out at one of the great defects of our time:

> It is good when common men are given every means and opportunity to rise to greater heights of excellence and achievement. But it is not good when the *common* becomes a norm of excellence and accomplishments, when the man of uncommon ability is resented and the person of uncommon performance is perpetually cut down to size. It is best for our traditions of faith and our institutions of freedom when citizens are inspired to seek *uncommon* heroism and *uncommon* stature, to avoid the merely common and to aspire after that which is more noble, more truly humane and more nearly divine.

Due to his excellence in delivering speeches and writing, Archbishop Cushing is very quick to discern these excellences in others. He has encouraged and helped young writers and has contributed many prefaces and introductions to many worthwhile books.

His public activities have brought him many honors. Numerous universities have showered him with doctors' degrees, and governments have honored him with medals, but he is just as proud of his certificates as honorary fireman or honorary president of the drum and bugle corps.

In 1953, a good part of Boston went to its knees with the announcement that Archbishop Cushing had gone to St. Elizabeth's Hospital for two major operations. In January 1954, he returned to his residence, and in spite of his doctor's pleading, refused to take a vacation from his heavy schedule.

In 1954, Cushing celebrated his first ten years as Archbishop of Boston. He seemed disposed to forget the fact, but priests and people showered him with gifts and praise. Nor did Pius XII forget the anniversary; in July 1954, His Holiness appointed Archbishop Cushing, Assistant at the Pontifical Throne with the title of Count of the Apostolic Palace and Court of the Lateran.

This ancient title—which ranks immediately below the cardinalate and usually points to it—dates back to the time when the pope lived at the Lateran Palace and his court was composed of these assistants. They usually took their turns in waiting on him. They were also closest to the papal throne on great occasions, and unlike lesser dignitaries who had to wear wool or cotton, were permitted to wear the silk.

Most people were surprised when the Archbishop of Boston was not named a cardinal at the Great Consistory in 1946, in which thirty-two bishops were elevated to the purple. Totally unconcerned, Archbishop Cushing proceeded with the complete reorganization of every society in the archdiocese.

In the Archdiocese of Boston, there are now the following Eastern Rites: Armenian, Byzantine Slavonic, Maronite, Melkite, Byzantine and Catholic Ukrainian. All are in a vigorous and thriving condition, due to the help and encouragement they received from Archbishop Cushing.

He has also helped handicapped and subnormal children. Beginning with the Kennedy Hospital, which ministers to children with disabilities, a whole phalanx of the most modern homes for children came into being.

Another significant change took place in the archbishop's thinking. He had hardly gone farther afield than the eastern seaboard, but after the war, all of this was changed when he led thousands of pilgrims to Ste. Anne de Beaupré, Lourdes, Fatima and the other shrines of Europe.

"It goes without saying," as Bishop John J. Wright of Pittsburgh testifies, "that these religious pilgrimages in lands still bearing the evidences of war had their intended effect in helping to bring together the people of divided nations. In due course, the governments of France, Italy, Germany, Portugal and Ireland were to pay their tribute to the work of international friendship by which Archbishop Cushing had made his own people so proud."

Archbishop Cushing has a manly and cavalier way of doing things that often completely surprises and enchants people. A sterling example of this was to be seen in June of 1951, when 40,000 members of the Holy Name Society gathered in Fenway

Park for a Holy Hour. Almost without warning, a torrential downpour began. A great many bishops would have canceled the meeting and their appearance as well. Instead, the archbishop appeared in full ecclesiastical pomp, wearing his *cappa* and followed by a trainbearer. He was greeted with a great roar of applause and laughter as he circled the entire park, drenched to the skin, gaily waving his biretta at the crowd and smiling like an amiable Buddha. It was only one of the occasions in which he had inspired the Holy Name Society. Actually, he has made the society a power in the archdiocese.

Archbishop Cushing has not only strengthened the network of guilds founded by Cardinal O'Connell, but he has added to them all along the line. Among the many innovations is the creation of a reading clinic that has done an immense amount of good for all those whose future was conditioned or imperiled by their inability to cope with the written word. The blind, the deaf, the handicapped and the troubled are all equally served and cared for. Nor does Archbishop Cushing forget the weak willed or misdirected. Every day some 700 men from skid row are given a hot meal.

After the death of Pius XII on October 9, 1958, there were many changes made in the hierarchy throughout the world. Boston was jubilant on November 17, 1958, when banner newspaper headlines proclaimed that the Archbishop of Boston had been elevated to the Senate of the Church. With him were named Archbishop O'Hara of Philadelphia, and Archbishop Cicognani, who had served the Church so faithfully and well for longer than any delegate in the history of the nation.

Everyone who knew and loved Archbishop Cushing was anxious to participate in the ceremonies attendant upon his being raised to the cardinalate. The list was finally cut down to a reasonable number, and on the 10th of November four planeloads of officials, friends and the press took off for Ciampino Airport in Rome.

The days of the consistories were a happy time for Cardinal Cushing and his friends. From the reading of the *biglietto* at the North American College until December 18 when he received the red *galero* in the splendid ceremony at St. Peter's, the cardinal and his friends lived in a current of happiness that showed plainly in all the pictures of the occasions that we have. The cardinal was particularly delighted with his titular Church, Santa Susanna, on the Via Venti Settembre. It is the American Church in Rome, staffed by the Paulist Fathers, who have long been special friends and enthusiastic helpers of His Eminence.

Upon his return to Boston, when the banquets and celebrations were over, Cardinal Cushing quickly returned to his work. Honors continued to fall upon him, including that of being the first cardinal to give the invocation at the Inauguration of a President of the United States.

With the calling of the Vatican Council in 1962, Archbishop Cushing played a prominent part in all those movements which will help to bring the liturgy—especially the Mass—closer to the people.

Before the closing of the first session of the council, the cardinal's health made it necessary for him to ask Pope John for permission to return to Boston. *Time* magazine reports an amusing exchange between the Pope and Cardinal Cushing at this final meeting. "Warmly sympathetic," says *Time,* "the Holy Father recommended to the cardinal a little bicarbonate of soda before going to bed.

" 'Your Holiness,' " replied Cushing, " 'thank God you're not infallible when prescribing medicine. That's the worst thing you can take for ulcers.' "

The joke is reminiscent of the famous story about Cardinal Gibbons, who upon his return from the first Vatican council was asked if the Pope was infallible in *everything.* "I don't think so," Bishop Gibbons replied, "he called me Mister Jibbons."

In his own quiet way Boston's cardinal goes on working for the archdiocese and the whole world. A recent splendid example of his charity was the $1,000,000 ransom which he personally raised for Cubans captured in the abortive Bay of Pigs invasion.

The message of Archbishop Cushing's tenth anniversary, in 1944, has been amply borne out and enlarged in the twenty years since that time. Especially true are the words: "To you, dear people, the history of the past ten years is yours, not mine. To you, after God, be all its glory."

The cardinal's days have been filled with service, without counting the cost to himself or taking pride in himself. He exemplifies Gibbons' sentiment: "It is not the cardinal that ennobles a man; it is the man that ennobles the cardinal." There is no better-loved prelate in the land, and it is not only Boston that will say Amen to that.

John Cardinal O'Hara

JOHN O'HARA was born in Ann Arbor, Michigan, on May 1, 1888, the son of John W. O'Hara and Ella Thornton O'Hara. Looking back, it seems almost symbolic that he should have been born on the first day of Our Lady's month, because his life was in every sense a practical poem to her honor, and his high regard for her—expressed again and again in so many moving passages of prose—was summed up in the motto of his coat of arms, "Following her you shall not go astray."

Most of John's boyhood was spent in Peru, Indiana, about midway between South Bend and Indianapolis, a scattered, slow-moving small city of about 6,000 on the banks of the Wabash River.

John first attended St. Charles Borromeo Grade School, but there is no indication that he displayed any special aptitude at this time or later when he went on to the public high school in Peru. He loved sports, especially swimming. His friendly nature led him to participate in the varied social affairs with which the Midwestern boy of his time tried to brighten the unexciting rhythms of the year.

The family circumstances were comfortable. John's father ran a small newspaper and was respected as a forward-looking man in community affairs and Republican councils. It was this modest eminence and thoughtful outlook that earned him entry into the foreign service at a time when Teddy Roosevelt was trying to strengthen the bonds between South America and the United States.

Mr. O'Hara's first post was Montevideo in Uruguay, where he was American Consul from 1905 to 1907. John was seventeen when, after the long sea voyage, he caught his first glimpse of the towering Cerro Light and entered the spacious harbor on the Rio de la Plata Estuary.

The strangeness of the city intrigued him; the narrow streets of the "old city," containing the business district and the relics of colonial grandeur, culminated in the Plaza de la Constitución, with its statue of the liberator José Gervasio Artigas directly in the center.

The soft phrases of the strange language pleased the young man. Soon he learned to handle its grammar and intonations with ease at the Colegio de Sagrado Corazón (College of the Sacred Heart), Montevideo's best school, staffed and directed by the Society of Jesus.

Between sessions at the college, John served as secretary to the United States Minister to Uruguay, and had his first experiences with the routine that develops a successful executive.

John had never been robust, and the moist, hot climate of Montevideo had a bad effect on his lungs, forcing him to take a year's rest in Argentina, where the healthier air cured him.

In 1907, when his father was transferred to Santos, Brazil, John went with him to the coffee capital of the world. The perpetual aroma of coffee and the low-lying city with its gigantic sea wall proved unhealthy, so John returned to Indianapolis in 1908, one year before his father gave up the foreign service to practice law in Indiana's capital city.

In 1909, it was decided that John would finish his college course at Notre Dame University in South Bend. The cost of his tuition was small, because his experiences in South America enabled him to find a place on Notre Dame's faculty, teaching elementary Spanish.

January snow lay on the wide fields framing the university when John arrived for the second term. The poet in him thrilled at the sight of the golden dome crowned with the statue of the Virgin, herself more pure than the dazzling whiteness mantling her demesne.

The campus was still small; students and faculty were like one big family. The dorms huddled around the church were severe and barnlike; only Sorin, with its towers, had a pretension to French château style, as if looking toward a more opulent future.

John found an appealing friendliness among the Holy Cross priests. They made him feel at home, and their active zeal for souls suited his own mentality and taste for doing things rather than talking about them. At morning Mass in the drafty administration chapel, he felt himself drawn ever closer to the religious life. When May came, the evening Rosary at the Lourdes Grotto under the splendid old trees kindled a love in him that was never to be erased.

Outwardly he gave no sign; his jocose manner and quick repartee were in keeping with the spirit of the time and place. Classes were sometimes rowdy affairs, and every boy on the campus was fanatically interested in football. The early coaches were priests, who brought to the game a quiet ferocity. One of them is reputed to have said, to a young man who showed some timidity in getting into the melee, "Whaddya standing there for, doing nothing? If you see a leg sticking out of the pile, break it off." It was no atmosphere for sissies.

John's students discovered an amiable toughness in their tall, slim, fair-haired teacher. They found themselves drawn to him because he seemed so near to them in time and spirits.

The scant two years of study passed all too quickly. Almost before it seemed possible, the June of 1911 and the week of graduation were upon him. The band played on the high porch of the Ad building every night. Young men who had spent much time kicking against the strict discipline now found themselves nostalgic as they walked through the fragrant June dusk and spoke of departure.

With his bachelor of philosophy degree behind him, John gave long hours of consideration to his future. Did he have a vocation to the priesthood? he asked himself. Was his health good enough to stand the novitiate of the Holy Cross Fathers, still informed with French piety and severity?

For a year he tested himself by remaining at Notre Dame as a lay teacher, and at its close made up his mind quite humbly that Notre Dame was his future home and the place where he could do the work he loved best. The novitiate would be the active test of God's call.

It proved to be just that. By nature, John was quick and inventive and did not find it easy to accept menial tasks and minute corrections laid down by rule and tradition. At last he saw through to the heart of the matter—obedience was not a fact that concerned himself and his superiors, but himself, his superiors and God. He had long loved prayer, and after that it was easy.

Studies came naturally to John, and he found a good natured bonhomie among his fellow novices. The physical exercise did him good, particularly the hours of swimming in the bracingly cool waters of the two small spring-fed lakes on the campus.

There was the excitement of football too. It became a mad passion for everyone when little-known Notre Dame defeated the powerful Army team in November 1913. The defeat was made possible by the brilliant passing of two young men by the name of Knute Rockne and "Gus" Dorais. It was their exploits and continuing fame which attracted many excellent students to the university and provided the current funds for the progress of the school—a fact that some people seem inclined to forget.

The day of John's ordination by Bishop Chartrand, September 9, 1916, in the cathedral at Indianapolis, was a memorable one for him and his family. They bent their heads with a kind of awe for his first blessing, but once they were all at home, John's engaging grin and sly jokes made them content and happy.

John had creative ideas, and his superiors had a use for them. A year's study of history at the Catholic University and courses at the Wharton School of Commerce at the University of Pennsylvania prepared him for the work he wished to do. In September 1917, he returned to Notre Dame. Father John J. Cavanaugh was president at the time, and his undeniable scholarship and brilliant skill as an orator had earned him the complete devotion of faculty and students.

Two signs that Father O'Hara was a coming man were evident in his appointment as faculty secretary and temporary head of the newly established school of commerce. It was a difficult time for Notre Dame. The First World War disrupted campus life and all the old pieties. Young men of the Students Army Training Corps came to the school by the thousands in 1918, and for a few brief months played havoc with the orderly beauty of the campus. Father O'Hara, who had also been appointed prefect of religion, found himself at full stretch trying to take care of his motley crew. With the armistice on November 11, 1918, everyone, including Father O'Hara, breathed a sigh of relief. Most of the student army had been released by Christmas.

The end of the war brought new opportunities for Notre Dame. Father O'Hara became dean of the College of Commerce and journeyed to South America for the establishment of exchange scholarships with the noted universities of the southern republics, rounding out his work with the establishment of courses in South American history.

Nearest to his heart was his job as prefect of religion, a position that he built up with enormous shrewdness. Many who had held the job before him had seemed more pious than realistic. John O'Hara's long hours in the confessional had taught him that the boys he dealt with were anything but angels, but he was amazed and inspired at their capacity for good. To channel and use that good was the very essence of his task.

The football team was a legend. On campus, the men in the leather helmets were almost completely idolized, and Knute Rockne's name was breathed with the hushed tone usually associated with the mention of the saints.

Obviously the place to begin the religious channeling and inspiration was with the team. Father John began to cultivate the players assiduously. With his completely manly qualities and casual sense of humor it wasn't too difficult, and his appearance among footballers came to be welcomed whether they were at play or practice. The players found themselves cleaning up their language, and it wasn't long before they were cleaning up their lives. Day or night, Father O'Hara was available for advice or confession.

The small mimeographed bulletin which he began to issue in 1921 did much to inspire team and students with the fervor for daily Mass and Communion. Father O'Hara didn't scruple to use either heavy sentiment or clichés, as long as they made his meaning clear and touched the generous hearts of the students.

Careful statistics were kept and quoted, and in time the habit of daily Communion became something of a crusade. From his bare room in Sorin Hall, not far from the tower room of Charlie Phillips—one of the best-loved teachers of the time— Father John kept his finger on the pulse of the university. Directness, simplicity, complete devotion were his watchwords, and whether among the faculty or students, his casual humility was memorable. Anyone who saw him at work could only marvel.

By 1933, when he became vice-president under Father Cavanaugh, he had brought about a more or less complete renovation in campus religious life which in turn paved the way for the intellectual future of Notre Dame. There were still occasional minor scandals and tragedies, but by and large the whole tone of student life was raised, with no sacrifice of the virile qualities Notre Dame prized.

The influence was not felt on the campus alone; prefects of religion from other schools came to South Bend to study Father O'Hara's methods, and his religious bulletin went out to hundreds of schools and colleges.

It was a boom period for Notre Dame. Many new dormitories were being built and the student body was growing rapidly. It was more than a build-up of quantity. A new type of student hungry for learning began to predominate, and all the

new currents of literature and art were discussed acrimoni-
ously.

The tragic death of Rockne in 1931 brought an end to an
era. Football would be played after him, sometimes making
the old flashy headlines, but never with the same following
among priests and students. The dedication of the new football stadium was the splendid realization of a long-cherished
dream. News and sports celebrities came from all over the nation for the event which had all the glamour of a film *premi-
ère*. The presence of G. K. Chesterton in the audience (he was
giving a six-weeks course of lectures at the time) and the universal interest in him on this great night indicated the new
trend in Notre Dame's life.

When Father O'Hara was appointed president of Notre
Dame in 1934, he understood every aspect of campus life. Under his administration the graduate school was strengthened
and began to play a more important part in the tone of the
school. The emphasis on science under the distinguished
Father Nieuland, who invented a base for synthetic rubber,
was to grow and become more important during Father
O'Hara's term of office. Though he now traveled with distinguished authors and educators most of the time, Father O'Hara
lost none of his simplicity. On early summer afternoons he
could be found taking the sun and swimming in the midst of
various student groups or alumni members back on the campus
for a week's celebration. It was Father John's cheerful humanity that knit ever closer the bonds between the old school and
its graduates and moved them to give or promote gifts for its
expansion.

The erection of new buildings went on apace. Dormitories
were all filled faster than they could be built. The science
building and the Rockne Memorial were a big step toward the
newly studious Notre Dame.

Honors for the work he was doing came to Father O'Hara
in abundance. President Roosevelt appointed him a delegate
to the Lima Conference, which in turn led to an invitation by
President Lopez Contreras of Venezuela to head a social-service

mission to that country. On both occasions Father O'Hara used every minute of his leisure time in making a survey of the South American school system on all levels.

The start of the Second World War, with the Polish blitzkrieg of 1939, warned Archbishop Spellman that American participation in the conflict was almost inevitable. That would mean an enormous enlargement of the military ordinariate and a competent staff of men to run its world-wide responsibilities.

With canny shrewdness, Archbishop Spellman, who had long admired Father O'Hara, appointed him military delegate and Auxiliary Bishop of New York. The consecration of the lean bishop of Mylasa took place in Sacred Heart Church on the campus of Notre Dame on January 15, 1940. Cardinal Spellman was consecrator, assisted by Bishops Chartrand and Noll. It was like a family affair; all the bishops were old friends, and students and Holy Cross nuns who knew and loved Father John packed the church.

Bishop O'Hara soon fell into the rhythm of his new work. He brought to it a complete dedication and friendly outlook that established close personal relations between himself and American chaplains around the world. One of the secrets of his success with people was an exceptionally tenderhearted concern for those in trouble. Tears would mist his eyes, even though his approach to a problem was logical and practical. Every chaplain received a letter from the delegate once a month, and he asked them questions about their problems and how to solve them. Visits to the tremendous camps all over the country kept him constantly on the go. Though he drove himself without mercy, baptizing, confirming, listening to gripes, his immediate approach to the endless responsibilities was easy and humorous, as though he had all the leisure in the world.

Living quarters had been found for Bishop O'Hara at St. Caecelia's Church, staffed by the Redemptorist Fathers, on 106th Street. Children had always been a magnet to Father John. The jests he made with them and his imaginative understanding made him as young as they were. St. Caecelia's was no exception, and when Bishop O'Hara found that the parish included a large number of Puerto Ricans, he somehow found time to chatter with the children in Spanish and to begin the work of instructing them and their parents.

Everyone was pleasantly surprised when President Roosevelt appointed Bishop O'Hara to the board of visitors of the Naval Academy at Annapolis. It was the first time a Catholic bishop had been named to that job.

As the war in Europe drew to a triumphant close in March 1945, word came that Pius XII had appointed Bishop O'Hara to the Diocese of Buffalo, as successor to Bishop John A. Duffy, who had died a few months earlier.

Cardinal Spellman installed his friend in St. Joseph's on May 8, 1945. Outside the crowded church the lilacs were beginning to bud and people were shouting, dancing and acting more than a little zany, because it was V-E Day.

The citizens of the lake city found the new bishop much to their taste. With his commanding presence and ability to see and define issues in direct and forceful speech, he graced any occasion. His jocosely serious treatment of feuds between the foreign minority groups in his diocese terminated many vendettas, and his humble way of treating priests and laity earned him universal affection.

One of his forward-looking moves was the progressive elimination of special schools and churches for Negroes. It wasn't so much integration as elevation through the recognition that color of skin has nothing to do with the complete equality of all the children of God.

The bishop spent much thought and effort on the Catholic school system. New schools were built, old schools were modernized and enlarged, a progressive plan for increasing the number of high schools was initiated.

By the end of the first year, the diocese and the nation had already begun to appreciate the quality of their new bishop. His appeal for Catholic charities was so entirely real in its approach that the large sum asked was oversubscribed and continued to be each year that he remained Bishop of Buffalo.

In 1946, Bishop O'Hara and Bishop Michael J. Ready were sent to Japan to make a report on the condition of the Church in that devastated nation. In the ruins of Nagasaki, once a prominent Catholic center, the bishop looked sorrowfully at the complete horror of modern war.

Bishop Duffy had inaugurated the custom of bringing babies from all parts of the diocese for an annual service of blessing at St. Joseph's Cathedral. Bishop O'Hara continued the custom which he immensely enjoyed. In the midst of the cooing, gurgling and squalling, his red-robed figure went through the crowd with words of admiration and a wide smile for everyone.

Honors and degrees continued to fall on his balding head through the Buffalo years, culminating in his appointment in 1951 as vice-president of the permanent committee on the international eucharistic congresses, an oblique tribute to the ardent love of the Eucharist and his ability to make people share in that love.

Four months later, news came from Rome that Bishop O'Hara had been elevated to the Archbishopric of Philadelphia. Looking back, it all seemed like a dream; he had only wished to be a priest and serve God's people. The titles given him had meant very little, because he was anything but a proud man and he was skilled in seeing through glossy surfaces to the universal lowliness of all mankind. Occasionally he had been ill and tired, and now at sixty-three he was taking on the responsibilities of one of the largest dioceses in the United States, after the thirty-three-year reign of a distinguished administrator. Squaring his shoulders, he prepared himself for the new tasks with the old staff of prayer.

At the brilliant installation services in the massive basilica-style brownstone cathedral of SS. Peter and Paul, he looked pensive and pale. When he rose to speak at last, after thanking Apostolic Delegate Amleto Giovanni Cicognani and his brother bishops who had come to honor him, Archbishop O'Hara spoke in words as simple as the Gospel and himself.

"I have no program to announce, nothing to reach but the

love of God. Recognizing my utter unworthiness to follow in the footsteps of such magnificent leaders as Cardinal Dougherty and his eminent predecessors, I only ask leave to second and encourage your efforts. If you will kindly tell me your needs, I shall do my best to meet them. I know no other way to serve. Working together with the assistance of God's grace, we can help one another save our souls."

The simple pronouncement was roundly appreciated in the City of Brotherly Love—more astonishingly still, it was found to correspond with the ensuing reality.

Cardinal Dougherty had been austere and distant on many occasions; the new archbishop was different. Almost always he cloaked the core of his profound depth and seriousness with a jocose and casual manner. Priests and laity who came with their problems went away from their visits encouraged and consoled.

One of the first things the priests noticed was that the palace at 5700 City Avenue was now a home. If summoned there for a meeting, they were astounded to have the archbishop answer the doorbell and go to the door with them after the visit. He usually held their coats for them as they prepared to depart. As he had always done, he preferred to move men through persuasion and liking, not through protocol and command.

Priests and people came out to the cathedral in large numbers on May 12, 1953, to see their archbishop receive the pallium symbol of his archepiscopal rank from the hands of Cardinal Spellman.

In the modest chancery (with its austere walls and red carpets) north of the cathedral, Archbishop O'Hara started to work on a survey of diocesan needs. Education was his first concern. He did not confine it to a mere paper approach, as was evidenced by his constant journeys to all parts of the diocese— making friends as he went—for a first-hand grasp of what needed to be done.

What he found was vastly encouraging. Cardinal Dougherty, a genuine scholar and a man of vision, had built well. At his death he could boast that there were Catholic grade and high schools for every child in the diocese, in which the parishes as units bore the entire expense of the children's education. But over the years and with the explosive growth of Philadelphia's population at the close of the war, many of the schools urgently needed enlargement or renovation. What Archbishop O'Hara achieved in his almost nine-year reign is nothing short of miraculous.

Between 1952 and September 1961, sixty-one new schools were opened. Of these, seventeen were high schools. One of the outstanding high schools is named for Cardinal Dougherty. It enrolls 3,000 boys and 3,000 girls. Their classrooms are in separate wings, but both are under the same administrative supervision. It is probably the largest high school in the world. The enrollment of all the schools at the end of Cardinal O'Hara's reign was 894,000. In addition to the fabulous new buildings, older structures were enlarged. In 1961 alone, 222 new classrooms were added to the existing structures.

Nor did the archbishop forget to encourage higher education, a field in which he was an outstanding expert. Three new women's colleges were opened, and Villanova attained university status. In 1961, the eleven colleges and universities of the diocese had an enrollment of nearly 20,000 students. One of the most appealing pictures ever taken of the archbishop, at Immaculata College graduation in 1956, expresses far more than any words could the complete interest and delight he showed when in the midst of his children.

Archbishop O'Hara, as an enlightened and practical educator, was interested in more than the bricks-and-mortar aspects of his responsibility. In a series of vigorous editorials in *The Catholic Standard and Times,* he summed up his views of Catholic education vis-à-vis Federal aid and control. The editorial gave unblinking proof of the tremendous gift Catholics were offering public education in the United States, and adroitly spotlighted the injustice of the double taxation that would fall upon Catholics in the plans for any stepped-up aid to public schools which did not include all religious schools in its thinking.

Shortly after the archbishop came to Philadelphia, he interested himself in the archdiocesan newspaper, *The Catholic Standard and Times,* which was making a name for itself under the competent editorship of Monsignor Anthony Ostheimer. The paper was functioning in the basement of a very old building. When the heavy, outmoded presses rolled, the whole structure shook, and frightened visitors expected the worst.

Archbishop O'Hara surveyed the plant and made his usual droll comments. A modern office and printing plant was built at 1818 Cherry Street. The façade is of particolored brick employed in the modern manner which the famous Benedictine architect Dom Bellot had used with memorable distinction in Quarr Abbey. It's a strictly functional building, but no less a delight to the eye. Housed in its fine new quarters, the paper began—with the powerful assistance of the archbishop—a period of expansion and promotion which increased its circulation to over 100,000.

The archbishop and the jovial editor worked in the closest possible harmony, witty badinage often characterizing their meetings. Monsignor Ostheimer, of solid German lineage, has a way of replying to priests or people who question him, "Well, as my Irish grandmother used to say . . ." concluding with some well-know saw.

Apparently the archbishop heard of this, and on one solemn occasion as they were going into the cathedral Archbishop O'Hara leaned over and whispered to the monsignor, "By the way, how's your Irish grandmother?" Monsignor Ostheimer had a difficult time maintaining his gravity. People liked and respected the other archbishops of Philadelphia, says Monsignor Ostheimer, but Archbishop O'Hara was loved.

One of the strongest indications of the love that begets love is to be found in his work for mentally retarded children. Five special schools were founded for this, enrolling 685 children who were solidly and patiently grounded in the simple beliefs they could comprehend. In time, along with other training, this enabled them to receive the Sacraments with fervor and understanding. To these children and those helped by the establishment, the St. Lucy's School for the Blind, and the enlargement of the Archbishop Ryan School for the Deaf, Archbishop O'Hara was something of a saint. Watching him moving among them was a touching sight; patience, complete manly sympathy, tenderness and joy were mirrored on his expressive face in turn.

As he had at St. Caecelia's in New York, the archbishop showed a fond regard for the Spanish emigrants who had come to Philadelphia, mostly from Puerto Rico. A center, Casa del Carmen, was founded for their religious, social and cultural activities. The newly ordained priests who were to work among them were sent to Puerto Rico for a year's training in the language, customs and mentality of their people.

From his experience in Buffalo, the archbishop brought to Philadelphia the graceful custom of blessing the children during the month of May. In the cathedral and in certain large parishes of the archdioceses, children and their parents came to receive the blessing of their bishops and were drawn closer to Christ.

The archbishop's loving concern for the family went far beyond the picturesque days of blessing. A committee for Christian home and family was carefully organized in every parish. When a new child was born, the parish women of the committee called upon the mother, congratulating her in the name of Archbishop O'Hara and presenting the child with a medal.

Every three months after this event until the child is three years old the ladies return with a leaflet outlining progressive religious training. Finally the mother is presented with a booklet for the further religious training of the child. The ladies of the committee, most of whom are mothers, keep themselves in good spiritual condition by frequent days of recollection and retreats.

Archbishop O'Hara initiated another practical program for strengthening family life—the premarital instruction program sponsored by the Family Life Bureau. In fall and spring, one night a week for four weeks, specially trained doctors and priests give instructions and answer questions on every aspect of married life. Over 55,000 couples have attended the lectures in the first eight years. For two years after marriage, the Family Life

Bureau follows up the initial instructions with a series of letters to newlyweds, giving practical pointers for a happy marriage.

Archbishop O'Hara always loved God's house. He was quick to note that the Cathedral of SS. Peter and Paul had grown shabby and crowded over the years. He announced its renovation and enlargement in 1955. Funds poured in and the work started in 1955 and continued for almost two years. The splendid interior of the cathedral today is enduring proof of Archbishop O'Hara's loving care for every aspect of Christian worship.

The archbishop ardently promoted daily Communion and frequent reception of the Sacraments. The results of his interest were soon apparent and brought great joy to a mind that had always seen through statistics to people and God.

In promoting the charities of the archdiocese, Archbishop O'Hara truly achieved wonders. The first organized appeal in 1958, which had a goal of $1,600,000, was oversubscribed by more than $300,000, and the two years following brought still more amazing results.

There were no narrow boundaries to John O'Hara's charity. Missionaries from the whole world were received warmly, and the archbishop's friendly approval of their cause sent them back to the missions encouraged in heart and pocket.

On November 16, 1958, word came from Rome that Pope John XXIII had named Archbishop O'Hara a cardinal. "How do you feel about it?" he was asked.

The cardinal grinned. "The news makes me numb all over," he replied. On being first made a bishop, he had observed: "The only purple I ever expected was on my confessional stole." With characteristic self-deprecation, he admitted that his brothers and sisters, who still called him "Father John," were astounded at the new honor. "After all they're sensible people," was the way he phrased it.

When Bishop O'Hara came to Philadelphia, he already was a sick man. The heavy burden he assumed and his perpetual activities, in which he refused to spare himself if he could stand on his feet, had made him a gaunt specter of his former self.

In flying to Rome for the ceremonies from December 15–18, he envisaged the possibility that the trip might mean his death, but he emplaned with the charming crooked grin that always meant he was laughing at himself. He went through the complex ceremonies in Rome like a good soldier, but between times he stayed out of the public eye and prayed hard to endure.

The barriers were up in the square outside his cathedral when he returned on a cold, blustery day. Thousands had braved the weather to greet their leader. There was a smile on his pallid face and a warm light in his eyes as he waved to them and they all laughed at his simple summing up. "It's great to be home," he said.

In the two remaining years, the cardinal fought for his life and his people. Several operations and long months in Misericordia Hospital kept him out of circulation but failed to dim his interest in being a good shepherd. From his sick bed, he kept his finger firmly on the pulse of the archdiocese by daily consultation with his secretary, the chancellor, and other officials.

There were always flashes of the old humor. On one occasion when he was taking twenty-two different kinds of pills at varying intervals, he complained, with a broad smile, "I don't mind all the different kinds of pills, it's the mathematics involved that gets me down."

On Saturday morning, August 27, 1960, word went out from the chancery to the 439 parishes that Cardinal O'Hara was gravely ill. Priests and people began to offer prayers for the man they loved. He died quietly the following morning at 3:06 A.M. He had long known that his days were numbered, and he looked forward to release.

Priests and prelates came from all over the United States for his funeral. Cardinal Spellman sang the final Pontifical Mass. The inspiring eulogy was delivered by Cardinal McIntyre of Los Angeles. Both had known him closely in New York; both admired him and loved him as a friend. Messages by the thousands paid tribute to the dead cardinal. Admiration for his deeds were in all, but the chief accent fell on the fact that he was sincerely loved by all who knew him.

In keeping with his simplicity of heart and dress, his will stipulated that he should be buried in the Holy Cross Cemetery on the grounds of Notre Dame. Though he had been the first priest of his community to be raised to the Sacred College, he had wished to rest inconspicuously under the greensward of the place he loved best, in the company of his old companions.

His wish was not fully granted. Because of his high cardinal-itial dignity, Rome thought it more fitting that he should be buried in Sacred Heart Church.

A tomb was hurriedly prepared in the chapel on the Gospel side of the main altar as he lay in state while Fathers and Sisters of the Holy Cross, professors and old friends, filed by. The final entombment took place on September 7, 1960. Archbishop Schultz of Indianapolis sang the Pontifical Mass and gave the final absolution.

The school term had not yet begun, it was a quiet time on the campus. The last farewells were in keeping with Cardinal O'Hara's simplicity of outlook and devoted love of community and friends. The red hat, symbol of his exalted office, would hang in the cathedral in Philadelphia until it fell to pieces. That was all behind him now as he took his rest in the spot he loved and hushed voices spoke in praise of "Father John."

Aloisius Cardinal Muench

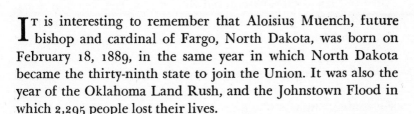

I T is interesting to remember that Aloisius Muench, future
bishop and cardinal of Fargo, North Dakota, was born on
February 18, 1889, in the same year in which North Dakota
became the thirty-ninth state to join the Union. It was also the
year of the Oklahoma Land Rush, and the Johnstown Flood in
which 2,295 people lost their lives.

The comfortable Muench home where the future cardinal
grew up was in north Milwaukee, at 2945 North Tenth Street.
Aloisius' father Joseph was an employee of the Northwestern
Store Equipment Company; his mother was a pillar of St. Boniface Church and was noted for her deep piety, good cooking and
sterling common sense.

Though the Muenches spoke English, German was the first
language of the family. They used it almost entirely in conversation, prayers and songs at home, and on Sundays at St. Boniface Church at West Clark and North Eleventh streets they were
sure to hear a solid sermon in impeccable German. In fact, later
on as Bishop of Fargo, Muench took some English 'essons in
order to overcome the traces of his German sentence structure.

St. Boniface School, to which Aloisius went in 1906, was
staffed by the School Sisters of Notre Dame. Under their excellent instruction, young Muench got a solid foundation in the
three R's and was encouraged in his mother's piety which was
both knowledgeable and sentimental.

Aloisius was a sturdy boy. He loved baseball, fishing and hunting, but all games and sports took second place to his love of religion and the Church. He declared his intention of becoming a priest early in life, and his mother skillfully encouraged him in a manner that at once moved him to humility and perseverance.

A picture of fourteen-year-old Aloisius, taken on his First Communion day in 1903, shows us a self-possessed young man, neat in dress and surrounded by all the romantic atmosphere of the occasion. Already the young man was taking extra lessons in Latin from Father Henry Niehaus, the saintly chaplain of Notre Dame's mother house.

By the time Aloisius entered St. Francis Seminary in 1904, the family had grown to six children. He had two brothers, Frank and Joseph, and three lively sisters, Teresa, Dorothy and Mary.

Muench was popular at St. Francis. His love of study, good marks and quiet ways endeared him to his professors, and among the students he was noted for his sly sense of humor and his interest in sports.

In the spring of 1913, Aloisius prepared for his final exams and ordination, which took place in St. John's Cathedral on June 8. Archbishop Stephen J. Messmer was the ordaining bishop. Touches borrowed from the South German homeland were added to the official procession at his first Mass—the little flower girls, and his sister Dorothy dressed as a bride, symbolizing the Church to which the young Levite was wedded.

Father Muench served as assistant to Monsignor Sebastian Bernard at St. Michael's from 1913 to 1917. It was with pained surprise that the young priest saw the emergence of a virulent anti-Germanism in Milwaukee during those years in which the United States drifted toward war. Fortunately for him, he was moved to an easier and better-informed atmosphere at the University of Wisconsin, in Madison, where he was assistant to Father Hengell, the vigorous chaplain of the Newman Club.

The chaplaincy at St. Mary's Hospital was added to Father Muench's work at St. Paul's Chapel. With his studies for his master's degree, his instructions and hospital duties, he was constantly on the go. Yet he was able to make frequent visits to his home and to the lakes and forests of Wisconsin, and even the briefest holiday was a delight.

Archbishop Messmer was pleased when his student priest received his master of arts degree with high honors at Wisconsin in June 1919. Father Muench elected to go to the ancient University of Fribourg in Switzerland in pursuit of his Ph.D.

He found the climate of Fribourg much like that of Milwaukee. His excellent grasp of German proved to be of tremendous value, both in the classroom and socially. Soon he was hard at work on his thesis, "Compulsory Health Insurance Projects in the United States."

In the early years of his priesthood Father Muench had been active in the *Central Verein*. As the midterm vacation approached in 1919, he was asked to go to Munich as its representative and to arrange for the distribution of relief supplies gathered in the United States for "starving Germany."

He found the usually gay city gloomy and in the midst of a panic in which Reichsmarks were worth less than the paper on which they were printed.

In searching about for a guarantee that the central *Verein's* aid would be distributed justly, Father Muench went to the apostolic nunciature. There he met the tall ascetic nuncio Eugenio Pacelli. The usually reserved nuncio warmed appreciably at the news Muench brought. They chatted away in German about details of the gift, and Father Muench departed with a fervent blessing. The encounter bore astonishing fruit years later when Germany lay in ruins and the Pope was looking for an American prelate who could handle the job of nuncio in occupied Germany.

Two years of study at Fribourg were sufficient to complete work on the thesis. In his final oral examination, Muench acquitted himself so brilliantly that he was given a *summa cum laude* citation. With his doctorate of laws safely achieved, Father Muench spent a further two years surveying advances in the social sciences at the Sorbonne and the Catholic Institute in

Paris. He also attended a series of lectures by outstanding social theorists in London, in Louvain, Belgium, and at Oxford. At Oxford, particularly among the Dominicans and Jesuits, Father Muench found a lively dialogue on social subjects and came into close touch with the outstanding Catholic authorities in the field.

However, theory alone did not engross the young student completely. At Basle, he assisted in the postwar reorganization of the International Association of Labor Legislation and also became a charter member of Pax Romana, a student organization to promote peace. There was still time to attend lively and sometimes acrimonious conferences on social and economic questions in Germany, Switzerland and France.

After arriving in Milwaukee in the summer of 1922, Father Muench, who might have been a brilliant teacher of social subjects, found himself appointed to teach dogmatic theology at St. Francis Seminary. He spent long hours reviewing dogma, and it was with a secure mastery of his subject that he began to teach his courses in September. Somehow he found time to write an occasional article for *America,* and he always found time to join in the sports activities at the seminary. Needless to say, he was one of its most popular professors.

After seven years of teaching, Father Muench became Rector of St. Francis Seminary. Those seven years had been filled with incessant activity—he was spiritual director of several women's organizations, a judge of the archdiocesan matrimonial board, chairman of the board of examiners for the junior clergy, and treasurer of St. Michael's priest fund. As Rector of St. Francis, Father Muench became chairman of the Catholic Action Committee of the Wisconsin branch of the *Central Verein,* and took on duties too numerous to mention, among the most important of which were vice-president of the seminary section of the National Catholic Education Association, and membership in the legislative committee of the Wisconsin Credit Union League.

Early in 1935, Father Muench was elevated to the prelacy with the tile of Right Reverend Monsignor and was invested with the purple on January 22. In August of 1935, Monsignor Muench received a letter from the apostolic delegate, telling him that the Holy Father, Pius XI, intended to appoint him Bishop of Fargo, North Dakota. Before making his decision, Monsignor Muench was perfectly free to discuss the matter with his Ordinary, Archbishop Stritch.

At first Monsignor Muench was moved to refuse the honor; he was honestly convinced that he lacked the practical qualities for a bishop and felt he could do more as a seminary instructor in preparing young men for the priesthood. He told this to Archbishop Stritch, who heard him out with a smile. Then he said one sentence in his soft southern voice: "One does not say no when the Holy Father beckons." Monsignor Muench needed no further persuasion; it was his duty to accept.

On August 12 the news was out. The people of Fargo rejoiced in having such a scholarly man for their bishop. Fargo had just barely weathered the Depression to become part of the disaster area known as the Dust Bowl, and its people were aware of Bishop Muench's background in the field of economic and social questions.

The new bishop was consecrated by Archbishop Stritch in St. John's Cathedral on October 15. A picture taken outside St. Boniface's Church on October 20, on the occasion of Bishop Muench's first pontifical Mass, shows a benign young bishop with a kind of homespun friendliness that is extremely attractive. He was installed in St. Mary's Cathedral in Fargo on November 6, 1935. Because the cathedral seated only 800, most of its space had to be restricted to the bishop's family, friends, visiting bishops, and nuns and priests of the diocese. Outside— a typical Fargo touch—the weather was near zero, the ground covered with four inches of snow.

It was an unfriendly welcome to the bishop's wide demesne, but the succeeding years gradually made up for it. In time Bishop Muench came to love the flat prairie lands of his diocese. The winters were long and bitterly cold and the wind howled perpetually, but in the spring, when the first grass blazed up spangled with wild crocus and red mallows and the meadow larks sang their plangent music, the prairies were beautiful. They were equally lovely in late summer; a sea of waving golden wheat to the far horizon. After the harvest came the duck and partridge shooting, and north in Canada the deer shooting. The bishop was a superb shot and loved the life of the woods, the hikes over rough country in the crisp weather, the open fires and sparse creature comforts.

One of his first acts was a quick survey of his 34,000 square miles of territory. The years of poor crops had left nearly all the parishes saddled with debts and helpless to further parish development. Almost at once the bishop began the collection of the Catholic Church Expansion Fund of the Diocese of Fargo, which in Muench's eleven years there had financed the building of churches, schools, convents and rectories costing many millions of dollars.

It was obvious to him that the fierce winter weather and bad roads made attendance at Sunday Mass practically impossible for many isolated families. Some radical new approach had to be found in teaching the people and their children the truths of their religion. With this in mind, the bishop organized the Confraternity of Christian Doctrine. It became such an active society that it soon embraced 11,000 members. Needless to say, the most active member was the bishop himself, who imported the Sisters of Service from Toronto to conduct correspondence courses in religion for the children in the most isolated sections.

The widely scattered parishes were another source of worry. "We need more priests," the bishop said, "and we need more churches." A little inquiry led him to conclude that many vocations were lost because of poverty—the sheer inability of families to clothe, educate and do without the earning power of the one with the vocation.

"We must provide help and scholarships to supplement the seminary collection," he said. People smiled a little at the idea of ever being able to assemble a scholarship fund, but the bishop trusted in God and people. Slowly the fund grew as conditions on the farms improved with government aid and the life in the town quickened anew with the flow of ready cash. How well

Bishop Muench built is amply evident. In the first ten years the number of vocations almost doubled and in the second decade it completely doubled again.

The early years were not all work and no play. There were fishing and hunting during vacations, and in 1938 his silver jubilee of ordination took place in St. Mary's Cathedral. Many bishops came, but best of all was the presence of his mother, his brothers and sisters and their children.

In the same year, he played host to the national convention of the Catholic Rural Life Conference. The bishop grinned a little to think that a city boy like himself should be host to experts in farming, but, as one of his biographers says: "The bishop was eager to learn, not so much the science of farming as the art of living on a farm according to Christian principles and ideals." A careful study of rural sociology and economics prepared him in mind and heart for advising his people. He was elected president of the conference twice. With the aid of Monsignor Ryan and Monsignor Mulloy, he compiled a "Manifesto on Rural Life." It is still one of the best expositions of Catholic rural philosophy.

Another precedent was the convening of a diocesan synod in 1941. The bishop welcomed his priests with an engaging cordiality that was one of his finest qualities. All the problems of the diocese were discussed with good sense and humor and were summed up in a synodal book that attracted considerable attention.

The great plans for financing the parish expansion were halted by the Second World War, but it is significant that in the five years after the war the bishop's plans brought into existence 7 hospitals, 49 new churches, 6 schools, 15 rectories and other smaller units.

In 1946, Bishop Muench was invited to join the party of Archbishop Stritch, who was going to Rome for his red hat. Muench found Rome interesting and was prepared to enjoy the magnificent ceremonies to the hilt when suddenly he was given an astounding surprise. Monsignor Montini summoned Bishop Muench to the Secretariat of State and informed him that the

Holy Father had selected him for a special mission to Germany. It would be his duty to make a complete visitation of the Church there and personally report his findings to the Holy Father. Apostolic Visitator was to be his title, and he could expect to be absent from his diocese from eight to fifteen months.

He was completely dumbfounded. Strangely enough, he was perhaps the only bishop in the world who could have carried out the duties he was asked to perform. He spoke English and German with equal facility, he was a man's man who knew how to make himself at home in rough circumstances, and his easy approach to people almost invariably led to friendship. Once again, from his memories of a young priest who represented the *Central Verein* in 1919, Pius XII had been inspired to select the man perfectly fitted for the task in hand.

After the great consistory was over, Bishop Muench hurried back to Fargo to make arrangements for his absence in Germany. On June 27, 1946, he started back to Rome from Washington in an old Army plane that island-hopped to Paris by way of Bermuda and the Azores. The bishop was entitled to government transport because he had just been given the title of "liaison consultant for religious affairs to the military governor"—a Pentagon triumph of circumlocution.

Back in Rome, he spent two weeks in hectic conferences; he was carefully briefed on the details of his mission and the extent of the task before him. Finally he was summoned to a private audience with the Pope, in which he learned in burning phrases how extensive the damage in Germany was, how pitiable the state of the Church and the condition of the German people. As a favorable introduction to his mission, the visitator was to head a large convoy of trucks carrying medical supplies from the Vatican to Frankfurt, Germany. The Pope graciously allowed himself to be photographed on the scene as the last trucks bearing the N.C.W.C. War Relief Services insignia were loaded and blessed.

The bishop had need of every blessing in the book. The long trip had to be made over bombed-out roads and bridges. There were almost no supplies of gasoline, and no repairs except in car pools of the United States Army.

By the time the long convoy had traveled through Northern Italy and over the Brenner Pass, Bishop Muench felt as if he had been on the road for years. He had used every ounce of his double authority as a bishop and liaison consultant. The Pope had envisaged Bishop Muench as an "angel of mercy"; the bishop only wished that the title had the wings that went with it. Western Austria . . . Bavaria . . . somehow the convoy lumbered through the endless ruins and arrived at Frankfurt.

The visitator was by this time more than a little appalled by the magnitude of the task before him. Germany was one vast heap of ruins; churches, schools, convents and rectories had suffered immense damage. Yet almost at once he began a systematic visitation of Western Germany. He had hoped to go to the Eastern Zone, but was refused permission to do so by the Russians.

The written reports of the visitator and the laudatory letters written about him by German bishops to the Pope and the Secretariat of State impressed Pius XII so deeply that on January 18, 1947, he was moved to issue to the German bishops the following rare letter in praise of Bishop Muench and his work:

> Our decision to send a special Apostolic Visitator to Germany, as well as the choice of the person fitted for this work, were determined by the conviction that the lack of a clear view of the first postwar years and of the real and juridical complications springing from it would lead to a situation in the religious field in which the presence of a far-sighted representative of the Holy See, standing aside and above the controversies of the day, would be conducive to the general good.
>
> With satisfaction We learn from your letters that the office itself as well as the person charged with it, and no less the manner in which he has conducted its affairs, have met with your undivided acclaim and esteemed approval.
>
> Furthermore, We know with what warm devotion and generoushearted love the Apostolic Visitator, designated by Us, follows the call to go to Germany. We know, too, with what zealous, objective, and benevolent impartiality he strives to

enter into the purpose and duties of his important but also grave and at times thorny mission, and labors to rise to the hopes which Holy Mother Church and the Church of Germany place on his endeavors.

In his visits throughout the ruined country, Bishop Muench impressed his hosts with his amiable energy and his ability to make himself thoroughly at home in any and all circumstances. During the winter cold he often slept in unheated rooms which were the best bishops and priests could offer him, shared their poor food, and often as not offered his Mass in partly ruined churches.

It was not until February that he got back to Rome. The warmth of his welcome amazed him. Even the usually reserved Pope embraced him while voicing sentiments of delight, and then listened to his report with extreme concentration. The private audience lasted well over an hour.

At its close, Bishop Muench asked the Pope: "Holy Father, how long will I be asked to stay on in Germany?"

The Pope smiled sadly. "Indefinitely, my son," he said.

"But, Holy Father, I have a diocese in North Dakota that I must worry about."

The Pope's reply was short and prompt. "The needs of the Church in Germany are more critical than in North Dakota. We have decided to appoint an auxiliary bishop in Fargo to administer the diocese during your absence."

The next day, with a speed that amazed the already stunned visitor, Bishop Leo F. Dworschak, Coadjutor of Rapid City, was recalled to Fargo as auxiliary bishop.

Bishop Muench returned to Germany completely convinced that his greatest life's work would be there for many years to come. It was fortunate for him and for Germany that he was capable of driving himself without mercy. As visitor, he accomplished tremendous things, not the least was his infusion of a note of optimism in the minds of all classes of German Catholics by attending every important meeting, youth rally, religious anniversary and bishop's meeting, at which he usually spoke bringing messages of religious hope and practical common sense.

During the American occupation, the bishop was very busy with his job as liaison consultant for religious affairs. The bishop and General Clay worked with complete harmony, and the general discovered that his conferences with the bishop saved him a great deal of frustration and embarrassment in handling German Catholic affairs at a time when there was no responsible government.

The reverse side of the coin as liaison consultant was his office as vicar delegate for American Catholics in the armed services, and later for their dependents.

These three jobs, which Bishop Muench handled with great devotion, might have used up a stronger person, but he had another still more demanding. He was administrator of the Vatican Mission, originally founded by Monsignor Walter Carroll, which, with the cooperation of General Dwight Eisenhower, was attempting to sort out and repatriate the thousands of refugees who had been brought into Germany as slave labor during the last years of the war—people who had survived unspeakable prison camps or escaped the horrors behind the Iron Curtain. It was a heartbreaking task that required a strong stomach and infinite patience.

It is remarkable, if not outstanding, that the visitator should have become one of the most loved and admired personalities in Germany. We can partly understand this if we remember the engaging nature of Bishop Muench, his wide learning, and the ease with which he wrote and spoke the German language. Another circumstance, which was quite accidental, was a tremendous help to him. In his Lenten pastoral for the Diocese of Fargo in 1945, he had chosen as his subject "One World in Charity." In it he pleaded for a Christian treatment of our enemies and roundly condemned the harsh Morgenthau plan of reducing Germany to a pastoral economy. Unknown to Bishop Muench, someone had taken this letter and translated it into German. Thousands of copies were made by mimeograph or by hand and were circulated widely throughout Germany before the bishop ever came there as visitor. As a result, Bishop Muench found himself already famous and well-known when he arrived in Germany, and the Germans' love and admiration for him grew the more they saw of him.

We can gain some idea of his importance and popularity from the conversations which Bishop Dworschak had with Cardinals Frings and Faulhaber. Cardinal Frings was eloquent in his gratitude to Bishop Muench and almost lyrical in praise of his accomplishments. Bishop Dworschak said: "All of us in Fargo have known from the beginning that the bishop is a great man. That is why we are all so anxious to have him come home soon."

Cardinal Frings looked up in shocked surprise. "What! Back to Fargo! That is utterly unthinkable. Germany needs him."

Two days later, at the close of a Munich visit with Cardinal Faulhaber, the cardinal took Bishop Dworschak aside for a short interval and spoke to him with great feeling of Germany's debt to the apostolic visitor. Bishop Dworschak repeated the same praise of Bishop Muench that he had used in conversation with Cardinal Frings. Cardinal Faulhaber's reaction was even more emphatic: "No! No! Not back to Fargo ever! We have already made our wishes known in Rome that if and when Germany can re-establish diplomatic relations, Bishop Muench will be appointed nuncio without delay."

In 1949, when the phenomenal progress of Germany made it evident that she could shortly look forward to independence from the occupying powers, Pius XII named Bishop Muench regent of the nunciature. In November 1950, in preparation for Germany's freedom, Pius XII conferred upon Bishop Muench the personal title of archbishop, as a preliminary step to naming him papal nuncio to the Bonn Government on March 6, 1951.

As the Pope's representative, the nuncio was extremely active in his attendance at public meetings of every sort. We can get some idea of his popularity by recalling the public Mass which he celebrated in 1958 in Berlin's Olympic Stadium—125,000 people filled the stadium to capacity. Before that, in August 1956 at the Cologne Catholic Congress, Bishop Muench offered

Mass before 500,000. He spoke the same afternoon, along with Chancellor Conrad Adenauer, to an overflow crowd of 800,000.

In 1957, the Bonn Government showed its appreciation for the nuncio when Theodore Huess, President of the West German Republic, conferred upon him the Grand Cross of the Order of Merit. Now there was time to enjoy social affairs and visits of ceremony at the charming nunciature in Bad Godesberg, and for the walks he enjoyed and democratic chats with children and grown people whom he met in the course of his exercise.

With the death of Pius XII and the election of John XXIII, there were many changes in the Roman Curia and among ambassadors of the Holy See throughout the world. No one was surprised when the Holy Father announced on November 16, 1959, that on December 19 he would confer the cardinal's hat on Archbishop Muench and seven others. More extraordinary still, one of the seven was Archbishop Meyer of Chicago. It was a long time since their happy days as teachers at St. Francis Seminary in Milwaukee.

Cardinal Muench found no difficulty in fitting himself into the Roman scene and his new function as a curial cardinal. He had always loved Rome and was no stranger to its life of ceremony and splendor. Yet when the twenty-fifth anniversary of his episcopal consecration came around in 1960, it was to Fargo that he returned for the big celebration on October 15. It was a family affair, and genuine love and affection overflowed in a torrent of praise about the great "Prairie Bishop."

In expressing his thanks, the cardinal said, in the *Catholic Action* "Bulletin":

> The Diocese of Fargo will always be of great interest to me. I shall watch the progress of the Church here very closely. The Bishop, the clergy, the religious, and the laity of this Diocese will always be in my prayers. I will ask Divine Providence to shower its richest blessings on you and yours in generous measure, and so long as I live I shall be grateful for the loyalty and the affection of the people of this Diocese which was demonstrated in such dramatic fashion this past week.

Among the praise that came from afar was a warm letter from Pope John XXIII. In it the Holy Father said:

> We dare not permit this auspicious occasion to go by without giving expression to the fatherly benevolence We feel towards you. We extend to you Our best wishes and congratulations. As Bishop of the Church of Fargo, you gave ample evidence of love and faith in carrying out your pastoral work. Among other things, We admire especially your zealous charity for the workers and those of humble rank. Learned as you are in the social sciences, a watchful and prudent shepherd, you devoted yourself completely to a social order that would be enlightened by right doctrine and promoted by effective action.
>
> In meetings of Bishops, your opinion on these matters was always sought, and when for a number of years you were president of the National Catholic Rural Life Conference, you accepted the challenge with noteworthy wisdom, diligence, and zeal. Later you manifested an even deeper concern for the needy and afflicted, when, after the last war, you were Apostolic Visitor and then Papal Nuncio in Germany. With your usual ingenuity and prudence in discharging heavy responsibilities, you lived up to the high expectations of the See of Peter.

To those who were nearest and dearest to the cardinal, the occasion was tinctured with a certain sadness in that they could see that he was in poor health and not likely to be long spared to them. Their fears were borne out on February 15, 1962, with the death of Cardinal Muench in Salvator Mundi Hospital in Rome.

Rome said her farewell on February 19, 1962, with appropriate splendor in St. Peter's. Pope John presided at the Vatican rites and gave the absolution following the Mass. The central ecumenical council postponed its opening session so that all the Fathers could attend the funeral. Many members of the diplomatic corps also were present.

Later the same day, the cardinal's body began its journey to the United States, accompanied by his secretary Father Raymond Lessard. On February 21, the body of Cardinal Muench reposed at St. John's Cathedral in Milwaukee. Archbishop William E. Cousins celebrated a Pontifical Requiem Mass. The following morning Bishop Leo F. Dworschak led the procession from the funeral home in Fargo to the cathedral and offered Pontifical Mass for the repose of the man he had admired so greatly.

At 8 P.M. the Office of the Dead was recited by the clergy and then repeated in English by the lay persons who attended. The final Funeral Mass, celebrated by Joseph Cardinal Ritter, took place on February 23, in St. Mary's Cathedral. Archbishop Karl J. Alter, Archbishop of Cincinnati, preached the panegyric. Many bishops from Canada and the United States were in attendance, as well as leaders of the state and municipality. The cardinal was buried in St. Mary's Cemetery.

Cardinal Muench might have had an ornate tomb in either Rome or Milwaukee, where he was so lovingly remembered. Instead, with a simplicity that characterized his whole life, he chose to rest in the spot he loved best in the world.

To many people it seemed a strange turn of fate that the bishop of one of the poorest dioceses in the United States should in the end have outranked his metropolitan and achieved the highest honors in the gift of the Vatican.

Actually there was nothing strange about it at all. Cardinal Muench was one of the most magnificently gifted and learned bishops in the world. It was a mark of his quality that he felt at home with popes and heads of government and equally at home with children and the simple-natured farmers of his huge diocese. Like Pius X, he preferred the quiet of a simple life, but a great intuitive pope lifted him out of it with a sure knowledge of his capabilities.

Albert Cardinal Meyer

IN 1892, Milwaukee was devastated by a great fire that burned over twenty-six acres and did some $5,000,000 worth of damage. At the turn of the century the new city that arose on the ruins of the old was a pleasant homey town noted for its beer gardens and the solid character of its citizens.

The Germans especially took their religion with great seriousness; they learned the truths of the faith thoroughly, were practical Catholics devoted to their Church, prayer and the Sacraments, and held their priests in high esteem.

Family life was close and affectionate and was tinged with the broad humor of South Germany and strong in its emphasis on character and respect for authority and learning.

It was in this orderly atmosphere of city and home that Albert Gregory Meyer was born on March 9, 1903, the fifth of a family of five children, three boys and two girls. Albert's father Peter and his mother Mathilda Thelen Meyer were respected parishioners of St. Mary's Church. Peter worked for a manufacturing firm. The family income was modest, but the kindly, self-respecting atmosphere of their home was wonderfully happy.

Albert went to St. Mary's School, staffed by the School Sisters of Notre Dame, a community widely respected for its solid teaching methods and devoted piety, whose old mother house —a great block of buildings on Wisconsin Avenue—was a powerhouse of learning and religion.

Albert, a tall lanky boy, was studious. The nuns soon singled him out as one to be pointed toward the priesthood. They gave him lacy holy cards as prizes and encouraged him in his devotions, especially love of the Blessed Sacrament and God's Mother. He was like a little bishop, they said as they watched him serving at Mass and benediction.

First Communion and confirmation were prepared for with great thoroughness; it was considered a disgrace if a child was unable to answer any question the priest or bishop might ask from the Catechism. A retreat preceded both great occasions, which were carried out with the utmost precision and solemnity after long hours of drilling and instruction. At home, too, First Communion and confirmation were great occasions celebrated with solemnity and good cooking. By the time Albert finished the eighth grade, he was sure of his vocation.

The times were filled with challenge and menace. The arrogance of the Kaiser was pushing the United States toward war as incidents against American rights and shipping mounted along with tempers. War was finally declared on April 6, 1917.

It was a bad time for Milwaukee; a hatred of all Germans swept the country, and feelings were bitter. The war, with its long casualty lists, brought great sorrows to which an influenza epidemic added further tales of woe. Topping it all, in 1919, the Eighteenth Amendment making Prohibition the law of the land put many out of jobs in the beer capital of the United States.

One year spent at Marquette Academy under the expert guidance of the Jesuits prepared Albert for early entry into St. Francis, the diocesan seminary where he distinguished himself as a student during the remainder of his high school and two years of college.

Life at St. Francis had a Germanic thoroughness in its respect for discipline and study, but there was a kind of fraternal family friendliness among professors and students which communicated a warm glow to seminary life, especially in the outdoor activities of baseball, tennis and hockey.

Summers were spent at home in the warm circle of the family.

Albert's two older brothers, Edmund and Norbert, were already self-sufficient; his older sister was a member of their beloved School Sisters of Notre Dame.

So excellent was Albert's record at St. Francis that Archbishop Messmer decided that the boy should take his philosophy and theology at the North American College in Rome.

Albert entered the North American College in 1921. Pius XI was beginning a brilliant pontificate that was to see the settlement of many vexing problems; Mussolini was "making the railroads run," and blowing hot and cold on Church questions.

At his classes in Propaganda, a whole new world opened up for Albert Meyer under skilled professors of the stamp of Cardinals Agagianian and Ruffini. Philosophy and theology provided many stranded paths into the complete understanding of God's world and the immortal democracy of the Church. Those lessons were amplified in the prayer life of Rome which was summed up in gorgeous ceremonies in St. Peter's or in a hundred other splendid churches. What the eye saw and the ear heard in beauty were intimately brought home to the heart in the religious life of the college, beginning with meditation in the morning.

Albert and the other students of his time were fortunate in having Monsignor Mooney as their spiritual director. Looking back from his own eminence later on in life, Albert would be able to say:

"My recollection of Cardinal Mooney goes back to the days when I was a student at the North American College in Rome. He was the revered and greatly beloved spiritual director there. In this capacity he left an indelible mark on all the students, inspiring them with his great learning and his solid spiritual guidance."

Rome and Italy were a fascinating object lesson of some of the greatest moments in history, art, architecture and every outstanding achievement of man's genius. Everything came alive; everything intensified the interrelationships of all learning and the wisdom beyond it. Summers at the Villa Santa Caterina were an added revelation of nature's splendors in blue lakes and snowy mountains.

In July of 1926, Albert's life in the Holy City came to its climax of examinations, retreat, and at last the great day of ordination by Cardinal Basilio Pompilj in the ancient Dominican Church of Santa Maria Sopra Minerva. The body of Catherine of Siena is buried there; it was an added note of happiness for Father Meyer to be ordained in her church.

His first Solemn Mass in Milwaukee brought him another kind of pleasure. In the happy faces of his family and friends he could measure how good the church had been and how lucky he was in the call God had given him.

The aging Archbishop Messmer was pleased with the record Father Meyer had made in achieving his doctorate in theology. As a mark of his pleasure, the archbishop sent him back to Rome in 1927 for three years of study at the Pontifical Bible Institute, which was to bring him his licentiate in sacred scripture and an immeasurably deepened knowledge of the antiquities of Rome and the Holy Land.

He was first assigned to St. Joseph's Church in Waukesha. Barely had he adjusted himself to his duties in the parish and school when, to the disappointment of all who were attracted to the dark-haired affable priest, he was assigned to teach in St. Francis Seminary in the fall of 1931.

Father Meyer had been saddened by the death of Archbishop Messmer in the summer of 1930. The archbishop had been a real friend and benefactor, but the new Archbishop Stritch, who seemed so young on first meeting, was a noted alumnus of the North American College who demonstrated how shrewd his judgment was in moving Father Meyer to a professorship at St. Francis Seminary. It is some indication of the young professor's width of learning that he taught religion, Greek, Latin, and Biblical archaeology and later on dogma and scripture.

The heavy teaching load might have cramped the style of one less energetic and extroverted. Soon after settling into his new quarters, Father Meyer took on the responsibility of looking after a group of Italian families in the district. They were happy to find a priest who knew their language and who was sympathetically at home in their culture and customs. Delight at finding such a man took concrete expression in a missionary chapel in which their religious life could be centered and fostered.

Father Meyer's speaking ability and his ease in applying the age-old wisdom of the Church to the practical solution of modern problems brought him to the attention of the Milwaukee Catholic clubs. Among these, the Serra Club was delighted with the young priest and asked him to be its first chaplain and adviser.

One of the joys of being at St. Francis was the cordial friendship that sprang up between Father Meyer and the seminary rector, Monsignor Muench. They both loved learning and had a special interest in rural problems, literature and the liturgy, all of which they discussed with a spirit that kindled a heightening of interest among the students. A further bond between them was a liking for sports and the outdoors.

The first years of Father Meyer's professorship were depression years; Milwaukee suffered severely. The year 1932 was the worst of all, but there was a glimmer of light as President Roosevelt took desperate measures to restore the shattered economy. Things began to improve, particularly in Milwaukee, when Prohibition was repealed in 1933 in a great wave of celebration, and the big breweries went into full production.

In 1935, Monsignor Muench became the third Bishop of Fargo, North Dakota. Professors and seminarians gave him a boyishly romantic torchlight farewell and with hardly less joy welcomed Father Meyer as their new rector in 1937. Further celebration came with Father Meyer's elevation to the rank of domestic prelate on March 15, 1938, with the title of right reverend monsignor.

The multiple tasks of teacher, rector, club chaplain and pastor, did little or nothing to slow down the monsignor's studious pursuits. One of his outstanding achievements was the translation and annotation of the Epistles of St. John for the new confraternity edition of the New Testament, sponsored by the United States bishops.

Nor did the monsignor forget his family at any step of his career. He loved to go home for weekly visits with his father and mother and to family celebrations with even the more distant members of the Meyer clan in Chicago. A marriage or a christening was sure to get a lift through Monsignor Albert's smiling presence.

Archbishop Stritch was moved up to the greater responsibilities of Chicago in 1939, and was succeeded by Bishop Moses Kiley of Trenton the same year. The new archbishop soon came to appreciate the gifted Monsignor Meyer who so warmly loved Milwaukee and so thoroughly understood its problems.

As the United States drifted into war, and during the war years, both the archbishop and the Rector of St. Francis threw themselves into the complicated problems of those terrible times. All the priests in the diocese were heavily burdened because of the large number of priests who were permitted to join the chaplain service and partly because of the huge number of Army trainees moving in and out of the bases in the Milwaukee area. Monsignor Meyer was one of the most active priests during those years of perpetual motion and tragedy.

No one in the Milwaukee area was really surprised by the news that Monsignor Meyer had been named Bishop of Superior on Washington's Birthday, 1946. At least they were going to keep him in Wisconsin for awhile.

The Meyer clan assembled in force for the consecration of their favorite son in St. John's Cathedral on April 11 of the same year. Archbishop Kiley was the chief consecrator, assisted by Bishop Muench of Fargo and Bishop William P. O'Connor of Madison. Many midwest bishops were in attendance to honor a man they had come to admire for his humility and scholarly eminence.

Fortunately it was not until the bright spring weather of May 10 that the new bishop was installed in his Cathedral of Christ the King by Archbishop Kiley. The winter had been severe, and the cold wind coming in off the lake would have discouraged anything but fur-lined pageantry.

The people of Superior liked their new bishop at once. His commanding presence in the celebration of the liturgy, fatherly interest and simplicity of manners were all commented upon.

The bishop found his diocese vexed with many problems. Superior had seen great days when the iron mines of the Mesabi Range had poured streams of ore through Superior and its twin sister Duluth, across the bay, and the long knifelike ore boats were lined up in the bay like herds of elephants. Now, especially after the desperate effort of the war years, the mines had practically petered out. There was no longer great wealth in the city.

Bishop Meyer built where he could and as money and circumstances allowed in the first years of scarcity after the war. With characteristic simple friendliness, he visited all parts of his large diocese, encouraged the building of schools, and quietly fostered missions and retreats that were instrumental in bringing numerous converts into the Church.

Winters were fierce and long, but the mild summers along the shore of the great lake were delightful. As an archeologist, the bishop took lively interest in the Apostle Islands off the coast near Bayfield. They had been a missionary center in the brave old days of Recollets and Jesuits who had explored the country and brought the faith to the Indians.

The tall bishop had always enjoyed a good game of tennis, in which his height (6 ft. 2 in.) had given him an advantage. Now he succumbed to the lure of fishing in the lovely lakes of the diocese, and when asked about his interests in sports, always replied with wit: "I used to be fond of tennis but now I like fishing. It's the apostolic recreation, you know."

In 1951, five years after his arrival, the entire diocese assisted Bishop Meyer in celebrating his silver jubilee with liturgical pomp and appropriate gifts. Orators spoke of his virtues and accomplishments, and these were obvious to all who loved and valued him and hoped that he would be their shepherd for years to come.

The Holy See thought otherwise. Soon after the death of Archbishop Kiley, Bishop Meyer was named Archbishop of Milwaukee on July 21, 1953. This time he would not have the pleasure of seeing his mother's face light up in welcome; she had died the preceding year.

Apostolic Delegate Archbishop Cicognani installed Archbishop Meyer in his cathedral on September 24, and called attention to the tradition of youthful bishops who had ruled the see, notably Archbishop Stritch, who was only forty-three at the time of his elevation. At fifty, Archbishop Meyer was still in that tradition of youth, since bishops seldom become metropolitans before the age of sixty.

Milwaukee received its new archbishop with the special enthusiastic affection reserved for home-town boys. It stood loyally behind him in a vigorous building program that made his five years there as archbishop an outstanding achievement.

The vigorous youth of the new archbishop was apparent. Though he had a relaxed manner of working and a half-shy way of avoiding the center of the spotlight if anyone else could be praised, Milwaukee began to find permanent evidence of his spiritual and executive forcefulness.

During his five-year reign, 34 new churches were built and 13 others were in the planning stage. In addition to this lightning expansion, 74 school buildings, 20 additional auditoriums and classrooms, 3 hospitals, 40 new convents and 12 rectories, as well as additions and expansions of older plants, were built.

All the colleges in the diocese were encouraged to expand and build, which they did with alacrity, and St. Francis Seminary was enlarged and modernized at a cost of $3,000,000 raised in a little over a three-year period.

Archbishop Meyer's religious and civic leadership was remarkable. Members of women's clubs and guilds found themselves charmed and moved into important programs; the Holy Name Society, Catholic Youth Organization, and other men's clubs grew in numbers and influence; the retreat movement took on new fervor and importance.

The archbishop also played important roles on the national

scene as president general of the National Catholic Educational Association, episcopal chairman of the important educational department of the National Catholic Welfare Council, and Vice-Chancellor of the Extension Society.

So outstanding was his achievement that few were amazed when he was chosen to be Archbishop of Chicago after the tragic death of Cardinal Stritch on September 24, 1958. Chicago gave Archbishop Meyer a neighborly welcome and Milwaukee bade him good-bye as if he was merely on loan to its bigger neighbor. Its citizens begrudged his going, because they knew his worth and admired his talents, but they took pride in a home-town boy's advancement.

Archbishop Meyer's ceremonial entry into his new responsibilities was marred with tragedy sixteen days after his formal installation in Holy Name Cathedral in the flash fire at Holy Angels School, which took the lives of 87 children and 3 nuns.

The archbishop, cut to the heart, outdid himself in spiritual consolation, and with a stern face began a crash program of school modernization throughout the entire diocese.

He streamlined the diocesan matrimonial court so that its pending cases would be dealt with more speedily. Along with these improvements, the archbishop caused something of a stir by banning Bingo. His reason for the ban was a moral one. Bingo was illegal in Chicago, and the bishop didn't think it correct or moral for pastors and organizations to expect the police to wink at transgression of the law.

He also stood out boldly for social justice in a statement presented to the President's civil rights commission in May of 1959, in which he criticized racially segregated housing and appealed to all responsible members of the community to cooperate in solving the problem.

A little over a year after Archbishop Meyer was installed in Chicago, Pope John XXIII nominated him to the College of Cardinals on November 16, 1959. Chicago rejoiced at the news in its usual robust fashion.

The archbishop was personally pleased with the honor because his old friend Aloisius Muench was raised to the purple on the same day. It was a signal honor for St. Francis that two of her most noted sons were named cardinals at the same time; no other seminary in the United States could point to such a coincidental distinction.

But the newly nominated cardinal whose whole career had been anchored with the deepest spirituality took this occasion to point up the meaning of the gift in the light of eternity:

> Our Holy Father, Pope John XXIII, has most graciously deigned to bestow a great honor on the Archdiocese of Chicago. In naming me to the Sacred College of Cardinals he has given a singular mark of His paternal benevolence to all of us. I am profoundly moved by the realization that this honor especially touches me and my position towards you as your Archbishop. In your name, as well as in my own name, I have expressed to His Holiness our sense of deep gratitude and appreciation. May I ask you to join with me in fervent prayer for His Holiness as we renew to Him our filial devotion and work with Him for the welfare of the Church and the cause of religion here in our beloved Archdiocese?
>
> I am confident that this new honor for Chicago will not prompt us to thoughts of vanity or pride. Rather, we will strive to realize that it represents a renewed challenge to devote ourselves even more unselfishly to the advancement of the Kingdom of Christ in our midst. Rightly we rejoice in the extraordinary vitality of Catholic life here in our great Archdiocese. We should not rest on our laurels, however, when so much remains to be done. When I came into your midst a year ago as your Archbishop, I earnestly asked you to give me the full measure of your cooperation as I pledged myself to spend and be spent for the welfare of your souls. As I renew this dedication of myself I ask you to join with me in the work that is mutually ours. In this we need above all the grace of God, which is given to us in full measure if we ask Him in humble confidence.
>
> I want to thank all of you for your many messages of congratulations. It is physically impossible for me to answer all these greetings personally. Will you please accept this expression of my profound gratitude for your wonderful spirit of cooperation during the past year, and the promises of your continued help expressed in your messages of good wishes. May we all

continue to work together so that we may worthily carry these new honors for the glory of God and the salvation of souls. May the Sacred Hearts of Jesus and Mary be with you all as I again thank you most warmly and extend to all of you my blessing and the assurance of my prayers.

The huge jet plane carrying the cardinal-elect, his lay and clerical friends and relations, left Chicago on December 10, 1959. Between 2,000 and 3,000 people had gathered for the occasion. The League of Loreto presented the smiling cardinal-elect with a medal of Our Lady of Loreto, patroness of airways. He then blessed the block-long machine, and it soared off into the sky. En route over the ocean, the cardinal-elect spent the hours chatting and praying with his friends, among whom were his two brothers Edmund and Norbert and their wives, and his sister, Sister Mary Therese, C.S.A.

The archbishop was met at the Rome airport by Cardinal Ottaviani and Bishop Muench. The two old friends clasped each other in a wide embrace. After assuring himself that all was in order for the comfort of his guests, Archbishop Meyer went to St. Mary of the Lake for some much needed rest, though he still appeared bright and refreshed. Cardinals-Elect Muench and Meyer received their *biglietti* of nomination at the splendid new North American College on the Janiculum on December 14, 1959.

The red biretta came to Cardinal Meyer from the hands of jovial Pope John XXIII in the Hall of Consistories on December 16. The following morning, in the magnificent public consistory in St. Peter's, the red *galero* was placed on Cardinal Meyer's head. Later that afternoon at St. Mary's of the Lake, he received his red hat from a representative of the Holy Father, who expressed the Pope's warm congratulations to the new prince.

Visits of ceremony to the cardinal dean and other members of the Curia followed. Cardinal Meyer was pleased to receive St. Cecelia in Trastevere as his titular church. This fabulous church, which goes back to early Christian times, is supposed to be built above St. Cecilia's house, and the body of the saint rests behind the main altar. Many times remodeled and enriched, the church is a fascinating study for anyone interested in antiquity, architecture or holiness.

Though the courtyard and inner church are beautiful, the outer wall of the compound is nudged by slum buildings usually festooned with strings of laundry. The Rector of St. Cecilia's, Monsignor Umberto Dionisio, a brilliantly learned man, is widely admired by Americans for his charm, humor and hospitality.

In taking possession of his church, the cardinal found it decorated with festive brocades. Monsignor Dionisi, clad in a splendid cope, met his new patron at the door of the church, offered him holy water and the cross to kiss, after which—to the triumphant strain of *Ecce Sacerdos Magnus*—he was escorted to his throne, passing en route the crypt shrine of the saint, with its touching recumbent figure of St. Cecelia.

The monsignor welcomed the cardinal with graceful words of praise; the cardinal replied with equal warmth and felicity. There were dinners and festivities celebrating the new honor, culminating in a private audience with Pope John for Cardinal Meyer and his entire party. Everyone was charmed with the jovial simplicity of the Pope, who embodied the qualities Cardinal Meyer had particularly stressed throughout his life. "All honor must take second place to that of being good priests and pastors of souls."

The cardinal's plane had been expected to land in Chicago on December 20, at 9:30 P.M. The airport was buffeted with gusts of high winds, snow and sleet, and those who had braved the weather—some 400 men and women—were genuinely worried as they waited in the brightly lighted lounge. Reassuring bulletins came from time to time. Finally after two hours the powerful jet put its wheels down on the slippery field. The waiting group milled about their new prince, kissing his ring, congratulating him, wishing him well.

Cardinal Meyer offered his first public Low Mass on December 22, at Columbus Hospital which had been founded by Mother Cabrini. The cardinal had always been devoted to this towering social saint; she had spent so many months of her busy lifetime in Chicago, and had died in Columbus Hospital in 1917.

Holy Name Cathedral blazed with lights and flowers on Christmas Eve of 1959, in preparation for the cardinal's Solemn Pontifical Mass. The distinguished congregation was one vast smile of pleasure as the liturgical procession appeared to the thunder of the organ and it watched the cardinal's tall splendidly clad figure walking down the center aisle to the high throne in the sanctuary.

He was a prince indeed, but he had labored always to show people the spiritual beauty of life, and his motto, "Thy kingdom come," blazoned on the back of his throne, explained his belief that the power and the glory reflect on no man but on Christ the world's Saviour. As the Christmas liturgy unfolded with its notes of heavenly glory and divine humility, the watchers savored for a moment the full meaning of what the cardinal had sought to teach them.

When all the amiable celebrations with their torrents of praise and commendation were over, priests and laymen were inspired by the devoted way in which Cardinal Meyer plunged into the work of his vast diocese, the largest in the United States. In the year 1960, over $10,000,000 were spent on charity alone, of which $5,000,000 went for the care of children in foster homes and ten institutions.

Cardinal Meyer did not look on his diocese of 2,000,000 souls complacently. As he went about for confirmations and the dedication of five new schools and buildings, he constantly stressed the necessity of "mission mindedness, the practical expression of the divine plan for the spread of Catholicism through human instruments." Catholics should be apostles in word and work, yearning for souls as Christ did when he commanded the Apostles to teach all nations.

One cannot go to Rome, even for a red hat, without feeling uplifted and moved by the democracy of the Church in action. The son of a peasant sat on the throne of Peter. Assembled around him were his distinguished sons in the Senate of the

Church, most of them coming out of circumstances as humble as the Holy Father's.

In Chicago, the cardinal saw how different things were in the occasional explosions of religious hatred, particularly where Negroes were concerned. Perhaps it was with this in mind that His Eminence called a clergy conference for September 20 and 21, 1960, to discuss outstanding race problems.

The conference, attended by 25,000 priests, met in Resurrection Auditorium at 5052 West Jackson Boulevard. Cardinal Meyer, in simple direct prose, gave the outstanding speech. It has since been published in pamphlet form under the title "Mantle of Leadership," and shows that the cardinal is still a great teacher. He told his priests that they and all Catholics should feel it a matter of justice to assist the Negro "in attaining his rights and equality in every way possible, not thinking of his conversion but of his human dignity." "The Mantle of Leadership" demands that we show all people that the church really loves them, as Christ loved and died for all humanity. Words are not enough; we must show our sincerity by deeds.

Thoughts and deeds do provide convenient measuring sticks. Measured by both, Cardinal Meyer's life and works demonstrate his capacity of greatness, enhanced by his approachable and attractive humanity. Priests and people admire him; more important still, they love him. Many observers are convinced that in learning, vision and executive brilliance, he is curial timber. Few would deny that conclusion, except in the interest in keeping him in Chicago.

Joseph Cardinal Ritter

THE town of New Albany, Indiana, nestles in a bend of the
Ohio River, across from the industrial city of Louisville,
Kentucky, famed for its whisky, tobacco and horse racing. In
1892, the year in which Joseph Ritter was born on July 20, New
Albany was a quiet town bowered in trees and largely in-
habited by solid German families, self-respecting, pious and
industrious.

Benjamin Harrison was President of the United States, but
before the year ran out he was to be defeated for a second term
by Grover Cleveland and an Illinois lawyer named Adlai Ste-
venson. The Gay Nineties were just getting under full steam;
everyone was singing a bouncy, tear-jerking ballad, "After The
Ball"; George W. J. Ferris had designed a new thrill known as
the Ferris Wheel; and John L. Sullivan had lost his boxing
crown to James J. Corbett.

Joseph's father Nicholas was a baker of modest means. His
mother, Bertha Luette Ritter, was of good German lineage
and had the humorous motherly qualities and the placid house-
wifely genius that make a happy home.

Religion centered in the solid collection of buildings clus-
tered about the round-topped steeple of St. Mary's Church on
Eighth Street. It was there that the future cardinal was baptized, made his First Communion, and was confirmed.

Gradually the roly-poly form of the boy lengthened out into
the spare muscular frame of a young man of medium height. In

the process, he experienced all the stimulation that goes with living on a great river in a community in which the bright face of nature and native ingenuity provide innocent and delightful pleasure.

Joseph's three older brothers, Harry, Frank and Edwin, took good care of him and taught him the manly, self-reliant outlook that distinguished even his earliest years.

At an early age, Joseph demonstrated his fondness for everything connected with the Church and its services. As devoted altar boys, he and his best friend Herman Emlinger cheerfully got up in the gray dawns of winter to serve early Mass, and even enjoyed returning to the church on Sundays for the long slow rhythm of Vespers, culminating in Benediction of the Blessed Sacrament in which the light of the candle-lustered altar and glittering monstrance was reflected on their ecstatic faces.

In May, they made ornamental altars to the Blessed Virgin, and they looked up to her with delight as their patron and immortal Mother, powerful in everything.

Both boys enjoyed the favor of the two parish priests: Father Faller, the pastor, had a dignity that went with his job and demanded respect; Father Borries was younger and more humorous—friendship with him was easy and rewarding. The direction of the boys' hearts was clearly evident in the fact that they often played at saying Mass, taking turns at being priest and server and emulating, quite without satire, the mannerisms and orotundities of their two heroes at St. Mary's rectory.

So sure of their vocation were Joe and Herm, that in the seventh grade they told Father Borries of their desire to begin studies for the priesthood after they passed the eighth grade.

The Ritters joyfully gave their permission to Joseph. It had been evident to Mrs. Ritter for many years that he was inclined toward the priesthood. She felt absolutely sure that the desire wasn't a passing fancy. Such a destiny was a high one, but he was a fine boy and the grace of God would do the remaining work of perfecting him. It would be the crown of her ardent belief and many prayers.

Herm's experience with his parents was quite different. They felt that he was too young to make up his mind about such a serious step. He would have to wait until he finished high school.

The two boys graduated from grade school in 1906. (It was the year of the San Francisco earthquake, and many pious people were saying it was a judgment on the wicked city.) The Ritters sat through the long exercise with placid satisfaction—delighted to see their slim blue-eyed son pointed out as an honor student.

After a last happy summer, part work and part play, the two friends parted with reluctance when Joe took the train for St. Meinrad's Abbey at which he was to finish his high school and college work.

The Benedictines at the Abbey received Joseph with the sincere but homely courtesy that distinguished St. Meinrad's at the time. The piety of the great house had a solid German weave; studies were serious and thorough, and discipline was strict.

Joseph had his moments of loneliness at first, but his inquisitive mind was soon intrigued with reading and study. And he had other rewarding experiences which were to influence his life in all the years to come.

The first of these was a love of the liturgy. Assisting at Mass in St. Mary's Church had always been a moving experience to Joseph. This was intensified at St. Meinrad's, where the Mass and the Holy Office were mounted with a splendor he had never imagined possible; the rich flow of the chant, the beauty of lights and vestments, the sonorous measures of the Latin, all spoke to his impressionable heart with immortal beauty.

Joseph also learned to appreciate the country and country life, and he came to understand why the monks said: "To labor is to pray." Even in its coarsest aspects, there was a purity in living close to the earth and a feeling of health and exaltation in the changing seasons as the earth renewed itself and as man watched and assisted in field and forest.

Discipline was strict, but it was also informed with quick kindness, broad understanding and humor. There were picnics and sports for occasional relief, visits from the family, too, and interludes in the warm atmosphere of his home.

All these were magnified when Herm, true to his purpose, arrived at St. Meinrad's in 1910. Joseph found an exciting happiness in showing his friend the sights of the abbey and the lovely countryside and in coaching him in the customs of the place.

By 1911, Joseph had finished high school and junior college. Taft was President, but Teddy Roosevelt was threatening to run against him at the next election. Everyone was mad about speed and the new autos that were breaking all the old records.

A complete and thorough grounding in the classics had prepared young Ritter for the study of philosophy, a field that fascinated him and opened his mind for the luminous truths of theology.

The last four years at St. Meinrad's, which now seemed like a second home to the young man, passed quickly. He was so eager to perfect himself for the priesthood that he learned everything with great thoroughness. When he began to practice saying Mass in preparation for the great day, he brought the same devotion to the rubrics that he had always given his studies. Only, in this case a little fear shook him in thinking of his terrible responsibility in calling down the Son of God each day.

But it was completely without doubt that he gave himself to God in the subdiaconate. Like the young Samuel, he said: "Here I am, Lord."

On May 30, 1917, Joseph Ritter was ordained to the priesthood in the abbey church. Bishop Chartrand anointed Joseph's hands, and then the newly ordained priest joined his fellows in co-offering Mass with the bishop. Father Ritter was so happy that he went through the first days in a sort of delighted trance: the first blessings for family and friends, the happy tears of his mother, his first Mass, the banquet at St. Mary's, the reception at home, all seemed part of a pleasant dream. What a fortunate man he was, doubly happy in the joy reflected in the faces of his parents, his four brothers and the baby sister Catherine they all loved so well.

After a much-needed holiday, Father Joe received his assignment as an assistant at St. Patrick's Church in Indianapolis. He had hoped that he might have a chance to study in Rome, which his scholastic record merited roundly. Bishop Chartrand was unwilling to spare the young priest, and from what ensued it appears that the bishop valued him, urgently needed him, and had his own plans for his advancement.

Father Ritter had hardly begun to find himself at St. Patrick's when he was moved up to be second assistant at the Cathedral of SS. Peter and Paul. Bishop Chartrand lived in the cathedral rectory with apostolic simplicity, and he soon noted the tonic effect of his new assistant. It wasn't only that he had a talent for making things run smoothly, his sermons were excellent and the religious life of the busy parish began to show the effect of his presence. In addition, the people liked him, and he had an easy, humorous manner in all that he did.

When the first assistant, Father Alphonse J. Smith, later Bishop of Nashville, was sent to found a new parish, Father Ritter succeeded him as first assistant to Bishop Chartrand.

Little by little, the bishop began to give Father Ritter a larger share in the control and governance of the parish. Wide powers were delegated to him in May 1924. Everyone rejoiced when Holy Father Benedict XV also made Father Ritter an honorary doctor of sacred theology in recognition of his studious eminence, and devoted labor in advancing the spiritual condition of the cathedral parish. The following year, Bishop Chartrand, in a further burst of generosity, relinquished his title of cathedral pastor to Father Ritter.

The bishop, whose saintly life and devotion to the Blessed Eucharist were widely admired, had always preferred to rule the diocese as a father rules his home. This admirable quality had served well for many years, but with the increase of the Catholic population in the diocese and the social demands of the times, it was becoming increasingly difficult for any one man, however devoted, to look after the multifarious details that cried for attention and solution.

In the eight years after Father Ritter was named pastor of the cathedral, the bishop found himself looking more and more to him for advice and quick decision. The times were distinctly out of joint. First, the Church came into violent collision with the Ku Klux Klan, which had its headquarters in Indianapolis. Bigotry and active violence were stirred up all over the country; sheeted cowards and the ignorant marched, burned their crosses, and bullied until the time when public scandals exposed the kind of sorry rascals they were.

Bishop Chartrand and Father Ritter had met the threat with prayer and careful instruction, but hardly had the Klan disappeared from the scene when the Depression struck.

Once more the two men betook themselves to prayer and scraped together every penny of personal and diocesan funds for use in active charity. By 1933, a new mood of hope had begun to take shape. Conditions were better. People were beginning to find jobs and incomes again.

Many people had wondered why Father Ritter was not a monsignor. As if in answer to that universal question, the aging bishop asked Rome for an auxiliary. Father Ritter's name headed the list of possible candidates.

There was wide rejoicing on February 3, 1933, when the news was released that Father Ritter was to be Auxiliary Bishop of Indianapolis. The phone in the rectory rang incessantly, messages of congratulations poured in, modest gifts multiplied.

The consecration took place in the cathedral, below the massive Calvary group ornamenting the main altar. Bishop Chartrand was consecrator, assisted by Bishop Ledvina of Corpus Christi, Texas, and Bishop Alphonse J. Smith of Nashville. It was a homey affair. The new bishop's entire family proudly watched the long, slow ceremony in which their Joe became a recognized leader in the Church. It was the crown of Bertha Ritter's life.

In keeping with the austerity of the times and conditions in the diocese, the banquet after the ceremony—Cardinal Ritter recalls—cost $1.25 a plate. This also included the cost of the music.

Two days after the consecration, Bishop Ritter was appointed vicar general of the diocese. It was obvious to all that Bishop Chartrand was nearing the end of his life. The new bishop was only forty-one years of age. Bishop Chartrand died in December 1933, making a bleak but busy Christmas for Bishop Ritter, who had long loved the saintly old man as a true father in Christ.

Until March 24, 1934, Bishop Ritter ruled the diocese as administrator. On that day news came that the Holy See had appointed him to succeed Bishop Chartrand as Bishop of Indianapolis. The announcement caused considerable surprise in ecclesiastical circles, because an auxiliary bishop seldom succeeds to the rule of a diocese, though that had not been true in the earlier days of Church history in the United States. Archbishop John T. McNicholas, of Cincinnati, came to install the new bishop on his baroque throne in the cathedral on April 24, 1934.

The initial task facing the young bishop was the reorganization of the diocese according to the needs and demands of modern times. He proved to be an excellent executive. He was alert, brisk, readily delegated authority, and made instant decisions without losing his simplicity or sense of humor. The Catholic Charities were reorganized and made more efficient, and all the other diocesan bureaus were streamlined to give prompt service.

With homespun realism, Bishop Ritter prepared the way for the closest possible cooperation between clergy and laity. Knowing full well the driving power of good women, he organized a diocesan unit of the National Council of Catholic Women. With their help, the Legion of Decency began to exert its influence in such a fashion that it attracted attention all over the United States.

The bishop did not forget the youth of the diocese. A unit of the Catholic Youth Organization was set up and became extremely active, not merely in athletics but on spiritual, social and cultural levels of approach aimed at the whole man.

In 1936, the financial condition of the diocese was so much improved that Bishop Ritter decided to finish the cathedral. Work on its classical façade was begun at Easter and finished in time for the midnight Mass on Christmas morning, to the pride and joy of the entire diocese.

With canny wisdom, Bishop Ritter also established a diocesan home missions board which channeled funds from the wealthier parishes to those which were poor or in need. As an adjunct to this active and provident charity, he organized a street-preaching unit composed of priests and laymen. It was their task to go into the small or backward communities to spread the faith and bring back to the Church those weak sheep who through ignorance, sloth, or the pressures of modern life, had strayed from the fold.

Bishop Ritter also played a prominent part nationally by his active participation in the liturgical and rural life movements. He was so busy and so available for any and all occasions that advanced the good of the faith and the good of souls that some wags in the diocese good-temperedly credited him with bilocation.

There was promise, too, for the determined and careful way in which he attacked the diocesan debt. In this instance he consulted business experts and followed their advice humbly.

A census taken by the Catholic Women's League showed that the diocese was growing swiftly and had a population of 173-463. This was reflected in more than a score of new parishes and schools organized and blessed in the years before the Second World War. Among the outstanding gains was a quiet integration of the parochial schools.

The year 1941 brought both joy and sorrow to the busy bishop. He blessed a new shrine in the cathedral. It was dedicated to the Blessed Virgin, and centered in the superb gift of Bellini's "Madonna of the Forest," presented by Mr. and Mrs. William Thompson of Indianapolis. Bishop Ritter also pontificated at the last Mass in the Church of St. Mary Magdalen. The United States Government had condemned the property as a part of the area set aside for the testing of explosives. The occasion was a sad one for all the Catholics of Indiana. St. Mary Magdalen had been established in 1830, and the church which was to be razed had been built in 1861, at the outset of the Civil War.

A second sorrow, nearer still, touched him in the death of his mother on December 13, 1941. She had done much to inspire his life, and the bishop realized that never again would any person be as interested in his welfare and progress.

The dedication of a Negro church, St. John's, in Evansville, in May, and the splendid new St. Thomas School in Indianapolis, rounded out the year.

With the attack on Pearl Harbor on December 7, 1941, all building stopped as the United States girded herself for war. Within a year, Bishop Ritter had released twenty-three of his much-needed priests for service as chaplains in the armed forces. He vigorously participated in all the war drives and did his utmost to comfort his people as the long casualty lists began to appear.

Sorrow once again struck the bishop in the death of his father Nicholas; his long life and sterling virtues had helped his sons toward the realization of their best.

The following year, on November 17, 1944, an exciting bit of news shared the war headlines. The Diocese of Indianapolis had been elevated to the rank of an archdiocese. Two new Indiana dioceses, Evansville and Lafayette, had been created. Bishop Ritter became the new archbishop and was installed with austere pomp and a minimum of celebration, in keeping with wartime regulations.

June 1945 saw the archbishop at his smiling best in the dedication of the De Paul Center for the cultural and recreational activities of Catholic Negroes of Indianapolis. Confirmations were heavy, among them those of twenty-eight converts in the disciplinary barracks at Fort Benjamin Harrison, an occasion that touched the bishop deeply.

As 1946 dawned, the archbishop might well have envisaged his entire tranquil future in the capital city of Indiana; he loved his state and was happy with his people, who responded with such generosity to his ministry and dreams.

Everything pointed to his stability in his present post when on March 27 he was invested with the Sacred Pallium, his insignia of Metropolitan dignity, by the Most Reverend John F. Knoll of Fort Wayne, Indiana. Among those present on the occasion were the two bishops of the newly created dioceses, Bishop Gummelsman of Evansville, and Bishop Bennett of Lafayette.

In April, Archbishop Ritter was tremendously pleased with the response to his appeal for the Bishop's War and Emergency Relief Fund. Almost $20,000 was collected, and that tidy sum was inestimably augmented in May with the opening, under the direction of the Propagation of the Faith Office—under the direction of Victor Goosens—of a mission salvage bureau, the second of its kind in the United States.

In the following month, with its crowded schedule of confirmations and commencement exercises, the archbishop announced the formation of three new parishes in Indianapolis: St. Anthony's, Holy Spirit and the Immaculate Heart of Mary.

In whatever free moments presented themselves, Archbishop Ritter drove out to Lake Maxinkuckee, where he had a modest refuge offering him the joys of fishing, boating and sun. His old love for the country was still enshrined in his heart, and he was never more happy than in the midst of the simplicities of sky and water.

On Sunday, July 21, 1946, the day after the archbishop's fifty-fourth birthday, he drove through the wilting heat to the chancery at 128 West Georgia Street. Entering the warm quiet of his office, he unlocked the box that held his private mail. On top of the pile of letters was one from the apostolic delegate in Washington. It informed Archbishop Ritter that Pius XII had selected him to succeed Cardinal Glennon as Archbishop of St. Louis.

There was time to pray about it, and the bishop did, fully realizing that it would wrench his heart to depart from the homespun atmosphere and the people he loved for a larger diocese where his responsibilities would be multiplied enormously. Yet the Pope had honored him and selected him—it was inconceivable that he should refuse the heavier burden.

The public announcement of his appointment was given to the press by the apostolic delegate on July 26. The people were sorry to lose their bishop. He had paid off over $3,000,000 of diocesan debts, and they could see and feel the vigorous force of the Church in every aspect of their lives—a tribute to the bishop's zeal, spiritual inspiration and hard work.

The priests of the diocese were even sorrier. The bishop had never stood on ceremony with them; he was quick to praise, slow to blame, and if they were sick or in trouble, he was the first to give them encouragement and practical help. Priests and people felt it significant that his last act among them was the closing of the Forty Hours Devotion at the cathedral, at which he was the celebrant.

In St. Louis, the announcement of Archbishop Ritter's appointment led to considerable activity among the newspapers. Journalists found nothing whatever about Bishop Ritter in the morgues of the local papers, and at first considered it strange that the Holy Father had selected for the venerable See of St. Louis a prelate whose entire education had been obtained on the Indiana prairies where he had spent his entire life.

Starting with his arrival at Union Station, the welcoming throng of Church and civic dignitaries began to find practical evidence of the Pope's wisdom in selecting Archbishop Ritter for the new post.

The smiling prelate apologized to Mayor Kaufman for coming to town at such "a busy time"—the opening of the world series between the St. Louis Cardinals and the Boston Red Sox.

The archbishop went on to tell the assembly: "I am happy to be here and I hope God will bless my work among you . . . my job, as I see it, is to do my best to advance the cause of religion and the civic and social welfare of the community."

Next morning Archbishop Ritter was formally enthroned in

his splendid new cathedral by the apostolic delegate, the Most Reverend Amleto Cicognani. The great cathedral was crowded, and many priests and visiting prelates were present.

Some Monday-morning quarterbacks later found it prophetic that the archbishop's first public appearance after his enthrone-ment was at a conference on Negro welfare held on October 16 in the Visitation School, the only integrated school in the dio-cese.

For almost a year Archbishop Ritter studied the records and prayed for guidance. Cardinal Glennon had begun the work of integration cautiously, with a letter to certain pastors, ask-ing them to start the work of enrolling Negroes in their schools. So far, only the Visitation had completely complied with the suggestion.

With the approach of the school term in 1947, Archbishop Ritter issued a directive to all the schools of the diocese, order-ing them to end segregation at once. There was an immediate flare-up of animosity and resentment in various communities. A committee of laymen was appointed to oppose the move. It went first to the archbishop. In his quiet way, he explained that the Church makes no distinction between men because of their color; it is the positive duty of all Christians to agree with the mind of the Church in this matter, which is based on the Bible and moral and logical principles, not on feeling or prejudice.

The committee did not agree, and next took its case to the apostolic delegate, who sided with Archbishop Ritter, giving sage advice but no satisfaction.

News broke that the committee would now seek a court ban against the bishop's order. This information was relayed to Archbishop Ritter in Perryville, where he had gone to confirm a large group at Assumption Church. The archbishop at once telephoned to the chancery in St. Louis, and dictated a letter to be read in all the churches of the diocese at all Masses on the following Sunday, warning those who threatened civil action that execution of such measures would merit automatic excom-munication from the Church.

The law of the Church (canon law on which all civil codes

were originally based) forbids Catholics to institute civil suits against their lawful superiors, and Archbishop Ritter was well within his rights in calling this to the attention of the committee.

The letter was read on September 21, 1947. As a result, the committee dissolved itself and integration took place. Six and a half years later, the Supreme Court ordered segregation ended for the whole United States. Archbishop Ritter had proved to be an important pathfinder for social justice.

Equally in advance of his times was his creation of an archdiocesan expansion fund in an Easter Letter of 1949, which directed that the unusually large collection on that day, formerly retained in each parish for expenses, was to be sent to the chancery to help poor parishes and build schools, churches and other institutions.

Some idea of the magnitude of this move can be estimated by looking at the amount spent on the diocesan building program from 1950 to December 1955—the astonishing total of $48,500,000.

As a tribute to Archbishop Ritter's leadership, he was asked to give the midterm baccalaureate address at Notre Dame University. He was given an honorary degree of doctor of laws at the graduation exercise, along with a solemn-faced young Senator named John Fitzgerald Kennedy.

The catholicity of the archbishop's mind also made news. The Archbishop Ritter World Mission Exhibition in May 1953, was a bombshell to the parochial-minded by its revelation of the extent and diversity of the Church's missionary activity the world over. The differing rites, colors of the participants, and the splendid sampling of the Church's works of mercy, art and education, were a revelation to many in and out of the Church.

As a practical corollary to this demonstration, the archbishop sent a group of six carefully prepared priests of St. Louis to La Paz, Bolivia, for work in the missions.

As had happened in Indianapolis, it fell to Archbishop Ritter to finish the decoration of his cathedral in St. Louis, one of the largest and finest cathedrals in the United States. The golden mosaics in the vestibule, paying tribute to the life of the great St. Louis, find artistic amplification in the lovely Beatitude mosaics in the nave, and in the dome over the altar in which the Twelve Apostles cluster with some of the splendor to be seen at Ravenna in the Church of Sant' Apollinare Nuovo.

Yet the challenge of decorating a cathedral he did not build is not the real test of Archbishop Ritter's esthetic subtlety; it is rather to be found in the new chancery next door to the cathedral rectory on Lindell Boulevard.

The cathedral is a massive edifice in which the dome is the outstanding feature. In building the modern chancery, the chief problem was to select a form that would harmonize with the domal character of the great church.

The archbishop elected to build his chancery on the land adjoining the massive gray stone cathedral rectory. It is a graceful circular building with a generous basement and two spacious stories. The delicate arches that support the frames for the wide panels of glass are as modern as a building by Frank Lloyd Wright. Inside, the visitor enters a semicircular hall terminating in a long wall against which a receptionist's desk stands. The entire floor is paved with delicately pink-flecked white marble, and the eye is carried up two stories to the domed ceiling of stained glass in jeweled blues and reds.

The wall behind the receptionist's desk marks off the beginning of the cardinal's office which is the center of the building. Surrounding it is the outer curve with the chancellors' offices on one side and a board room and reception rooms on the other. The second floor contains offices and reception rooms for the auxiliary bishops, and the basement has a small theatre for large meetings, and ample filing facilities.

Some idea of Archbishop Ritter's endless activities may be seen in the constant school expansion plan in the opening of new parishes, in the $5,000,000 Glennon Hospital for children and the new $14,000,000 St. John's Hospital. Yet the general welfare of his city and all its people has been well served by his endorsement of public school bond issues and his active co-operation in the civic work of neighborhood rehabilitation.

If this general sampling of his activities is set in its proper frame of meetings, confirmations, speeches, and personal appearances, one can see at a glance how much he has accomplished and how hard he works for his people.

The archbishop's worth is recognized widely outside his own diocese. On November 11, 1956, Pius XII named him assistant at the pontifical throne, an honor that gives him a place in the Pope's household and ranks only a step below the cardinalate. In 1952, he was named president of the National Catholic Educational Association. The following year he was appointed a member of the governing board of the Catholic Welfare Conference. In 1958 he headed the new liturgical apostolate, and in 1959, became head of the N.C.W.C.'s legal department. These are but a few of his responsibilities in the nation and the world.

The busy archbishop found a letter from Pope John XXIII in his mail of Wednesday, December 14, 1961. It informed him that he was to be made a cardinal, but enjoined secrecy until the announcement was made in Rome on Friday, December 16.

The news caused genuine excitement in St. Louis and the nation. Reporters were given their due at an hour's conference in the cardinal-elect's library at 4510 Lindell Boulevard, in which he answered questions patiently and allowed himself to be photographed from every angle.

The visitors, the messages and the necessary preparations took endless hours, but the archbishop went through every item on his regular schedule, despite the new demands. It is pleasant to record that on his last Saturday in St. Louis, before going to Rome, he presided at the cathedral choir boy's party, and with warm words and many jests, presented each boy a pin.

On the following morning, January 8, 1961, he pontificated at the annual meeting of the Holy Name Union. As he walked through the emblazoned banners of the Holy Name units lining his way from the cathedral rectory to the entrance of his cathedral, the beaming smiles of the men were reflected on his own happy face.

The chartered jet was blessed by the cardinal-elect and took off on January 10, 1961, with his friends and relations, among whom were his sister, now Sister Mary Catherine, S.C.N. The cardinal's oldest surviving brother Harry, a Louisville physician, was unable to make the trip.

After a safe journey lasting twelve hours and three minutes, the plane arrived at Ciampino, Rome's airport. The cardinal-elect and his secretary Monsignor Adrian Dwyer took up their quarters at the North American College; his guests and entourage were quartered at the Grand Hotel where the cardinal had dinner with them almost every evening.

He received his *biglietto* of nomination under the gaily painted ceiling of the college refectory on January 16. Over 400 people were present. Speaking in Italian, which he had learned quickly at the Berlitz School in St. Louis, where he had also learned to speak Spanish, the cardinal paid graceful compliments to the Pope and the people of St. Louis. There was constant applause. Calls of ceremony of distinguished cardinals of the Curia filled out the day.

The reception of the red biretta of his rank took place at the semipublic consistory of January 18. In a public consistory the following day, Pope John conferred the red hat on Cardinal Ritter, who thanked the Pope in his own behalf and that of the other cardinals raised to the sacred purple with him.

On Sunday the cardinal took possession of his titular church, the Church of St. Alphonso, on the Via Merulana, which contains the original and fabled picture of Our Lady of Perpetual Help.

St. Louis welcomed her distinguished resident in a series of brilliant ceremonies. The new cardinal was careful on all occasions to refer the honor to the Pope's benignity, the people of the diocese, and the merits of his predecessor, Cardinal Glennon.

Once the ceremonies were over, he settled back into his simple life of work and the never-ending round of consultations and personal appearances.

Most of the time he lives quietly at his small country place at Creve Coeur, on the lakes of the Illinois, where in an old windbreaker and beat-up hat he works on his grounds and in his greenhouse. He takes long walks, too, and has the full swinging stride of one who enjoys walking. It is said the cardinal has a green thumb for both flowers and vegetables and is particularly proud of the home-grown tomatoes displayed on his table at Christmastime. Occasionally he goes to baseball games; he now has a double reason to root for the St. Louis Cardinals.

He knows that as America's seventeenth cardinal he is a symbol as well as a busy archbishop. Though he has kept his simplicity, humor and modern outlook, he carries himself with superb dignity and alert kindness. He has constantly demonstrated his intelligent liberalism at the Vatican council.

Recently a journalist went to St. Louis to secure material for writing a profile of the cardinal, having arranged the preliminary details by telephone with the amiable assistant chancellor, Father Michalski.

While waiting in the extraordinary lobby of the chancery with its beautiful stained-glass ceiling, the journalist had an unexpected meeting with His Eminence. Father Michalski emerged from his office, and seeing the two men in animated conversation, was momentarily thrown off stride. "He's here," he said of the journalist, "to get the clippings on Your Eminence's canonization." Obviously he meant the cardinal's elevation to the Sacred College.

A ripple of merriment spread over the cardinal's expressive face as he asked, with a hearty laugh, "Aren't you a bit previous?" His Eminence gave the journalist a broad wink.

BIBLIOGRAPHY

Arakelian-Ryan, *Richard Cardinal Cushing: An Appreciation*. Cambridge: Mekhitarist Publications, 1959.

Bennett, William H., *Catholic Footsteps in Old New York*. N.Y.: 1909.

Blunt, Hugh F., *Readings From Cardinal O'Connell*. N.Y.: 1934.

Boucher-Tehan, *Prince of Democracy: James Cardinal Gibbons*. N.Y.: Doubleday & Company, Inc., 1962.

Brann, Henry L., *History of The American College*. Rome, N.Y.: 1910.

Brusher, Joseph, S.J., *Popes Through the Ages*. New Jersey: D. Van Nostrand Co., Inc., 1950.

Buherle, Marie Cecilia, *Cardinal Stritch*. Milwaukee: The Bruce Publishing Company, 1959.

Ellis, John Tracy, *American Catholicism*. Chicago: University of Chicago Press, 1956.

Farley, John Cardinal, *The Life of Cardinal McCloskey*. N.Y.: Longmans, Green & Company, 1918.

Finn, Brendan A., *Twenty-Four American Cardinals*. Boston: Bruce Humphries, Inc., 1947.

Gannon, Robert I., *The Cardinal Spellman Story*. N.Y.: Doubleday & Company, Inc., 1962.

Hayes, P. J. Rt. Revd. Msgr., D.D., *John Cardinal Farley* (Privately printed).

Kelly, John Bernard, *Patrick Cardinal Hayes: One of Ourselves*. N.Y.: 1939.

Lavelle, Rt. Revd. Msgr. Michael J., *Cardinal Farley*. N.Y.: The Paulist Press, 1919.

Maynard, Theodore, *The Story of American Catholicism*. N.Y.: The Macmillan Co., 1942.

Morgan, Thomas B., *Speaking of Cardinals*. N.Y.: G. P. Putnam's Sons, 1946.

North, Rt. Revd. Monsignor William E., Ph.D., *The Flight to Rome*. Los Angeles: Kellow Brown Company, 1953.

O'Connell, William Cardinal, *Recollections Of Seventy Years*. Boston: Houghton Mifflin Company, 1934.

Sexton, John E., *Life of Cardinal O'Connell*. Boston: 1926.

The Catholic Directory. N.Y.: P. J. Kenedy & Sons, 1961-1962.

The Catholic Encyclopedia (15 Vols.). N.Y.: 1907-1922.

Thornton, Francis Beauchesne, *The Burning Flame: Life Of Pope Pius X.* N.Y.: Benziger Bros., 1952.

Thornton, Francis Beauchesne, *Cross Upon Cross: Life Of Pope Pius IX.* N.Y.: Benziger Bros., 1955.

Will, Allen Sinclair, *Life of Cardinal Gibbons.* N.Y.: E. P. Dutton & Co., Inc., 1922.

OFFICIAL PRESS AND JUBILEE VOLUMES

Cushing, Richard Cardinal, Introduction to *Welcome To Boston.* Boston: The Pilot Publishing Company, 1962.

Fifty Years of Notable Achievement in the Life of His Eminence Dennis Cardinal Dougherty (1890-1940), Official Jubilee Volume. Philadelphia: 1940.

Elevation and Investiture of His Eminence James Cardinal Francis McIntyre Archbishop of Los Angeles, Official Jubilee Volume. Los Angeles: *The Tidings,* 1953.

A Tribute on The Silver Jubilee of Aloisius Joseph Cardinal Muench (Episcopal Consecration). Fargo: 1960.

N.C.W.C. News Service Biographical No. 142-A (Revised), *His Eminence Richard Cardinal Cushing: Archbishop Of Boston.* Washington, D.C.: 1958.

Elevation and Investiture of His Eminence John Cardinal O'Hara Archbishop of Philadelphia (Official Press Book). Philadelphia: Prepared by *The Catholic Standard and Times* (1953).

NEWSPAPERS AND MAGAZINES

Catholic Action News, Fargo, North Dakota.

The Catholic Bulletin, St. Paul, Minnesota.

The Catholic Herald Citizen, Milwaukee, Wisconsin.

The Catholic News, New York City, N.Y.

The Catholic Standard and Times, Philadelphia, Pennsylvania.

The Catholic World, New York City, N.Y.

The Fargo Forum, Fargo, North Dakota.

Life, New York, N.Y.

The Michigan Catholic, Detroit, Michigan.

The Minneapolis Star, Minneapolis, Minnesota.

Newsweek, New York, N.Y.

The New World, Chicago, Illinois.

The New York Times, New York, N.Y.

The Pilot, Boston, Mass.

The St. Louis Review, St. Louis, Missouri.

The St. Paul Pioneer Press, St. Paul, Minnesota.

Saturday Evening Post, Philadelphia, Pennsylvania: Jack Alexander, Sept. 12, 1953.

The Tidings, Los Angeles, California.

Time, New York, N.Y.

Index